King's Dream

King's

YALE UNIVERSITY PRESS   NEW HAVEN & LONDON

Dream

Eric J. Sundquist

A Caravan book. For more information, visit www.caravanbooks.org.

Set in Janson type by Integrated Publishing Solutions.
Printed in the United States of America.

Library of Congress Cataloging-in-Publication Data

Sundquist, Eric J.
King's dream / Eric J. Sundquist
p.   cm. — (Icons of America)
Includes bibliographical references and index.
ISBN 978-0-300-11807-0 (cloth : alk. paper)
1. King, Martin Luther, Jr., 1929–1968—Oratory.   2. King, Martin Luther, Jr., 1929–1968. I have a dream.   3. King, Martin Luther, Jr., 1929–1968—Language. 4. King, Martin Luther, Jr., 1929–1968—Political and social views.   5. African Americans—Civil rights—History.   6. Civil rights movements—United States— History.   7. Equality—United States—History.   8. United States—Race relations.   9. Southern Staes—Race relations.   I. Title.
E185.97.K5S864 2008
323.092—dc22   2008014499

A catalogue record for this book is available from the British Library.

This paper meets the requirements of ANSI/NISO Z39.48-1992
(Permanence of Paper).
It contains 30 percent postconsumer waste (PCW) and is certified
by the Forest Stewardship Council (FSC).

10 9 8 7 6 5 4 3 2 1

For my grandchildren

Contents

Contents

Introduction

Had he not departed from his prepared text and spoken so eloquently about his "dream" of racial justice in America, the speech given by Martin Luther King, Jr., at the March on Washington on August 28, 1963, might still have been a landmark in American history. It might still have played an indirect role in the historic civil rights legislation passed soon thereafter—the Civil Rights Act of 1964 and the Voting Rights Act of 1965—and it might still have added to the renown that led to King's being awarded the Nobel Prize for Peace in 1964. Not least because it was the high point of what King rightly called in his opening words "the greatest demonstration for freedom in the history of our nation," the speech would still be studied for its evidence of his unwavering belief that equal rights for African Americans entailed nothing more—and nothing less—than returning to the nation's founding ideals.

Absent King's reiterated affirmation of "I have a dream," however, one may wonder whether the speech would have attained the iconic status that it enjoys today—"the greatest speech given since

[Abraham] Lincoln's time," according to Garry Wills, the very best of the one hundred best political speeches of the twentieth century, according to a survey of the leading scholars of public address. Where schoolchildren once recited Lincoln's Gettysburg Address, they now grapple with the Dream speech, just as Martin Luther King, Jr., Day now rivals Presidents Day in public consciousness. By the late 1980s, according to a study by the National Endowment for the Humanities, high school seniors more often correctly identified the source of "I have a dream" (88.1 percent) than the opening words of the Gettysburg Address (73.9 percent) or the Declaration of Independence (65.7 percent); by 2008 recognition of King's words among American teenagers had reached 97 percent. The speech's most famous lines have become shorthand not only for King's life but for the whole of the civil rights movement and even the 1960s itself—a kind of "rhetorical Woodstock," in the words of Greil Marcus—and it is incumbent upon preachers and politicians, especially presidents, to claim King's message as their own.

Along with the numerous biographies of King and studies of the civil rights movement, both scholarly and popular, that followed his assassination in 1968, memorial photographic compilations such as *I Have a Dream: The Story of Martin Luther King, Jr., in Text and Pictures* (1968) and collections of his words such as *"I Have a Dream": The Quotations of Martin Luther King, Jr.* (1968) made remembrance of King synonymous with remembrance of his "dream." The speech and its best-known phrases were cited frequently during debates over the proposed federal holiday and helped to raise King into the ranks of great Americans. King insisted that America be "as good as its Declaration of Independence, as good as its Bill of Rights," said Representative Thomas P. ("Tip") O'Neill, who recalled hearing the Dream speech in person. Changing the nation "not by force of arms but by moral force," King asked us to "make the words of the Founding Fathers . . . come alive for all people." After President

Ronald Reagan signed the bill creating the holiday in 1983, despite his own reservations about King's loyalty to the nation, the commission charged with issuing guidelines for its first celebration in 1986 titled the results of its work "Living the Dream."

It quickly became evident, however, that there was no general agreement as to what King's dream actually was. On the occasion of the first holiday, Motown Records founder Berry Gordy placed a full-page laudatory ad in the *New York Times*: "By wisely choosing its heroes, a country shapes its destiny. Thank you Dr. Martin Luther King, Jr., for making an impossible dream come true." Yet on that same day Jesse Jackson lamented the nation's preoccupation with the Dream speech at the expense of King's more radical vision—his denunciation of economic inequality at home and abroad, his opposition to the Vietnam War, his advocacy of affirmative action—and implied that King had been murdered as part of an FBI or CIA conspiracy. "The so-called 'I Have a Dream' speech," declared Jackson, a former aide to King and recent presidential candidate, "was a speech describing nightmare conditions. . . . Dr. King was not assassinated for dreaming but for acting and challenging the government."

Notwithstanding his suspicions about King's death, Jackson remained true to King's vision of brotherhood and nonviolent social change. But King's values were by no means universally shared, even by African Americans. The slain King had been compared to Gandhi, Lincoln, and Christ, and canonized along with President John F. Kennedy, another assassinated "dreamer," in the pop singer Dion's hit "Abraham, Martin, and John." Within a matter of years, however, the outlaw heroes of black nationalism, especially Malcolm X and Muhammad Ali, had eclipsed King in popularity among many black youth—in fact, among American youth in general. The music video "Fight the Power," hip-hop anthem for Spike Lee's 1989 film *Do the Right Thing*, opened with familiar black-and-white newsreel

3

footage of the March on Washington, pausing on King's image before cutting to Public Enemy's combative lyrics accompanying a "Young People's March on Brooklyn to End Racial Violence," whose leader announced, "Word up, we ain't going out like that '63 nonsense." When Malcolm X merchandise flooded America's streets and malls amid the glamorization of black gangsters in the 1990s, King's dream seemed quaint.

In a 1997 CNN/*USA Today*/Gallup poll that asked how much of King's dream had been fulfilled, those responding *all of it* and *none of it* were tied at 1 percent each, while 20 percent thought *a great deal*, 53 percent *a moderate amount*, and 23 percent *not very much*, a nearly exact bell curve that revealed nothing at all, since the dream was undefined and, perhaps, indefinable. Appropriations of his image and words having long since been spread across the political and cultural spectrum, King himself had become a kind of Rorschach test on the meaning of racial equality in America. If true believers turned him into "Holy Martin," a figure beyond reproach, others turned him into an "elastic fetish" conveniently stretched to fit any cause.

For those on the political Left, King's dream became associated less with colorblind "equal opportunity," what was once the core value of democratic liberalism, than with race-based (and sometimes class-based) programs designed to achieve diversity, usually defined as proportionately equal outcomes, the new core value of democratic liberalism. The concept of King's dream and slogans such as "Keep the Dream Alive" were soon pervasive in educational and social programs aimed at minorities. In the case of the I Have a Dream Foundation, for example, low-income, predominantly black and Hispanic grade school students designated as "Dreamers" are adopted by sponsors who provide extra tutoring, mentoring, and counseling, then pay college expenses for those who graduate from high school, a program that has aided more than ten thousand students to date. When *Newsweek* titled a 1995 article about the legal retreat from race-based affirmative action "Rethinking the Dream," the editors seemed to find the content of King's dream self-evident.

By the same token, those on the Right have routinely cited the Dream speech—specifically, King's hope that "my four little children will one day live in a nation where they will not be judged by the color of their skin but by the content of their character"—in support of an ideal of colorblind justice, and conservatives, no less than liberals, have presumed to know where King would stand on hot-button issues such as affirmative action, reparations for slavery, and school vouchers. Along the way, King has been recruited for causes that might have surprised him. Randall Terry, the head of Operation Rescue, which has employed tactics of civil disobedience and public protest to disrupt the operation of abortion clinics, cited his inspiration by King alongside the precedents of the Underground Railroad and those who rescued Jews from Nazis. During the 2006 midterm elections, the National Black Republican Association ran a short-lived radio ad claiming King as one of their own. Once the party of segregationist Dixiecrats, today's Democrats have "bamboozled blacks" with racial preferences and an immoral social agenda said two women exchanging questions and answers, whereas King was "a real man"—a Republican.

Adaptations of King's famous phrase automatically play upon his integrity, his idealism, his altruism for one or another cause. The fund-raising campaign for the Martin Luther King, Jr., National Memorial in Washington, D.C., goes under the banner "Build the Dream." The slogan for the 2008 summer Olympics in China, "One World, One Dream," is but one of many international adaptations of King's phrase in recent decades, from South Africa to Poland to Pakistan. With the catchphrase "I Have a Dream . . . New Millennium, New Hope," for instance, UNICEF's Millennium Dream Campaign raises money for Ethiopian children orphaned or stricken by HIV/AIDS. Appeals to King's legacy were quickly apparent in the 2008 Democratic presidential campaign. Senator Hillary Rodham Clinton provoked a minor backlash when she remarked that "Dr. King's dream began to be realized when President Lyndon Johnson passed the Civil Rights Act of 1964," a comment some considered dismissive of King's own role. Appearing alongside Clinton's main opponent, Senator Barack Obama, Oprah Winfrey declared that "Dr. King dreamed the dream," but now people could "vote that dream into reality," which might have seemed a call for racial allegiance, rather than colorblindness, except for Obama's ability, as he put it in naming Lincoln and King as his predecessors, to traverse "the landscape of our collective dreams." No sooner had Obama clinched the nomination than pundits and op-ed cartoonists depicted the event as King's dream come true.

Not surprisingly, African Americans have been especially alert to the potentially acerbic ambiguity of King's phrase. When controversy erupted in 1996 over a proposal to teach "Ebonics"—vernacular black English—in the public schools of Oakland, California, a group known as Atlanta's Black Professionals ran a newspaper ad that borrowed from King's speech to condemn the plan: superimposed over the image of a well-dressed black man with his back turned to the viewer was the message, "I Has a Dream." The ad drove home its point by naming Malcolm X along with King among those who had "paid the price of obtaining our voice with the currency of their lives." Not just King's eloquence, which might have been written off as bourgeois by the proponents of Ebonics, but also that of Malcolm, the epitome of razor-sharp black nationalist discourse, was cited in contrast to the Oakland plan, which, according to the ad, would condemn black students to functional illiteracy and strip them of effective speech.

Solemnly recited on the King holiday and throughout Black History Month, the Dream speech is also routinely lampooned, whether

in the mock version appearing in the satirical newspaper *The Onion*
("I had a really weird dream last night. . . . Thank God, Almighty, I
am awake at last") or the blasphemous parody in Darius James's
1992 novel *Negrophobia*, in which Walt Disney, as the American
president, delivers a racist Dream oration in celebration of King's
assassination and the end of black culture in the United States. So
deeply ingrained in national consciousness is the Dream speech, or
at least fragments of it, that King's words haunt even his most ardent
enemies. Before being driven away in a brief storm of violence, Ku
Klux Klan members protesting the King holiday with a 1998 rally
in Memphis—they had to get permission to parade from a black
mayor and request protection from a black chief of police—were
thus treated to one speaker's pathetically unimaginative mimicry of
King: "I have a dream that one day little white boys and little white
girls will be playing in the parks and segregation will rule once again
in this country."

Sound bites and misappropriations of the Dream speech are everywhere imaginable, sacred and meaningless, a surfeit of dreaming
that led Michael Eric Dyson to propose a ten-year moratorium on
listening to or reading the Dream speech and prompted the four-
year-old son of a friend of mine to conclude, "No wonder they
killed him. He kept giving the same speech over and over."

King came of age along with television news, a medium he used
to masterful effect. Because it was also an age in which celebrities
became art (Andy Warhol's silk screens of Marilyn Monroe, a recent
suicide, appeared in 1962) and revolutionaries became celebrities
(Che Guevara was featured in a *Look* magazine cover story and
photo spread in 1963), it is no surprise that the martyred King and
his speech soon became iconic means to mark a time of national
transfiguration. In addition to its role in numerous civil rights doc-
umentaries and the 1978 television miniseries *King*, King's speech
has been inserted visually and aurally into films as various as *Ghosts*

of Mississippi, JFK, Contact, and *Undercover Brother.* Music inspired by King's dream is commonplace, ranging from Elie Siegmeister's 1967 cantata for mixed chorus and orchestra, *I Have a Dream,* to Josh Green's 1976 stage musical of King's life, *I Have a Dream,* starring Billy Dee Williams, to Max Roach's 1982 "The Dream—It's Time," in which excerpts from King's speech provide a counterpoint to Roach's solo drumming, to the rapper will.i.am's "Dream" in the 2007 film *Freedom Writers.* Commercial products imprinted with King's image and excerpts from his speech are not limited to baseball caps, T-shirts, coffee mugs, and cell phone ringtones but also include CafePress's pet apparel and the "Equality Martin Luther King Jr. Classic Thong," underwear for women and girls, featuring King's likeness and his famous line about his children being judged by "the content of their character."

Among more respectable commercial ventures, Apple Computer used King's image, along with those of Gandhi, Picasso, and Einstein, in its "Think Different" campaign, while a television ad for Alcatel Americas depicted King speaking to a vast empty space between the Lincoln Memorial and the Washington Monument, accompanied by the words "Before you can inspire, before you can touch, you must first connect." One of the most ingenious adaptations of the Dream speech appeared in a promotional ad run by the *New Republic.* Using a widely reproduced photograph from the March on Washington, shot from inside the Lincoln Memorial and behind Lincoln's statue looking out through the glare of camera lights toward the speaker's podium and the crowd beyond, the ad relied on the instantly recognizable iconography of King's speech, without naming it or portraying him, to associate his message with the magazine's content: "There will always be an audience for a powerful idea" (figure 1).

The Apple and Alcatel ads, among others, were licensed by the King family, the late Coretta Scott King and her four children, who not long after his death became intimately involved in protecting copyright to King's words and image—so much so, in fact, that controversy over their efforts to maintain private rights in one of the most "public" properties in modern history came to overshadow King's own legacy. The family filed successful suits against CBS and Henry Hampton, producer of the acclaimed documentary *Eyes on the Prize*, for using news footage of the Dream speech, and against *USA Today* for reprinting the text of the speech on its thirtieth anniversary. Even as the King family quarreled with the National Park Service over control of the visitors center in Atlanta's Martin Luther King, Jr., Historic District (comprising his birthplace; Ebenezer Baptist Church, where King and his father preached; and the Martin Luther King, Jr., Center for Nonviolent Social Change), their plan for a virtual reality interactive museum re-creating his role in the civil rights movement prompted the *Atlanta Journal-Constitution* editorialist Cynthia Tucker, a frequent critic of the family's ventures, to ridicule the project as "I Have a Dreamland." Whereas King's original speech inspired headlines such as "'I Have a Dream . . .': Peroration by Dr. King Sums Up a Day the Capital Will Remember" (*New York Times*) and "In Shadow of Abe Lincoln, a Voice Shouts for Freedom" (*Atlanta Constitution*), its merchandising has made it the subject of accusatory squibs such as "The Dream Defiled" (*Boston Globe*) and "The Dream—For Sale" (*Los Angeles Times*).

In purely rhetorical terms, the Dream speech may not have been King's best. His speech at the conclusion of the voting rights march from Selma to Montgomery in 1965 was arguably his most commanding, in part because it capped two months of tension and violence that ended with a victorious march to the very steps of what was once the capitol of the Confederacy. The anti–Vietnam War speech he delivered at New York's Riverside Church in 1967, a stinging censure of his nation's foreign policy and one that cost King a good deal of prestige and support, was thought by some to be his greatest. Ralph Abernathy, King's closest friend and longtime aide, believed that his wrenching, uncanny speech on the eve of his assassination in Memphis, raised to tragic intensity by the fate that awaited him, rivaled the Gettysburg Address and George Washington's Farewell Address. Yet Abernathy's reason for preferring the Dream speech was exactly right: it was "a prophecy of pure hope at a time when black people and the nation as a whole needed hope more than anything else."

King's greatness, as well as the greatness of his speech, lay in his ability to elevate the cause of civil rights and the cause of America at the same time. The nation had failed black Americans, no doubt, but it was not—contrary to the opinions of some raising the fist of Black Power—irredeemably corrupt and ripe for overthrow. Enlisting his audience in a crusade sanctioned equally by the Declaration of Independence and the Bible, King in no way rejected America's foundational values. Rather, he purified and consolidated those values by insisting that only when the revolutionary rights they guaranteed were shared by Americans of all colors, creeds, and nationalities would they truly *be* America's foundational values.

"All this probably hasn't changed any votes on the civil rights bill," said Senator Hubert Humphrey after the March on Washington, "but it's a good thing for Washington and the nation and the world." King's speech was indeed good for the nation and the world, but Humphrey may have underestimated its practical value. Although we will never know the fate of the civil rights legislation proposed by President Kennedy had it been he, rather than Lyndon Johnson, who fought to make it law, the Dream speech, which raised King to national stature and epitomized his leadership, set the stage in a way neither Kennedy nor Johnson could have done. Entering a convulsive debate about racial justice whose prime movers were the Supreme Court and Congress, King proved, through his catalytic personal witness in key civil rights campaigns and the majesty of his words, especially at the March on Washington, that the conscience of a nation, and ultimately its laws, could be changed by a single citizen.

King, of course, did not act alone, as one after another history of the civil rights movement has made clear. Without determining to what extent King made the movement or the movement made King, however, we can be certain that he was truly its *icon*—that is, an *eikon*, a reflection of the *eidos*, the *idea* of justice and equal rights driving the movement. He was rightly compared to Gandhi and Lincoln because, like them, he embodied, in transcendent distillation, the qualities of courage, compassion, and visionary idealism that had to be aroused in many in order for justice to prevail and equal rights to be achieved. On one occasion above all others, King put those qualities into timeless words.

King's Dream does not purport to tell the story of King's life or the civil rights movement, or even the March on Washington, except in broad outline. These subjects have been studied in searching detail by others, and, as I indicate in my reference notes, I have benefited enormously from previous biographies and histories. I have likewise benefited from a number of shorter commentaries on King's speech and from Drew Hansen's book *The Dream: Martin Luther King, Jr., and the Speech That Inspired a Nation* (2003), which is especially important for its careful reconstruction of the circumstances in which the speech was written and the process of revision through which it went. Even though no study of King fails to pay at least some attention to the Dream speech, however, it is surprising nonetheless how little sustained attention it has received.

There is no substitute for hearing King or, better, watching and listening to him. Fortunately, numerous recordings and videos, as well as Internet postings, make it easy today to hear and study those features of his style which cannot be captured by description alone. I take note of the visual and aural dimensions of King's appearance at the March on Washington, but my first interest here is in the significance of his words. Although *King's Dream* includes commentary on virtually every sentence of the speech, I do not provide a line-by-line analysis. My purpose instead is to place King's speech, through a series of interlocking essays that illuminate its vibrant range of historical and cultural reference, in both the context of the postwar civil rights movement and the context of American debates about issues of racial equality from the early republic through present-day Supreme Court rulings.

Insofar as King's articulation of his dream was by no means confined to his appearance at the March on Washington, this likewise entails looking for reflections and refractions of the Dream speech in other writings, sermons, and orations, while using them in turn to understand the magnificence of his single greatest oration. Notwithstanding the fact that he later spoke in a more radical voice, one can find in the Dream speech a nearly perfect lens through which to see King's lifelong philosophy. Through his overt or implicit reflections on the vital but unfulfilled promise made by the Founding Fathers, "the architects of our republic," in the Declaration of Independence; on the legacy of Abraham Lincoln and the Emancipation Proclamation in its centennial year of 1963; on *Brown v. Board of Education* and the question of states' rights; on the contemporary relevance of the Exodus, of the biblical prophets Isaiah and Amos, and of Daniel, an interpreter of dreams; on the power of Gandhian "soul force" in the face of fire hoses and attack dogs; on the meaning of national citizenship evoked by cultural artifacts as different as "America" and "I Thank God I'm Free at Last"; on the inspiring history of African American protest stretching from the days of slavery through the March on Washington, when King himself, not President Kennedy, would issue a "Second Emancipation Proclamation"—through all of this one can find in the Dream speech a panoramic account of the civil rights movement in its many dimensions.

Our challenge today is to recapture King's dream—not to relive, nostalgically, the elation of August 28, 1963, nor to pretend that he could or would give the same speech today. Rather, our challenge is to understand how perfectly, in grand poetry and powerful elocution, Martin Luther King, Jr., told the story of African American freedom and with it the story of the nation.

Dreamer—1963

"I started out reading the speech," recalled Martin Luther King, Jr., then "all of a sudden this thing came out of me that I have used—I'd used it many times before, that thing about 'I have a dream'—and I just felt that I wanted to use it here. I don't know why, I hadn't thought about it before the speech." Folk history of the March on Washington would record that Mahalia Jackson, who just minutes earlier had seized the audience's collective heart with her rendition of "I Been 'Buked and I Been Scorned," called out in the midst of King's oration, "Tell 'em about the dream, Martin!"

And so he did. "I was near my beloved Dr. King when he put aside his prepared speech and let the breath of God thunder through him," remembered Joan Baez, "and up over my head I saw freedom, and all around me I heard it ring." According to Coretta Scott King, the words of her thirty-four-year-old husband "flowed from some higher place," and "for that brief moment the Kingdom of God seemed to have come on earth." After King finished, reported Lerone Bennett, Jr., grown men and women "wept unashamedly." No doubt *Time* magazine could have chosen a more appropriate metaphor in reporting that King "enslaved his audience," but this was true even of those who feared his message. Because of its power to influence the masses, concluded the head of the FBI's Domestic Intelligence Division, King's "demagogic speech" made him the nation's "most dangerous Negro."

As was his custom, King began speaking in measured cadences, then gathered passion and exuberance as he proceeded. Although his colleagues had persuaded him to take more than the five minutes allotted each speaker—he ended up speaking for about sixteen minutes—it may be that King discarded his prepared text in favor of "this thing" about the dream because he realized he had not yet truly connected with his audience, despite the applause and shouts of approbation that greeted him throughout the first two-thirds of his speech. The result was a cascading vision, rich with historical resonance and contemporary significance, whose cumulative effect remains astounding and moving a half century later:

> I say to you today, my friends, so even though we face the difficulties of today and tomorrow, I still have a dream. It is a dream deeply rooted in the American dream.
>
> I have a dream that one day this nation will rise up and live out the true meaning of its creed: "We hold these truths to be self-evident, that all men are created equal."
>
> I have a dream that one day on the red hills of Georgia, the sons of former slaves and the sons of former slave owners will be able to sit down together at the table of brotherhood.
>
> I have a dream that one day even the state of Mississippi, a state sweltering with the heat of injustice, sweltering with the heat of oppression, will be transformed into an oasis of freedom and justice.
>
> I have a dream that my four little children will one day live in a nation where they will not be judged by the color

of their skin but by the content of their character. I have a dream today.

I have a dream that one day down in Alabama, with its vicious racists, with its governor having his lips dripping with the words of "interposition" and "nullification," one day right there in Alabama little black boys and black girls will be able to join hands with little white boys and white girls as sisters and brothers. I have a dream today.

I have a dream that one day every valley shall be exalted, and every hill and mountain shall be made low; the rough places will be made plain, and the crooked places will be made straight; and the glory of the Lord shall be revealed, and all flesh shall see it together.

Here is virtually the whole of King's repertory: the quotation from the Declaration of Independence, which appeared countless times in his speeches and sermons; the challenge to the descendants of slaves and slaveholders alike to live as brothers and sisters; the hallmark metaphors in which the oppressive weight of injustice, generation after generation, comes palpably alive; the hope that one's character, not the color of one's skin, shall be the basis of judgment and reward; the attack on states' rights framed in the daring terms of black and white children holding hands; the biblical injunction, here from the prophet Isaiah, to realize justice not only in God's heaven but on God's earth.

Rather than stumbling over his words, as it might have seemed during the awkward pause that is clearly audible after "I say to you today," King had begun improvising—much to his benefit, as Drew Hansen has shown, for the remainder of the prepared text, though suitable for the occasion, was pedestrian by comparison. Following an invocation of the book of Amos—"until justice rolls down like waters and righteousness like a mighty stream," one of his favorite scriptures—King had intended to conclude his speech with an ex-hortation to join nonviolent protest to political lobbying:

> And so today, let us go back to our communities as members of the international association for the advancement of creative dissatisfaction. Let us go back with all the strength we can muster to get strong civil rights legislation in this session of Congress. Let us go down from this place to ascend other peaks of purpose. Let us descend from this mountaintop to climb other hills of hope.

Instead, his spontaneous "I have a dream" refrain led to an even more stirring peroration, one he had also used before, that turned the words of "America"—"My country, 'tis of thee, sweet land of liberty, of thee I sing"—into a magnificent vision of racial justice spreading across the nation.

Because of his capacious memory and his fondness for particular stories and rhetorical constructions, King often repeated, sometimes off the cuff, especially effective passages from earlier sermons, speeches, and writings. Both as a speaker and as a writer, he also borrowed from many sources, sometimes consciously and sometimes unconsciously, sometimes with attribution and sometimes without. As King emerged as the nation's most prominent civil rights leader, his schedule of speaking engagements, often several a day, severely limited his time for writing and forced him to rely increasingly on his staff, as well as outside editors and ghostwriters, for assistance with his speeches, essays, and books. Even so, he was able to draw on an imposing body of his own writing, both sermons and more scholarly work, reaching back to his student days. Neither his borrowings nor the role played by others in his oratory and writing should diminish the fact that the words he spoke and those that appeared under his name in print were always the embodiment of a vision that was uniquely his own.

Especially in the case of the Dream speech, and not least because of his extemporaneous departure from the text, we can say without question that this was King speaking the exact words he wanted the nation and the world to hear. Along with members of his staff, King had worked late into the night before the March revising his speech—returning to ideas, metaphors, and passages that had been successful before and trying out new ones, seeking just the right tone, the right balance, the right cadences. And yet the parts of the speech for which he is most remembered were nowhere to be found on the pages before him. Speaking suddenly from the heart, he delivered a speech elegantly structured, commanding in tone, and altogether more profound than anything heard on American soil in nearly a century. In the midst of speaking, King rewrote his speech and created a new national scripture.

"Someday, I'm going to have me some big words like that," a young King told his mother after hearing an eloquent preacher. At Morehouse College, at Crozer Theological Seminary, in his graduate study at Boston University, and in the early years of his ministry, King worked hard on both his pulpit style and the content of his sermons. Like the black preachers of old described by James Weldon Johnson, he spoke a language "saturated with the sublime phraseology of the Hebrew prophets and steeped in the idioms of King James English." At the same time, his sermons included little of the straining, moaning, and whooping that constituted the performative essence of some African American preaching. King relied instead on an impressive combination of erudition, passages quoted or paraphrased from works he liked, and a beautiful baritone voice— "each syllable had the timbre of an African drum," according to one listener—which grew rich and darkly melodic, weary with the weight of prophecy, over time.

From the outset, his congregations, church women especially, loved his preaching. "When I hears Dr. King," said one of them,

"I see angel's wings flying 'round his head." Short on organizational skills, by some accounts, King was long on charisma, courage, and moral authority, and his leadership, thought Wyatt T. Walker, executive director of the Southern Christian Leadership Conference (SCLC) from 1960 to 1964, came from his ability "to get more warm bodies in the street at one time than anybody else we've ever seen in American history." Recalling how most southern blacks were resigned to segregation until King gave them hope for something different, Charles Gratton of Birmingham, Alabama, said that whenever he heard King talk "it seemed like he was touching me from the inside."

In addition to his inventory of speaking skills, observed the television journalist Dan Rather, King possessed a "well-honed ability to size up an audience," to know what to say and how to say it. For that same reason, said others, King's response to the disparate needs of his audiences made him a "conservative militant" who took a stance of "radical moderation." (Not moderate enough, objected King's own denominational leader, the president of the black National Baptist Convention Joseph H. Jackson, who considered the Dream speech a "dangerous, unwarranted protest.") Carefully crafted, perfectly modulated, King's performance at the March on Washington struck a precarious balance between insistence and reassurance, a feat difficult to repeat and impossible to sustain when he took his message to the slums of the urban North. "You just can't communicate with the ghetto dweller and at the same time not frighten many whites to death," King said in a 1966 interview. "I don't know what the answer is to that. My role perhaps is to interpret to the white world. There must be somebody to communicate to two worlds."

Like so many in the freedom movement, King fervently believed, in the words of the civil rights anthem "We Shall Overcome," that "God is on our side." Speaking in the vernacular of the black church and insisting that it was a "voice out of Bethlehem two thousand years ago [that] said all men are equal," King made God's covenant a covenant of racial justice, a message of liberation succinctly stated in his description of sit-in protestors in "Letter from Birmingham Jail":

> One day the South will know that when these disinherited children of God sat down at lunch counters they were in reality standing up for the best in the American dream and the most sacred values in our Judeo-Christian heritage, and thusly, carrying our whole nation back to those great wells of democracy which were dug by the Founding Fathers in the formulation of the Constitution and the Declaration of Independence.

When King addressed his audience as "children of God" or "God's children," as he did three times in the Dream speech, he made both a theological and a political argument. Not only were all human beings the children of God, but all Americans, regardless of skin color, were children of the nation's Founding Fathers.

Within his own lifetime, however, King grew despondent about his dream. In his Christmas Eve sermon of 1967, he looked back soberly: "In 1963, on a sweltering August afternoon, we stood in Washington, D.C., and talked to the nation about many things. Toward the end of the afternoon, I tried to talk to the nation about a dream that I had had, and I must confess to you today that not long after talking about that dream I started seeing it turn into a nightmare." He meant not only the Ku Klux Klan's bombing of the Sixteenth Street Baptist Church in Birmingham on September 15, 1963, which took the lives of four young black girls preparing for Sunday choir. He meant the riots in Newark, Watts (Los Angeles), Detroit, and other cities he could do nothing to stop. ("I had a dream, I had a dream," jeered one resident of Watts. "Hell, we don't need no damn dreams. We want jobs.") He meant the escalation of the Vietnam

War, which he opposed with much of his energy—far too much, his critics said—in the last year of his life.

King's peculiar locution—a dream "I had had"—which he repeated in Memphis on the eve of his assassination, made it seem that his hope for racial justice really *had* been a dream, that even its memory had begun to fade. One month before his death, King cited God's words of consolation to King David for the temple of which he had dreamed but which he had failed to build: "And the LORD said unto David my father, Whereas it was in thine heart to build an house unto my name, thou didst well that it was in thine heart" (1 Kings 8:18). The dream remained in David's heart, the house of justice unfinished, and the scripture's lesson, King concluded, was that "life is a continual story of shattered dreams."

■

Whether such a melancholy assessment was accurate depends on what one thinks King's dream was. One might say simply that each incremental step forward in the civil rights movement was a part of the dream coming true. "In a very real sense," said King when the jails of Birmingham filled with protestors for the first time in May 1963, "this is the fulfillment of a dream." Even better was the successful conclusion of his campaign of nonviolent direct action in that most segregated of southern cities. When Birmingham "discovered a conscience" and signed a desegregation agreement, King proclaimed, our "dream came true." Riding high on the activists' triumph in Alabama, the March on Washington itself then became the dream. "Mr. Randolph," said a jubilant Bayard Rustin to A. Philip Randolph, who had championed the event for more than two decades, "it looks like your dream has come true."

As though they might find the secret source of the Sermon on the Mount, biographers and scholars have tried to determine the origins of King's memorable phrase. It may have emerged from the movement's rank and file. James Bevel, one of King's colleagues in the SCLC, believed the inspiration for "I have a dream" must have come from a 1962 service he and King conducted in the burned-out remains of Mount Olive Baptist Church in Terrell County, Georgia, one of seven churches torched by arsonists in a two-week period. As a young woman prayed, Bevel recalled, she began to intone, "I have a dream," and soon the whole congregation, King included, was swaying to its rhythm. Equally certain she knew the source, SCLC staff member Dorothy Cotton remembers telling King about a white woman she heard say to a black woman, in Albany, Georgia, "I have a dream one day that my child can reach out and hold hands with your child . . . and that it won't matter."

It may be that the inspiration for King's dream descended from antebellum times. "I had dreams, horrid dreams of freedom through a sea of blood," recalled Frederick Douglass of his days as a slave. "But when I heard of the Anti-Slavery movement, light broke in my dark mind. Bloody visions fled away, and I saw the star of liberty peering above the horizon." Or perhaps it came from a more recent instance of the black jeremiad. "This is a wonderful world, which the founding fathers dreamed," remarked W. E. B. Du Bois in his *Autobiography*, "until their sons drowned it in the blood of slavery and devoured it in greed." Or from black literature. "Let America be the dream the dreamers dreamed," wrote Langston Hughes in his 1936 poem "Let America Be America Again." In *Killers of the Dream* (1949), King's friend Lillian Smith, a prominent white liberal, described the tragic divide between those southerners committed to integration, the dreamers, and those who denied the dream by any means necessary, the killers. "How many dead dreams will it take to destroy us all?" Smith asked in the preface to a new edition of her book in 1961, where she recounted the phone call a frightened King placed to Attorney General Robert Kennedy from the First Baptist Church in Montgomery, under siege by a white mob bent on attacking the civil rights demonstrators gathered within.

The source of King's dream was just as likely to have been spiritual. Some years later he told Harold DeWolf, his dissertation adviser at Boston University, that the dream existed first in the mind of God, and that he simply communicated it to the nation. In the speech itself, just moments after his dream catalogue, King alluded to one of Nebuchadnezzar's dreams in the book of Daniel—"With this faith we will be able to hew out of the mountain of despair a stone of hope"—a strange image interpreted by Daniel to mean that the kingdom of God will prevail over all the kingdoms of man. Like Daniel, King meant to offer a lesson in the ascendancy of divine justice—even, it may be, at the cost of his life. After his death, King would rightly be likened to another biblical dreamer, Joseph, who both interpreted the dreams of Pharaoh and was reviled, assaulted, and left for dead by brothers jealous of his own dreams of patrimonial favor: "Behold, this dreamer cometh./Come now therefore, and let us slay him, and cast him into some pit . . . and we shall see what will become of his dreams" (Genesis 37:19–20).

For participants in the civil rights movement, of course, dreams of freedom were omnipresent. Before his third attempt to enroll at the University of Mississippi, James Meredith composed what he later acknowledged was a kind of "last will and testament," to be released in the event of his death. "I dream of the day when Negroes in Mississippi can live in decency and respect and do so without fear of intimidation and bodily harm," he wrote. Where Meredith dreamed of inclusion, others embraced exclusion. "They have some kind of strange dream of a black nation within the larger nation," King remarked of the Nation of Islam in 1961. "At times the public expressions of this group have bordered on a new kind of race hatred." Black nationalism, though, arose in answer to white nationalism. The Georgia Council on Human Relations thus issued a pamphlet entitled "Albany, Georgia—Police State," which began: "The white majority in Albany is living in a dream—a one hundred year old, segregated dream" in which everyone is content. "Negroes are happy in their child-like singing and dancing. Whites are loving, understanding and paternal."

Any number of these sources may have fed into the "I have a dream" refrain, less robust and lucid versions of which King had already used in Albany, as well as in Rocky Mount, North Carolina, in 1962, and then again in Birmingham, Chicago, and Detroit in 1963, as though in unconscious preparation for what would prove to be his most resonant and widely remembered words.* With respect to its philosophical essence, however, King himself offered the most useful clue about his meaning when he said his dream was "deeply rooted in the American dream." Yet this explanation, seemingly transparent, raised the question: what, to King, was the American dream?

Throughout the twentieth century, especially in the post–World War II years, the American dream signified the "vaults of opportunity" and "vast ocean of material prosperity" that King, in the Dream speech, placed at the heart of the national experience. More broadly, it signified a colloquial notion of "freedom," the essence of the American way of life, whose best approximation may be found in what Abraham Lincoln referred to as the principle of "Liberty to all" embodied in the Declaration of Independence, a principle pre-

* No doubt the metaphor of the dream resonated for King's audience in part because it was also commonplace in the day's popular culture. From "All I Have to Do Is Dream," a chart-topper for the Everly Brothers in 1958 to the Temptations' "Dream Come True" in 1962 and Roy Orbison's 1963 hit "In Dreams," dreams were ever-present on the airwaves, to take note of only the years immediately preceding King's speech. Broadway contributed "I had a dream, a dream about you, baby," from *Gypsy*'s 1959 banner song "Everything's Coming Up Roses"—the 1962 film version was fresh in the nation's memory—as well as "To dream the impossible dream," the signature phrase of *The Man of La Mancha*, first heard in a 1959 teleplay that preceded its stage fame in 1965.

dating the Constitution and "entwining itself more closely about the human heart." Independence from Great Britain could have been declared and achieved without this higher principle, said Lincoln, but not something greater, something that "gives *hope* to all," for no oppressed people "will *fight*, and *endure*, as our fathers did, without the promise of something better, than a mere change of masters." Alluding to Proverbs 25:11 ("A word fitly spoken *is like* apples of gold in pictures of silver"), Lincoln offered a metaphor that made the wisdom of the revolutionary generation scriptural:

> The assertion of that *principle*, at *that time*, was *the* word,
> "*fitly spoken*" which has proved an "apple of gold" to us.
> The *Union*, and the *Constitution*, are the *picture* of *silver*,
> subsequently framed around it. The picture was made, not
> to *conceal*, or *destroy* the apple; but to *adorn*, and *preserve* it.
> The *picture* was made *for* the apple—*not* the apple for the
> picture.

Lincoln's "great soul," his "clearness of vision," and his "perfect capacity for sacrifice," thought Du Bois, derived not only from his self-schooling and his integrity but also from "his dreaming."

Understood as a matter of racial justice, the American dream likewise corresponded to the "American Creed" described in Gunnar Myrdal's pathbreaking 1944 study *An American Dilemma: The Negro Problem and Modern Democracy*. Not only whites but also blacks, said Myrdal, embraced this creed, compounded of "the essential dignity of the individual human being, of the fundamental equality of all men, and of certain inalienable rights to freedom, justice, and a fair opportunity." Because the American Creed remained imperfectly achieved, however, the nation was "continuously struggling for its soul"—a struggle joined by King and the SCLC, whose motto was "to redeem the soul of America."

Most certainly, the American dream was personified in the civil rights movement. By dramatizing "the immorality and irrationality" of Jim Crow, wrote the *Atlanta Constitution* publisher Ralph McGill, the students who sat-in at lunch counters and integrated schools brought the phrase to life: "The [American dream] ceased to be a cliché as the words of the Bill of Rights stood up from the printed page and became living symbols in the presence of the first Negro students to pass through the barriers of state laws and screaming pickets into the classrooms of schools and universities." Implausible as it may have seemed at the time, the American dream thus included, too, the promise stated by Robert Kennedy when he avowed that since his brother the Irish Catholic had now been elected president, surely in thirty years an African American could be president.

By the time there was a national holiday in King's honor, his dream had become virtually equivalent to the American dream. Those responding to a 1986 Roper poll that asked, "What individual, either living or dead, famous or not famous, would you say best exemplifies your idea of The American Dream?" mentioned only John F. Kennedy and Abraham Lincoln more often than King. "When I think of King," said the jazz musician Wynton Marsalis on the occasion of the King holiday in 1999, "I think of a man who . . . did the most to advance the meaning and feeling of the Constitution, the Declaration of Independence and the Bill of Rights" in the twentieth century. "He is the single most important person in the fight that America has to be itself." Like the American dream, King's dream *was* America—the original, as yet unrealized nation conceived by the Founding Fathers. Hence the tautological formulation of Langston Hughes, "the dream the dreamers dreamed," which had its own biblical overtones—as in Genesis 37:5 ("And Joseph dreamed a dream, and he told *it* his brethren: and they hated him yet the more") or Deuteronomy 13:1 ("If there arise among you a prophet, or a dreamer of dreams, and giveth thee a sign or a wonder . . . ")—and which King reiterated in a May 1963 sermon,

"What a Mother Should Tell Her Child," when he warned that America was doomed because "she has failed to live up to the great dream of America."

If it was not Mahalia Jackson who prompted King to proclaim his dream for the nation, it could have been Joachim Prinz, whose own speech at the March on Washington, demanding that all citizens act "for the sake of the image, the dream, the idea and the aspiration of America itself," may have triggered King's familiar train of thought. This conception of the dream, as a kind of self-verifying, self-evident truth, reached its most complete formulation in King's sermon "The Negro and the American Dream," preached in September 1960 in Charlotte, North Carolina, as well as in other variants before the Dream speech:

> In a real sense America is essentially a dream—a dream yet unfulfilled. It is the dream of a land where men of all races, colors and creeds will live together as brothers. The substance of the dream is expressed in these sublime words: "We hold these truths to be self-evident, that all men are created equal, that they are endowed by their creator with certain unalienable rights, that among these are life, liberty and the pursuit of happiness." This is the dream. It is a profound, eloquent and unequivocal expression of the dignity and worth of all human personality.

The dream was the nation and the nation was, in turn, the dream. It was the principle of "Liberty to all," on which Lincoln called when he issued the Emancipation Proclamation in 1863 and which King revitalized in its centennial year. It was the promise held in abeyance—the unredeemed promissory note about which King spoke with soaring passion—ever since "the founding fathers of our nation dreamed this dream." If so, added King, the Negro may be "God's instrument to save the soul of America."

■

Nineteen sixty-three was the year of Martin Luther King, Jr. In 1963, wrote King in *Why We Can't Wait*, his chronicle of the year's electrifying conflicts, its ugly brutality, and its beautiful triumphs, blacks "awoke from a stupor of inaction with the cold dash of realization" that one hundred years had passed since the pledge of freedom was signed by "the pen of the Great Emancipator." In 1963 King traveled some 275,000 miles and gave more than 350 speeches. He had acquired such prestige that his simple presence could be a galvanizing force. Admirers as well as detractors, especially younger activists jealous or skeptical of his power, called him "De Lawd." To his legion enemies he was "Martin Luther Coon," "Martin Lucifer King," "Martin Loser King," "Liver Lip Luther," or, according to one Ku Klux Klan newspaper, the "Right Reverend Riot Inciter." In 1963 one word sufficed to describe his dream and sweep his followers into a frenzy: "We will say Freedom, Freedom, Freedom, Freedom, Freedom, Freedom, Freedom, Freedom, to the world!"

Fresh from graduate school and still finishing his dissertation when he assumed his first pastorate at Dexter Avenue Baptist Church in Montgomery, Alabama, King quickly rose to prominence, at the unlikely age of twenty-six, when he was asked to lead the Montgomery Improvement Association, newly formed in December 1955 to challenge the city's segregated buses after a respected local seamstress, Rosa Parks, refused to relinquish her seat to a white man. In his first speech to the association, prepared with less than a half hour's notice and delivered in the Holt Street Baptist Church, King instantly struck a number of themes and spoke in the ornate metaphorical style that would characterize his oratory in sermon after sermon, speech after speech:

> And you know, my friends, there comes a time when a people
> get tired of being trampled over by the iron feet of oppres-

sion. There comes a time, my friends, when people get tired of being plunged across the abyss of humiliation, where they experience the bleakness of nagging despair. There comes a time when people get tired of being pushed out of the glittering sunlight of life's July and left standing amid the piercing chill of an alpine November.

We are here, we are here this evening because we're tired now. And I want to say that we are not here advocating violence. We have never done that. I want it to be known throughout Montgomery and throughout this nation that we are Christian people. We believe in the Christian religion. We believe in the teachings of Jesus. The only weapon that we have in our hands this evening is the weapon of protest. That's all.

And certainly, certainly, this is the glory of America, with all its faults. This is the glory of our democracy. If we were incarcerated behind the iron curtain of a Communistic nation we couldn't do this. If we were dropped in the dungeon of a totalitarian regime we couldn't do this. But the great glory of American democracy is the right to protest for right. My friends, don't let anybody make us feel that we are to be compared in our actions with the Ku Klux Klan or with the White Citizens Council. There will be no crosses burned at any bus stops in Montgomery. There will be no white persons pulled out of their homes and taken out on some distant road and lynched for not cooperating. There will be nobody amid, among us who will stand up and defy the Constitution of this nation. We only assemble here because of our desire to see right exist.

This was powerful enough for a largely extemporaneous speech, but King suddenly rose to a new level of eloquence and authority. In a signature use of repetition that elevated his message to a transcendent height, King made himself one with the greatest dreamer of them all:

> And we are not wrong, we are not wrong in what we are
> doing. If we are wrong, the Supreme Court of this nation
> is wrong. If we are wrong, the Constitution of the United
> States is wrong. If we are wrong, God Almighty is wrong.
> If we are wrong, Jesus of Nazareth was merely a utopian
> dreamer that never came down to earth. If we are wrong,
> justice is a lie. Love has no meaning. And we are determined
> here in Montgomery to work and fight until justice rolls
> down like water, and righteousness like a mighty stream.

For more than a year, despite the loss of jobs, arrests, cross-burnings, bombings, and court injunctions, Montgomery's black residents car-pooled and walked to work to protest the city's Jim Crow bus laws. The boycott's stunning success—the Supreme Court held the city's segregation ordinances to be unconstitutional in November 1956—proved that the strategy of nonviolent direct action, the philosophy of Mohandas Gandhi brought to the streets of the American South, could be as powerful as a legal brief.

Whereas the nation's oldest and most prominent civil rights organization, the National Association for the Advancement of Colored People (NAACP), preferred the courtroom strategies of its legal arm, the NAACP Legal Defense Fund, King and the SCLC, formed as an outgrowth of the Montgomery movement, advocated direct confrontation with the forces of segregation. In the wake of *Brown v. Board of Education* (1954), thought by many southerners to constitute an illegal usurpation of states' rights, much of the South undertook a campaign of "massive resistance" to evade the school desegregation ordered by the Supreme Court and to forestall it in other facilities and services. In response, said King at the first annual meeting of the Institute of Nonviolence and Social Change, "we must speed up the coming of the inevitable," even if it means facing "physical death," a price worth paying "to free [our] children from a permanent life of psychological death."

King concluded this speech, given a year into the bus boycott, as he did his more famous one at the March on Washington, with a sonorous quotation from "America"—"My country, 'tis of thee, sweet land of liberty, of thee I sing"—followed by an expansive, exhilarating command that "freedom must ring from every mountainside," from the "prodigious hill tops of New Hampshire" and the "curvaceous slopes of California" to "every hill and mountain of Alabama." Already, he had conceived of his campaign against the segregationist doctrine of states' rights in constitutional terms meant to embrace the whole republic and all its citizens.

Montgomery was only one step, but it resounded throughout the South and turned King, a handsome man with a beautiful voice, an unnerving self-assurance, and a calm demeanor, into a national figure. Whether or not King's victory in Montgomery could be compared to that of the attorneys who prevailed in *Brown*, said *Time* magazine when it put him on its cover in 1957, "King reached beyond lawbooks and writs, beyond violence and threats, to win his people—and challenge all people—with a spiritual force that aspired even to ending prejudice in man's mind."

During the next several years, however, King and the SCLC enjoyed only sporadic success. King returned to Atlanta, his birthplace, joining his father, Martin Luther King, Sr., as co-pastor of Ebenezer Baptist Church, which would remain his home church for the remainder of his life. He traveled extensively, speaking on civil rights and giving guest sermons throughout the nation; wrote and published his first book, *Stride toward Freedom* (1958), with the editorial assistance of Stanley Levison; visited India to find out more about Gandhi's methods of nonviolent protest; contemplated a strategy modeled on the evangelical crusades of Billy Graham; and cast about for a battle in which he could replicate the success of Montgomery. Even as King's allies worried about the movement's becoming too dependent on the magnetism of a single leader— "people have to be made to understand that they cannot look for salvation anywhere but to themselves," said Ella Baker, a longtime NAACP activist and executive director of the SCLC—other fronts were opening in the war for African American rights.

Although sit-in protests had been tried with limited success as early as the 1940s, they first became key weapons in the integration of public facilities—restaurants, parks, theaters, libraries, and other public venues—in 1960 after college students in Greensboro, North Carolina, endured days of harassment in attempting to be served at their local Woolworth's lunch counter. Exemplifying King's nonviolent direct action, the sit-in movement spread rapidly throughout the South, with tens of thousands of people, young people in particular, protesting segregated facilities in more than one hundred cities and towns by the end of 1960, in the process discovering an exceptional strength of purpose and independence. A student SCLC conference gave birth to the Student Nonviolent Coordinating Committee (SNCC), whose younger activists, led by John Lewis, strengthened the movement's organizational base but soon favored more aggressive tactics than the SCLC was ready to countenance. The following year, and renewing a form of protest that had first been employed by the Congress of Racial Equality (CORE) in the late 1940s, groups of young blacks and whites working together initiated the Freedom Rides, intended to integrate interstate buses and bus stations throughout the South. Riders were viciously attacked at several stops, and only reluctantly, after much bloodshed, did the Kennedy administration intervene to protect the protestors.

Despite his campaign promises, President John F. Kennedy had proved to be hesitant about black civil rights, preferring low-key action in support of voting rights and disclaiming the authority to use federal force until pressed to the extreme, as when federal troops were required to protect the Freedom Riders or to ensure the safe enrollment of James Meredith at the University of Mississippi in October 1962. Until the summer of 1963, Kennedy's prosecution of the Cold War rivaled his fear of alienating southern Democrats. (Kennedy has a plan to put a man on the moon in ten years, wrote King in the spring of 1962, but no plan "to put a Negro in the State Legislature of Alabama.") However much Kennedy wanted a civil rights victory that would show the world, especially nations in the throes of anticolonial revolt, that the United States, not the Soviet Union, offered true freedom, he also knew it could jeopardize his hoped-for reelection in 1964. Kennedy opposed the Freedom Rides and King's nonviolent direct action campaigns not out of principle, nor with confidence in his own legal position, but because black protest harmed him politically in the South and provoked reactionary white violence certain to make the United States look bad in the eyes of enemies and allies alike.

King had expected more from Kennedy. When King had been arrested at an Atlanta sit-in during the fall of 1960, what should have been a routine booking turned into a sentence of four months at hard labor in the state penitentiary, because King had forgotten that he was on probation for a previous traffic violation. Then in the final weeks of his presidential campaign against Richard Nixon, Kennedy used his influence to have King released, much to his political credit since it gained him the implicit allegiance of King and his father, a lifelong Republican. In a momentous reversal of black support stretching back to the days of Lincoln, the decided advantage enjoyed by Republicans among black voters, though it had begun to weaken in the 1930s, collapsed in the 1960 election. This political sea change, which would be felt for decades to come, was even more evident by the summer of 1963, when blacks supported

Kennedy by a 30-to-1 margin and only 10 percent continued to identify themselves as Republicans.

At a 1961 White House luncheon for civil rights leaders, King noticed an engraving of the Emancipation Proclamation in the Lincoln Room, prompting him to say to Kennedy, "Mr. President, I'd like to see you stand in this room and sign a Second Emancipation Proclamation outlawing segregation, one hundred years after Lincoln's. You could base it on the Fourteenth Amendment." Encouraged by Kennedy's seeming interest, King soon delivered to the president a leather-bound draft of such a proclamation, "An Appeal to the President of the United States for National Rededication to the Principles of the Emancipation Proclamation." King challenged Kennedy to make himself the "conscience of America," like Lincoln a century earlier—"The time has come, Mr. President, to let those dawn-like rays of freedom, first glimpsed in 1863, fill the heavens with the noonday sunlight of complete human dignity"—and he went so far as to request that the Lincoln Memorial be reserved for midnight ceremonies on New Year's Eve 1962. The president, however, was less receptive than he seemed. His participation in the September 22 centennial of the Preliminary Emancipation Proclamation at the Lincoln Memorial was limited to a taped message, and rather than issue any kind of proclamation on January 1, 1963, Kennedy staged a White House reception in honor of Lincoln's birthday the following month. King chose not to attend.

The symbolic value of 1963 as the centennial of the Emancipation Proclamation entered into virtually everything King did, said, and wrote at the time. If he did not find a way to capitalize on the centennial—to return to "the one moment in the country's history when a bold, brave *start* had been made" and resume "that noble journey toward the goals reflected in the Preamble of the Constitution, the Constitution itself, the Bill of Rights, and the Thirteenth, Fourteenth and Fifteenth Amendments"—it would be a great opportunity squandered. By the end of 1962, SNCC had eclipsed the SCLC in the sit-in movement, CORE had taken the lead in the Freedom Rides, and police chief Laurie Pritchett had outmaneuvered King in his effort to desegregate public facilities in Albany, Georgia. Lacking a clear sense of direction, King needed a challenge that could harness the movement's energy and keep it from being channeled into the greater militancy urged by SNCC, not to mention the antagonistic black nationalism and rejection of nonviolence espoused by Malcolm X.

When King, at the invitation of Fred Shuttlesworth, a local minister and leader of the Alabama Christian Movement for Human Rights, came to Birmingham in early 1963, he faced not only a newly elected governor, George Wallace, who in his inaugural speech had declared, "Segregation now, segregation tomorrow, segregation forever!" Nor did he face only a city whose reputation for the violent enforcement of segregation had earned it the nickname "Bombingham." He also faced the ire of the president and the attorney general, no less than the white ministers he addressed in "Letter from Birmingham Jail," all of whom considered his protests unwise and untimely. That, however, was precisely the point. Perhaps his actions were "ill-timed," King replied to Kennedy, reiterating his argument to the ministers. "Frankly, I have never engaged in a direct-action movement that did not seem ill-timed." Where the Kennedy administration counseled caution and deliberation, King believed, as he put it in the Dream speech, that this was "no time to engage in the luxury of cooling off or to take the tranquilizing drug of gradualism."

Although King and Shuttlesworth postponed their campaign long enough for a mayoral contest to be decided, they set it in motion immediately thereafter, despite the fact that the moderate candidate had won. Gandhi had taught King how to use protest to provoke a public crisis, even at the cost of violence unleashed against protestors, but Albany had shown him the importance of choosing his targets wisely. In Birmingham's hot-headed commissioner of public safety, Eugene "Bull" Connor, the defeated mayoral candidate, King was confident he had his man. Smaller-scale protests starting in 1962 had prepared the city's blacks for more aggressive action, and a carefully devised plan of escalation—"Project C" for "confrontation"—had been set forth by King's aide Wyatt T. Walker. The goal was to desegregate Birmingham stores and other facilities, as well as force the hiring of blacks by businesses and city services. The method was to fill the city's jails.

Initial results were disappointing, however, with the number of arrests too few to get significant national headlines or provide any leverage with the city. Seeking to make his own sacrifice galvanizing, King defied a court injunction against further protests and, on Good Friday, went to jail along with Ralph Abernathy and others. It was the thirteenth time King had been arrested in a civil rights protest. His solitary confinement over the Easter weekend produced his single greatest essay, "Letter from Birmingham Jail," written first on scraps of newspaper and then on paper smuggled in and out by his attorneys. Reprinted frequently in the weeks before the March on Washington, the "Letter," many of its ideas drawn from King's earlier sermons and speeches, helped prepare the way for his August success, but the April arrest that produced it failed to stir massive protest in his support.

The Birmingham campaign seemed close to collapse when James Bevel persuaded King to let students, including children as young as six years old, join in. Just when the media had begun to lose interest, Bevel's dangerous ploy not only turned the Birmingham campaign around; it also rescued King from what might have been a setback serious enough to end his leadership. What became known as the Children's Crusade brought thousands of young protestors into the streets—some twelve hundred of them would be arrested—and unleashed a furious response from Bull Connor. Unable to halt the waves of children streaming out of the Sixteenth Street Baptist Church, the staging ground that launched the young protestors through Kelly Ingram Park and toward downtown Birmingham, Connor ordered the use of truncheons, fire hoses, and attack dogs. "I want to see the dogs work," shouted Connor. "Look at those niggers run."

The vast majority of whites, as well as many blacks, condemned the use of children in the Birmingham campaign. To which Wyatt T. Walker replied, "Negro children will get a better education in five days in jail than in five months in a segregated school." Day after day, the children of Birmingham and the parents who joined them were brutalized and arrested—all so that they could try on clothing in a downtown store, eat in the same restaurants as whites, play baseball in the same park. When asked by a policeman what she expected to get by going to jail, a tiny girl replied simply, "F'eedom." "No Gabriel trumpet," wrote King of the incident, "could have sounded a truer note."

And the whole world was watching.

Having been denied the normal means of political redress through elected officials, as well as journalistic and public forums, King said later, blacks "had to write their most persuasive essays with the blunt pen of marching ranks." He might better have said the "blunt camera of marching ranks." Print media attention to the civil rights movement increased dramatically as a result of Birmingham and the March on Washington—*New York Times* coverage doubled in 1963 and then again in 1964, for example—but even though stories and photographs were powerful in their own right, televised coverage was all the more visceral. By 1963, when the three networks expanded their evening news from fifteen minutes to thirty minutes, more than 90 percent of American households had at least one television. Primetime may have been dominated by amusements such as *The Andy Griffith Show*, which evoked a tranquil southern world impervious to change, but that same year, according to a Roper poll, the majority of Americans for the first time ranked television, rather than newspapers, as their top source of news among various media. Said one reporter of the networks' civil rights coverage, with only some exaggeration, "we made it impossible for Congress not to act."

Beginning with the Montgomery bus boycott, King had a keen instinct for the galvanizing power of the media. His captivating personality and august speaking style were ready-made for television—in this regard he surpassed Kennedy, often hailed as the first politician to exploit the new medium—and he quickly realized how to use the media to the movement's benefit. "Public relations is a very necessary part of any protest [or] civil disobedience," King wrote to Harold Courlander in 1961. "Without the presence of the press," he said, "there might have been [an] untold massacre in the South." At the same time, however, his theory of nonviolent direct action—the cultivation of "soul force" through the deliberate creation of moments of highly publicized crisis—depended on provoking the very reaction that would make not just national but worldwide news. Only the "luminous glare" of photography and television, "revealing the naked truth to the whole world," King said of the nonviolent crusade of 1963, could make evident the riveting brutality of the South's response. "A newspaper or television picture of a snarling dog set upon a human being," commented CBS's Eric Sevareid, "is recorded in the permanent photoelectronic file of every human brain" (figure 2).

Not only was the nation at large, including many in the South, sickened by what they saw, so too was the president. Strained negotiations, punctuated by outbreaks of violence that led finally to Kennedy's federalization of the Alabama National Guard, lasted into June before a desegregation settlement, encompassing most of the protestors' demands, was reached. Segregation was dealt another serious blow when Governor George Wallace, who attempted personally to block the registration of two black students at the University of Alabama, thus physically enacting the doctrine of "interposition," was forced aside by federal authority (figure 3). The face-saving gesture permitted him by Kennedy did little to conceal Wallace's humiliation. If "segregation forever" had become an empty threat, however, this was far clearer in hindsight than it was in the summer of 1963.

Having quashed Wallace but facing bloody clashes that rippled through other cities, Kennedy decided to propose new civil rights legislation in a televised speech on June 11. In doing so, he effectively paid tribute to the power of King's nonviolent direct action as a component of the nation's legislative and constitutional deliberations. "Now the time has come for this nation to fulfill its promise," said Kennedy. "The events in Birmingham and elsewhere have so increased the cries for equality that no city or state or legislative body can prudently choose to ignore them." Returning home late that night, Medgar Evers, field secretary for the Mississippi NAACP, was murdered by a white supremacist. A near riot followed Evers's memorial service in Jackson, and subsequent violence in a number of cities set the uneasy tone for the summer to come, when the Department of Justice reported more than one thousand demonstrations in more than two hundred cities across three dozen states.

Nevertheless, on the eve of the March on Washington, King was so hopeful that he declared that "race and color prejudice will have all but disappeared in their most obvious forms in the next five years." Although his optimism would prove wildly unrealistic, it seemed corroborated by the mood among blacks. According to a *Newsweek–Brink-Harris* poll, an unprecedented number of blacks were willing to engage in protest: 40 percent of those surveyed said they had already participated in a sit-in, a mass demonstration, or the picketing of a store; 48 percent said they were willing to take part in protests even if it meant going to jail. Perhaps because of their new assertiveness, blacks also tended to be more optimistic than whites about where they would stand five years hence: 67 percent thought their pay would be better and 64 percent their work situation; 62 percent thought they would have better housing, while 58 percent thought their children would have the benefit of integrated education. If they were somewhat less optimistic about access to public accommodations and voting rights, a considerable 73 percent, as well as 93 percent of black leaders, expected white attitudes toward them to improve.

Indeed, they already had improved. Whereas near the end of World War II only 45 percent of whites believed that blacks should have an equal opportunity to compete for any type of job, by 1963 the figure stood at 80 percent. When *Time* magazine named King its "Man of the Year" for 1963, it proclaimed that the March on Washington "made irreversible all that had gone before in the year of the Negro revolution," which saw more gains than in any year since the end of the Civil War. King had begun his speech by standing in the "symbolic shadow" of Lincoln. In *Time*'s illustration, King now cast his own shadow (figure 4).

■

Everyone involved in the civil rights movement "now remembers having dreamed up the March on Washington, and in a way everyone is right," wrote Ralph Abernathy in his 1989 autobiography. Inspired by many motives and coalescing from many directions, "it was an idea that recommended itself." The germ of the SCLC's commitment to the March, according to Andrew Young, was James Bevel's proposal to stage a dramatic march of eight thousand people from Birmingham to Washington, D.C., a distance of twelve hundred miles, modeled on Gandhi's famous Salt March to the Sea. Only half-joking, Bayard Rustin told Thomas Gentile, one of the

March's first historians, that its real organizers were "Bull Connor, his police dogs and his fire hoses." In their meeting with Kennedy afterward, Roy Wilkins said the March proved that it was not the assembled leaders who were the moving force behind the civil rights movement but the "people from back home" who "dreamed up this civil rights business." Calvin Hernton surmised that the inspiration for the March came from disaffected urban blacks—"field Negroes in the ghettoes," as Hernton called them—who started talking about "storming the White House, tying up Congress, and even lying down on the runways of airports."

Since late 1962 A. Philip Randolph, head of the Brotherhood of Sleeping Car Porters and president of the Negro American Labor Council (NALC), and Bayard Rustin, a World War II pacifist and longtime civil rights activist, had been planning an "Emancipation March to Washington for Jobs" to be staged in October 1963, with the first day to be spent lobbying Congress and the White House and the second in a mass march. Randolph's proposed march garnered only lukewarm support from civil rights organizations, however, including neither the NAACP nor the National Urban League. King's success in Birmingham gave the idea new momentum and a new name, the "March on Washington for Jobs and Freedom," and his negotiations with Randolph pressured both the NAACP and the National Urban League into joining CORE, the NALC, the SCLC, and SNCC in backing the march. Official planning documents fittingly spoke of the March as "the climax to the people's commemoration of the Emancipation Proclamation of 1863."

Along with Randolph and King, the leaders of the other organizations constituted a planning group known as the "Big Six": Roy Wilkins, executive secretary of the NAACP; James Farmer, national director of CORE; John Lewis, chairman of SNCC; and Whitney Young, executive director of the National Urban League. To this group four others were eventually added, making it the "Big Ten":

Joachim Prinz, chairman of the American Jewish Congress; Eugene Carson Blake, vice chairman of the Commission on Race Relations of the National Council of Churches of Christ in America; Mathew Ahmann, executive director of the National Catholic Conference for Interracial Justice; and Walter Reuther, president of the United Automobile, Aerospace, and Agricultural Implement Workers of America, AFL-CIO. Bayard Rustin was named deputy director and given the enormous job of organizing the event. All ten leaders, as well as Rustin, would speak on August 28, but only one would be remembered.

Although there was some discussion of nonviolent demonstrations, such as a mass prayer vigil encircling the Capitol, and SNCC lobbied for civil disobedience that would paralyze the city, it quickly became apparent that such actions would be counterproductive. Anxious about the prospects for his civil rights bill, Kennedy told March leaders that he wanted no one in Congress to be able to say, "Yes, I'm for the bill—but not at the point of a gun." August 28 was chosen because Congress would still be in session before its Labor Day recess. ("Think they're listening?" asked Bob Dylan as he looked toward the Capitol during the event. "No, they ain't listening at all.") Eventual support for the March from a long list of labor and church organizations guaranteed that it would be carried out by a "bi-racial army," in a phrase appearing in King's prepared text but omitted in delivery, one that was about 25 percent white, according to most estimates. The ubiquitous lapel buttons depicting black and white hands clasped in unity were testimony to King's own interracial message at the March: "The marvelous new militancy which has engulfed the Negro community must not lead us to a distrust of all white people, for many of our white brothers, as evidenced by their presence here today, have come to realize that their destiny is tied up with our destiny. And they have come to realize that their freedom is inextricably bound to our freedom. We cannot walk alone."

In the words of one press release, the March on Washington was intended to be "a living petition—in the flesh—of the scores of thousands of citizens of both races," from all parts of the country, who would be orderly but not subservient, proud but not arrogant, nonviolent but not timid, outspoken but not raucous. As "the living, beating heart of an infinitely noble movement," in King's subsequent description, the March would be carried out by "an army without guns, but not without strength," its most powerful weapon being "love"—plus worldwide media attention.

From our vantage point, the March seems the symbolic culmination of black protest reaching back to abolitionism. At once peaceable and patriotic, it was also, like the whole of the civil rights movement, driven by a strong-willed, nearly martial faith. Think only of the movement's music, where marching was a central theme in any number of the slave spirituals and hymns reborn as civil rights anthems: "Onward Christian Soldiers" ("Marching as to war, / With the cross of Jesus going on before"), which reverberated through Holt Street Baptist Church the night King was chosen to lead the Montgomery Improvement Association; "Children, You'll Be Called On" ("To march in the field of battle," to be a "soldier of the cross"); "We Are Soldiers in the Army" ("We got to hold up the freedom banner, / We got to hold it up until we die"); "The Battle Hymn of the Republic," whose apocalyptic lyrics—

> Mine eyes have seen the glory of the coming of the Lord:
> He is trampling out the vintage where the grapes of wrath
>   are stored;
> He hath loosed the fateful lightning of his terrible swift
>   sword:
> His truth is marching on

—made the Civil War an agent of the nation's millennial salvation before they were recited a century later by King at the conclusion of the 1965 voting rights march from Selma to Montgomery; and "Ain't Gonna Let Nobody Turn Me Around" ("I'm gonna keep on a-walkin', Lord, / Keep on a-talkin', Lord, / Marching up to freedom land"), which was second only to "We Shall Overcome," which King called "the battle hymn of the movement," in filling activists with the courage to face police dogs, beatings, and jail.

Given new impetus during World War II, the very idea of the protest march promised liberation—one way or another. Once the war is over, "millions of marching blacks of the southland must pack up and move," wrote Adam Clayton Powell, Jr., in *Marching Blacks* (1945). "Freedom road is no longer an unmarked trail in the wilderness. It is a highway." The historic marches of the civil rights movement—the March on Washington itself, the voting rights march of 1965, James Meredith's one-man 1966 "March Against Fear," joined by King, Stokely Carmichael, and others after Meredith was shot and wounded—renewed the "American Exodus," as Powell called it, but with this difference. Rather than leave the South, marchers would stand and fight in the South. The Promised Land was no longer distant in time and place: it was *here* and *now*, if only the marchers, as Lillian Smith said of the Freedom Riders, had the courage to "climb into the unknown."

For many younger black activists, however, there was only a thin line, or none at all, between martial faith and martial action. When the chant of "Black Power" rose up in Greenwood, Mississippi, during the Meredith march, or when Malcolm X called for "a black nationalist army," not to mention when the Black Panthers began patrolling the streets of Oakland and the corridors of the California State Capitol with rifles and live ammunition, marching blacks might have seemed instead to incarnate the fearsome admonition John Adams included in an 1821 letter to Thomas Jefferson: "Slavery in this Country I have seen hanging over it like a black cloud for half a Century. . . . I might probably say I had seen Armies of Negroes marching and counter-marching in the air, shining in Armour."

King dreaded nothing more than that the March on Washington would turn violent. He was hardly alone. Bill Mauldin's syndicated political cartoon for August 24, 1963, depicted several long phalanxes of people, mainly black, converging on and then climbing up and into a large powder keg labeled "Washington, D.C." (figure 5). March security was provided by fifty-nine hundred District of Columbia police officers, seventeen hundred National Guardsmen, and three hundred police reservists. At nearby military bases four thousand soldiers and marines were on alert. Fears that any aspect of the March might appear to promote or justify violence led organizers to demand that SNCC representative John Lewis edit his planned speech, after Patrick O'Boyle, archbishop of the Diocese of Washington, D.C., who was to give the invocation, saw an advance draft and refused to participate were the speech not altered.

Incensed that the Kennedy administration was turning what was supposed to be a protest against the government's neglect of civil rights into an occasion to demonstrate its support, Lewis wanted to say that the president's proposed bill was "too little, too late" and ask "which side" the federal government was on. More than that, he intended to issue an ultimatum:

> We won't stop now. All the forces of [Mississippi Senator James] Eastland, [Mississippi Governor Ross] Barnett, [Alabama Governor George] Wallace, and [South Carolina Senator Strom] Thurmond won't stop this revolution. The time will come when we will not confine our marching to Washington. We will march through the South, through the heart of Dixie, the way Sherman did. We shall pursue our own "scorched earth" policy and burn Jim Crow to the ground— nonviolently. We shall fragment the South into a thousand

pieces and put them back together in the image of democracy. We will make the actions of the past few months look petty.

Compared to the rhetoric of Malcolm X—or even James Baldwin, whose best-selling 1963 book *The Fire Next Time* ended with a slave spiritual's prophetic warning, *"God gave Noah the rainbow sign, No more water, the fire next time"*—Lewis's words were not truly incendiary. Notwithstanding his coy use of the word *nonviolently*, however, his "scorched earth" challenge to the South's leading segregationists seemed preparation for war.

"I have waited twenty-two years for this," said a tearful A. Philip Randolph to Lewis, when he resisted making any changes in his speech. "I've waited all my life for this opportunity. Please don't ruin it." No one had a greater right to request that Lewis tone down his speech. The March on Washington, said the *Pittsburgh Courier*, might better be known as "A. Philip Randolph Day." Without him, there might still have been a March, but it would not have been the culmination of *his* dream, as in fact it was (figure 6). In response to Randolph's threat to lead one hundred thousand blacks in a march on the White House and Congress in June 1941, President Franklin Roosevelt had issued an executive order ending discrimination by governmental agencies and manufacturers with defense contracts. The order also created the Committee on Fair Employment Practices, which, although it was allowed to die in a matter of years, led later to the Equal Employment Opportunity Commission, initiated by President Kennedy's executive order creating a predecessor committee and given a mandate by the Civil Rights Act of 1964.

Although the demonstrations envisioned by Randolph never materialized—he also called off a planned march after President Harry Truman desegregated the military in 1948—the March on Washington Movement, as it came to be called, provided a model for the 1963 March on Washington. Mass demonstrations, wrote Randolph in 1944, because they can awaken common people and involve them in a crusade for justice, are "worth a million editorials and orations in anybody's paper and on anybody's platform." In his earlier "Call to Negro America," in fact, Randolph had spoken more in the spirit of John Lewis: "Negroes can build a mammoth machine of mass action with a terrific and tremendous driving and striking power that can shatter and crush the evil fortress of race prejudice and hate. . . . An 'all-out' thundering march on Washington, ending in a monster and huge demonstration at Lincoln's Monument, will shake up white America."

When King said of his Birmingham campaign that it was carried out by "a special army, with no supplies but its sincerity, no uniform but its determination, no arsenal but its faith," his language sounded familiar because it was the language of Gandhi fused with that of the African American church. It was also familiar, however, because it was the language of wartime and postwar black patriotism. "By fighting for their rights now," said Randolph in 1942, "American Negroes are helping to make America a moral and spiritual arsenal of democracy" as well as contributing to the "global war for freedom." Among the signs carried by Howard University students attempting to desegregate a Washington, D.C., cafeteria in 1944 was one that read, "Are you for HITLER's Way (Race Supremacy) or the AMERICAN Way (Equality)? Make Up Your Mind!" The March on Washington would be successful only if it was peaceful, but the very idea implied a force both disciplined and powerful, a martial force that linked the Civil War to the civil rights movement by finishing the wartime African American campaign for "Double V"—victory abroad over totalitarianism and victory at home over segregation.

When Gunnar Myrdal argued that if the United States would act on "the century-old dream of American patriots," it would acquire "the trust and the support of all good people on earth"; when Truman's Committee on Civil Rights concluded that "*the United States is not so strong, the final triumph of the democratic ideal is not so inevitable that we can ignore what the world thinks of our record"*; or when Kenneth Clark, whose experiments in the psychology of race were cited prominently in *Brown v. Board of Education*, contended that the achievement of equality for the nation's minorities would create "a stronger bulwark of democracy for all," each cast back to 1776 by way of 1863. Each, too, might simply have quoted Abraham Lincoln, whose objection to slavery grew in part from his belief that "it deprives our republican example of its just influence in the world—enables the enemies of free institutions, with plausibility, to taunt us as hypocrites—causes the real friends of freedom to doubt our sincerity."

"It is not Russia that threatens the United States so much as Mississippi," said W. E. B. Du Bois in a petition submitted to the United Nations for redress of African American "human rights" violations. The case was hardly so clear-cut, however, and Du Bois, speaking as a Soviet sympathizer at a time when *freedom* and *individualism* under capitalism were starkly opposed in mainstream American thought to *slavery* and *collectivism* under communism, was a voice in the wilderness. If World War II catalyzed the civil rights movement, the Cold War introduced a polarizing standoff. Civil rights advocates argued that segregation was a manifestation of un-American fascist tendencies and that discrimination pushed blacks toward communism, Du Bois being a case in point. Their opponents charged that agitation, not to mention federal action, on behalf of black rights played into the hands of communists both at home and abroad. When the Supreme Court ruled in *Shelley v. Kraemer* (1948) that state enforcement of restrictive housing covenants prohibiting the sale or lease of property to nonwhites was unconstitutional, Representative John Rankin of Mississippi thus declared on the House floor: "Mr. Speaker, there must have been a celebration in Moscow last night." Nor was the cause of the March well served, even fifteen years later, when Roy Wilkins received a congratulatory telegram from Chinese Premier Mao Zedong.

The frequent allegation by southern politicians that King was a communist or the tool of communists, an allegation abetted by FBI leaks and smears to that effect, was only the most glaring instance of the roadblock posed by Cold War politics. It made little difference to George Wallace or to FBI Director J. Edgar Hoover that King explicitly rejected communism. "Since for the Communist there is no divine government, no absolute moral order," King wrote in 1958, borrowing from a sermon by Robert McCracken, "almost anything—force, violence, murder, lying—is a justifiable means to the 'millennial' end." (In this, he was in line with Randolph, whose program for the March on Washington Movement condemned communism as "a pestilence, menace and nuisance to the Negro people," and argued that it was "suicidal for Negroes to add to the handicap of being *Black*, another handicap of being *Red*.") Responding to charges of communist influence among his staff, King had the temerity to say on the television program *Face the Nation* that, given the violence and discrimination they faced, it was "amazing how few Negroes have turned to communism." Yet only after he appeared to cut his ties to Jack O'Dell and Stanley Levison, two close aides suspected of being communists, could King be confident of Kennedy's support for the March on Washington.

■

When at last it came, the March on Washington came "like a force of nature. Like a whirlwind, like a storm, like a flood," wrote *Ebony* editor Lerone Bennett, Jr. What might easily have become a "meaningless gesture . . . a prayer said to the wind" was redeemed by the many thousands of people who traveled by bus, by car, by train, and by plane from Seattle, Los Angeles, Dallas, Miami, Las Vegas, Little Rock, Milwaukee, Detroit, and hundreds of other cities and towns.

More than nine hundred chartered buses and a dozen special trains arrived from New York City alone. Members of CORE's Brooklyn chapter walked to Washington. Eighty-two-year-old Jay Hardo bicycled from Dayton, Ohio. Ledger Smith roller-skated from Chicago. Among the 260 Alabamans leaving by bus from Kelly Ingram Park, site of the confrontations with Bull Connor, twenty-year-old Willie Leonard said, "I guess you could call me a combination freedom rider and tourist on this trip."

The logistics were staggering. In addition to its enormous security detail, the March required nearly three hundred portable toilets, twenty-one drinking fountains, thirty-two first aid stations, and sixty-four ambulances. Two hundred ushers were engaged. Volunteers prepared eighty thousand cheese sandwiches. Others painted signs with slogans, officially approved by March leaders, such as "We Demand Voting Rights Now!" "We March for First-Class Citizenship Now!" "End Segregated Rules in Public Schools," and "America Has a Century-Old Debt to Pay, Contracted on Emancipation Day" (figure 7). Rustin and his staff sent out thousands of pamphlets detailing how the March and its program were to be conducted and enlisted hundreds of marshals to oversee every aspect—travel, parking, marching orders, seating for dignitaries, sound systems, and trash cleanup. Celebrities both black and white, including Jackie Robinson, Marlon Brando, Lena Horne, Burt Lancaster, Charlton Heston, and Sidney Poitier, were much in evidence and much photographed, and some of the most popular singers allied with the civil rights movement—Joan Baez, Bob Dylan, Odetta, and Peter, Paul, and Mary, as well as the SNCC Freedom Singers—serenaded the crowd before and during the March. Other than those singing, however, women played a small role in the March, a fact that angered those who had been as much on the front lines in the southern struggle as the men. At the last minute, organizers added a short "Tribute to Negro Women Freedom Fighters" at which Rosa

Parks, Ella Baker, Diane Nash, and others were introduced, and Daisy Bates, a leader in the desegregation of Central High School in Little Rock, Arkansas, spoke briefly.

The official estimate of the crowd was 250,000, although the African American newspaper the *Chicago Defender* introduced its coverage of the event with a huge banner headline reading "300,000 March! Greatest Day in U.S. History," and some observers thought the crowd was up to a third larger. Despite the mammoth throng, there was virtually no disorder. A counterprotest by George Lincoln Rockwell and the American Nazi Party was squelched by police, and only four people, all white, were arrested: one neo-Nazi, two hecklers, and a health insurance employee who drove to work with a loaded shotgun. The size of the crowd made it more of a meandering stroll than a march. A large contingent wandered down the mall ahead of time, leaving the leaders struggling to keep up, and Marian Anderson, slated to sing the national anthem, was prevented by the surge from reaching the platform in time. In any case, it was a parade largely without spectators. Wary of traffic problems and disorder, most Washington residents stayed home, so that the protestors were effectively performing for themselves and, more important, for the media, a fact crucial to the success of the March and King's speech.

In a city that had in years past seen a number of large protest marches and would see many more in years to come, the March on Washington would still have been an impressive feat of orchestrated demonstration, whatever its audience.* Without television, however,

---

* The March on Washington was preceded by the unemployed workers' protest of Coxey's Army (1894); the Woman Suffrage Procession and Pageant (1913); the Veterans' Bonus March (1932); the Prayer Pilgrimage for Freedom (1957); and the Youth Marches for Integrated Schools (1958, 1959). It was followed by the Poor People's Campaign (1968); the Mobilization against the Vietnam War (1969); the antiabortion March for Life (1973); a twentieth-anniversary revival in the March on

it would not have been a spectacle remembered by millions almost as though they had been present. In this respect, the March conformed to Daniel Boorstin's definition, in his 1961 book *The Image*, of the "pseudo-event": the planned, rather than spontaneous, news event whose staging and packaging make it newsworthy. "What happens on television will overshadow what happens off television," wrote Boorstin. In addition to coverage of the March by all major American print and broadcast media, there were press corps from numerous countries—in the Soviet Union, the Communist Party organ *Izvestia* devoted its entire front page to the event, part of its relentless coverage of American racial strife—as well as film crews from Great Britain, Germany, Japan, France, and Canada. Broadcast live in its entirety by CBS, and in part by NBC and ABC, the mass pilgrimage to the most sacred site of the nation's civil religion was grand public theater, and its star performer was Martin Luther King, Jr. (figure 8).

Not just the event, therefore, but the way it was covered and distributed by the media, including several quickly released LPs, proved decisive.* Reporters and newscasters typically underscored

---

Washington for Jobs, Peace, and Freedom, attended by some three hundred thousand people (1983, with a less successful sequel in 1993); the abortion rights March for Women's Lives, which drew some five hundred thousand (1992); the March on Washington for Lesbian, Gay, and Bi Equal Rights and Liberation (1993); the Nation of Islam's Million Man March (1995); the Multiracial Solidarity March (1996); the pro–gun control Million Mom March (2000); and, in a final declension at century's end, the Million Mutt March, on behalf of unwanted dogs (2000). The Lincoln Memorial provided a backdrop to most of these events, as well many others, including rallies on behalf of military personnel missing in action, those suffering from AIDS, victims of drunk drivers, Americans held hostage in Iran, or human rights in China, Cuba, Pakistan, South Africa, and other countries.

*Competing recordings soon made the speeches widely available, even as they generated disputes over rights that foreshadowed disputes over the ownership of King's words that went on long after his death. King had agreed to let the Motown

the pacific, festive atmosphere. Veterans of the movement from the South projected a crusading zeal, wrote James Reston of the *New York Times*, but many others gave the appearance of attending "an outing in the late summer sun—part liberation from home, part Sunday School picnic, part political convention, part fish-fry." Although David Lawrence, writing in the *Birmingham News*, lamented the "public disgrace" of "government by mob" brought to bear on civil rights legislation, Kenneth Crawford, writing in *Newsweek*, thought the marchers were "the best mannered, best disciplined . . . petitioners for the redress of grievances" ever witnessed in Washington, a view shared by almost all newspapers outside the South, as well as most major magazines. The narrator of "The Big March," a *News of the Day* newsreel, reported that there had been many previous political marches in the nation's capital, but "none with so little bitterness, so little aggressiveness, or hint of coerciveness."

When the leaders finally made their way to the platform, they stood upon a stupendous stage set, with the Lincoln Memorial at one end, the Washington Monument at the other, and the Reflect-

---

producer Berry Gordy release a recording of the version of the Dream speech he had given in Detroit in June, with the royalties to go to the SCLC. The record had not yet appeared by the time of the March on Washington, however, and Gordy, seeing the opportunity for greater sales, cannily titled his Detroit record *The Great March to Freedom* and attached the title "I Have a Dream" to King's address. King then brought suit against Motown and two other labels, Mr. Maestro and 20th Century–Fox, for albums produced in direct competition with *The Official March on Washington* album, authorized by March leaders and produced by WRVR, a radio station affiliated with Riverside Church in New York. Either because he reached an accord with Gordy or because he chose not to pursue a black-owned company, King dropped his suit against Motown, which soon issued its own version. King prevailed in the other suits, the judge ruling that although his speech had been broadcast and reprinted widely, King's words were still technically "unpublished" and therefore not in the public domain. Deals were then negotiated allowing 20th Century–Fox to produce *Freedom March to Washington, August 28, 1963*, and Folkways to release *We Shall Overcome: Documentary of the March on Washington* in 1964.

ing Pool stretching between like an immense mirror bringing the blue heavens down to earth on a seasonably warm summer day (figures 9 and 10). Each side of the Reflecting Pool was filled nearly to capacity, with some spectators dangling their feet in the water and others perched in surrounding trees. Like the March itself, the prayers, songs, and speeches unfolded more or less according to script as Bayard Rustin nervously checked his watch and clipboard whenever the crowd's ovations threatened to prolong the program, especially when Mahalia Jackson sang.

Other than King, each of the speakers stuck closely to his prearranged text. Randolph spoke for jobs and justice, saying that those "who exhort patience in the name of a false peace are in fact supporting segregation and exploitation"; Blake and Ahmann outlined the support for civil rights to be found in Christian teachings; Lewis, having consented to revisions in his speech, promised more temperately to "march with the spirit of love and with the spirit of dignity" so as to "splinter the segregated South into a thousand pieces and put them [back] together in the image of God and democracy"; Reuther spoke for the interests of labor but also struck an international note in saying "we cannot defend freedom in Berlin so long as we deny freedom in Birmingham"; Floyd McKissick, reading the speech prepared by James Farmer, who had been jailed in Plaquemine, Louisiana, for participating in a voter registration drive, paid tribute to the many who had suffered and died in the civil rights struggle; Young, proclaiming that "our march is a march for America," focused on the plight of urban blacks; Wilkins announced news of the death of Du Bois the previous day and dwelled on the urgency of passing new civil rights legislation; and Prinz, recalling his days as a rabbi in Germany when Hitler came to power, cautioned Americans not to become "a nation of silent onlookers" in the face of racism. At the end of the day, preceding the benediction by Benjamin Mays but following King in an inevitable anti-climax, Rustin read the March's official petition of demands, a number of which would be codified in the Civil Rights Act of 1964.*

By the time King came to the podium, introduced by Randolph as "the moral leader of our nation," it was late in the day. Some of the crowd had already dispersed, and a good deal of momentum had been lost since Mahalia Jackson's performance of "I Been 'Buked and I Been Scorned," along with her unplanned encore, "How I Got Over," had energized the crowd earlier in the program. The event was actually ahead of schedule, however, and all those who remained, as well as those watching on television, including President Kennedy, witnessed a speaker and a speech without parallel in modern American history. Blacks heard a black man whose courage, dignity, and eloquence gave them hope few had ever known. Whites heard a black man, standing before them as their equal, preaching to them in the name of brotherhood and justice. All heard words rivaled only by those inscribed on the marble walls of the Lincoln Memorial rising in the background.

*WHAT WE DEMAND

1. Comprehensive and effective civil rights legislation from the present Congress—without compromise or filibuster—to guarantee all Americans

   access to all public accommodations
   decent housing
   adequate and integrated education
   the right to vote.

2. Withholding of Federal funds from all programs in which discrimination exists.
3. Desegregation of all school districts in 1963.
4. Enforcement of the Fourteenth Amendment—reducing Congressional representation of states where citizens are disfranchised.
5. A new Executive Order banning discrimination in all housing supported by federal funds.
6. Authority for the Attorney General to institute injunctive suits when any constitutional right is violated.

In his Second Inaugural Address, steeped in humility before the divine reckoning, Lincoln had spoken not of southern slavery but of "American slavery," on account of which God had given "to both North and South, this terrible war, as the woe due to those by whom the offense came." So, too, King addressed himself not to a region but to all of America. It was not the South alone but the nation that would continue to be shaken by "the whirlwinds of revolt"; it was the nation for whom it would be "fatal . . . to overlook the urgency of the moment"; it was the nation that had to be lifted up "from the quicksands of racial injustice to the solid rock of brotherhood." Like Lincoln, King spoke with reference to the Declaration of Independence and the Bible, but the moral authority on which he called to redeem the soul of America, to make the nation truly be what "the dreamers had dreamed," came from the deep waters of black history.

Raised up by the enthusiasm of the crowd, which frequently called out in response, King stated uncompromising demands in beautifully formed periodic sentences. His mesmerizing style—the undulating tones drawn from syllables unexpectedly prolonged or stressed; the lyrical, idiosyncratic diction and usage ("staggered by the winds of police brutality," "the Negro is still languished in the corners of American society," "the curvaceous slopes of California"); the aural enjambment of one sentence wrapping urgently into

---

7. A massive federal program to train and place all unemployed workers—Negro and white—on meaningful and dignified jobs at decent wages.
8. A national minimum wage act that will give all Americans a decent standard of living. (Government surveys show that anything less than $2.00 an hour fails to do this.)
9. A broadened Fair Labor Standards Act to include all areas of employment which are presently excluded.
10. A federal Fair Employment Practices Act barring discrimination by federal, state, and municipal governments, and by employers, contractors, employment agencies, and trade unions.

the start of the next, as in the "I have a dream" cadenza; the towering majesty of his concluding words—all of this was one with his message, which embraced the crowd he saw and the nation he envisioned. Even as he castigated America for its historic wrongs, King offered it grounds for atonement, transforming what was already a historic occasion, a mass petition to the president and the Congress, into an act of testimony and prophecy before the world (figures 11 and 12). The longtime activist Pauli Murray, although she was furious that women had been excluded from any important role other than singing, still marched proudly, and she remembered the event as "the nearest thing I've seen to Judgment Day . . . like the 'great gettin' up morning.'"

It is unlikely that King converted any ardent segregationists, but he very clearly touched hearts and minds ready to be touched. She had never liked King and "this civil rights stuff," a flight attendant told *Atlanta Constitution* editor Eugene Patterson as he flew home after the March. After watching him on television, however, the young woman had changed her mind: "I was proud of the Negro and proud of America. . . . He made my country seem so beautiful I felt like I wanted to shake his hand."

In retrospect, wrote David Halberstam, the March on Washington seemed "a great televised morality play," the final act in a melodrama of good guys and bad guys: "Lift up the black hat and there would be the white face of Bull Connor; lift up the white hat and there would be the solemn black face of Martin King, shouting love." In 1963 the media, television in particular, were the great allies of the freedom movement. Those things that could most easily be changed by exposure before the nation and the world, the rankest racism and inhumanity, were their perfect subject and the March on Washington the year's redemptive, if premature, climax. Surrounded by the leaders of black America, buoyed by the day's vibrant interracial optimism, and certain that she was "living and breathing history,"

Mahalia Jackson believed African Americans "were at the threshold of salvation" now that "the American people were beginning to fall into step with us." Among the millions who watched King on television was a seventeen-year-old southerner, future president Bill Clinton, who remembered the moment clearly almost three decades later: "I was home in Hot Springs, Ark., in a white reclining chair all by myself. I just wept like a baby all the way through it."

■

Soon it would be the age of the Free Speech Movement, when Mario Savio, fresh from voter registration work in Mississippi during the Freedom Summer of 1964, stood atop a police cruiser in Berkeley and raged against the university machine. Soon it would be the Age of Aquarius, when the "free gratification of man's instinctual needs" that Herbert Marcuse trumpeted in *Eros and Civilization* spread from communes to dorm rooms, and when Tom Wolfe, chronicling the acid-fueled expeditions of the Merry Pranksters, adverted to Hermann Hesse to capture the quintessence of the drug culture epiphany: "the freedom to experience everything imaginable simultaneously." Soon it would be the age of Woodstock, with Richie Havens's frenetic guitar-strumming, foot-stomping rendition of "Freedom"—*freedom, freedom, freedom,* repeated incessantly, punctuated by choruses from "Sometimes I Feel Like a Motherless Child"—and Jimi Hendrix's pyrotechnical "Star-Spangled Banner," with its cacophonic harmonics and screaming reverb simulating incoming artillery. Soon it would be the age of "Free Huey," when Huey Newton, a charismatic thug–turned–Black Panther, having been convicted of murdering an Oakland police officer, would be deemed a political prisoner by followers inspired by Frantz Fanon and Patrice Lumumba rather than Thomas Jefferson and Abraham Lincoln.

Soon, but not quite yet.

"Nineteen sixty-three," said King in his speech, was "not an end, but a beginning," and certainly this is true with respect to the land-mark legislation—the Civil Rights Act of 1964 and Voting Rights Act of 1965—that followed. Everything to date had been a re-hearsal, said John Lewis just before the March, but on August 28 "the curtain goes up on the first act of the revolution." But what kind of revolution—to what end, how fast, and with whose support?

King later identified the voting rights march of 1965 as the deci-sive turning point in the movement: "The path of Negro-white unity that had been converging crossed at Selma, and like a giant X began to diverge. Up to Selma there had been unity to eliminate barbaric conduct. Beyond it the unity had to be based on the fulfill-ment of equality, and in the absence of agreement [about how that was to be accomplished] the paths began inexorably to move apart." Just days after President Lyndon Johnson signed the Voting Rights Act, the Watts riot exploded. Although it was rival members of the Nation of Islam who killed Malcolm X, his 1965 assassination, the chant of Black Power spreading outward from Mississippi in 1966, and the wave of inner-city riots between 1964 and 1968 all seemed to mark the end of the King era, even before his own assassination on April 4, 1968. The findings of the National Advisory Commis-sion on Civil Disorders were not published until that year, just be-fore King's death, but its diagnosis that "our nation is moving to-ward two societies, one black, one white—separate and unequal" could have been made earlier, almost as early as the March on Washington. Even as King spoke, observed Roger Wilkins, looking back in 1973, "grim clocks were ticking in the wretched ghettoes of the North where nothing was changing."

The summer of 1963 was "a very, very optimistic moment, prob-ably the peak moment for my generation," recalled Richard Flacks, principal author of a Students for a Democratic Society manifesto titled *America and the New Era.* Americans were shocked that year by news photographs of Buddhist monks setting themselves on fire in protest of the United States–backed government of South Vietnam, but few were overly concerned about President Kennedy's dramatic increase in the number of military advisers stationed there. Nineteen sixty-three brought the publication of Charles Webb's novel *The Graduate*—far better known in its film version four years later—in which youthful rebellion was still far from deadly. Dominated by songs such as "He's So Fine" (the Chiffons), "It's My Party" (Leslie Gore), and "Surfin' USA" (the Beach Boys), the 1963 pop charts made just enough room for the mildly subversive messages of Pete Seeger's "If I Had a Hammer," covered by Trini Lopez (following upon the previous year's version by Peter, Paul, and Mary), and Bob Dylan's "Blowin' in the Wind," which appeared on his album *The Freewheelin' Bob Dylan* at virtually the same moment as the hit single released by Peter, Paul, and Mary. Whatever it owed to illusion up to that point, however, the nation's spirit of optimism was abruptly shattered by the assassination of President Kennedy in November. "From 1960 to 1963 the news people got from TV was essentially optimistic," said television producer Fred Freed of the rising mood of anxiety and discontent. "From 1963 on, it wasn't."

At the center of the youth-driven social revolution of the 1960s— sexual liberation, the drug culture, dissent over the Vietnam War, the scorn for "repressive" authority—was the issue of black rights, defined increasingly in terms alien to those King's age and older. Even among those gathered at the March on Washington, not everyone shared the dream. King "went on and on talking about his dream," complained Anne Moody, a young CORE veteran from Mississippi, but "I sat there thinking that in Canton we never had time to sleep, much less dream." Precluded from participating because of his arrest in Louisiana, James Farmer cried when he watched the March on television, but he also came to see it as the "beginning of the end of the civil rights movement." A middle-class demonstration that cut across racial lines, Farmer later said, the March relied for its public relations success on a strategy that excluded the poor of the urban North, who found little in King's message that applied to their lives and needs. With his usual gift for the damning pun, Malcolm X declared the March the "Farce on Washington," co-opted by the Kennedy brothers and scripted like the pageantry of the Kentucky Derby. Others dismissed the whole event, King included, as "a night-club act" (Amiri Baraka), "an abortion" (Michael Thelwell), or "a giant therapy session" (Julius Lester). The March's "gentle army," lamented C. E. Wilson, purposely screened out "the winos—the dope peddlers—the pool sharks—the failures—the unemployed—the uneducated."

King's limited ability to address problems that could not be solved by judicial decisions, television exposure, and equal rights legislation can be illustrated by two events held in Detroit in 1963.

The Detroit "Walk for Freedom," organized by local ministers C. L. Franklin and Albert Cleage, Jr., for the Detroit Council for Human Rights and staged on June 23, attracted upward of two hundred thousand people. The predominantly black crowd heard King deliver a rather more militant speech than the one he would give at the March on Washington. "Segregation is a cancer in the body politic, which must be removed before our democratic health can be realized," said King. "Segregation is wrong because it is nothing more than a new form of slavery covered up with certain niceties of complexity." One does not need an extensive vocabulary, he insisted, to understand three crucial words: "We want *all* of our rights, we want them *here*, and we want them *now*." The end of the Detroit speech seemed a dress rehearsal for the one King improvised in Washington, but his "I have a dream" refrain here focused specifically on the racial terrorism of the Ku Klux Klan and other white supremacists:

I have a dream this afternoon that one day, one day men will no longer burn down houses and the church of God simply because people want to be free.

I have a dream this afternoon that there will be a day that we will no longer face the atrocities that Emmett Till had to face or Medgar Evers had to face, but that all men can live with dignity.

According to a *Newsweek* poll of African Americans taken in July 1963, King ranked first among fourteen top black leaders from various walks of life, with an 88 percent favorable rating among everyday citizens and 95 percent among one hundred other black leaders. At the bottom of the list was Elijah Muhammad, leader of the Nation of Islam, with 15 percent and 17 percent, respectively. (As Muhammad's subordinate, Malcolm X was not included in the poll.) Yet the comparative weakness of King's appeal among blacks in the urban North became evident in November, when Franklin and Cleage had a rancorous split over plans for the Northern Negro Leadership Conference, with Cleage on short notice organizing a competing event, the Grassroots Leadership Conference, for the same weekend. Despite King's support for Franklin's conference, Cleage's drew a larger crowd and a number of more radical activists, who heard Malcolm X deliver his famous "Message to the Grass Roots." Ridiculing the March on Washington as "a circus, with clowns and all," Malcolm offered a provocative, if historically misguided, parable of the "field Negro," representative of the masses, and the "house Negro," characterized by fawning devotion to his master: "If the master said, 'We got a good house here,' the house Negro would say, 'Yeah, we got a good house here.' . . . Whenever the master said 'we,' he said 'we.'" The modern version of the house Negro who says "our government"—and here Malcolm meant King in particular—was simply "out of his mind." If Malcolm's brand of activism would have been fatal in the South, King's already seemed tepid in the North.

In 1963 "i / became black," wrote Haki Madhubuti in a poem entitled "Black Sketches," "& everyone thought it unusual; / even me." Madhubuti was in the vanguard. Whereas other speakers at the March used the terms *Negro* and *Negro American*, only John Lewis spoke exclusively of *blacks* and *black masses*. King used *Negro* repeatedly and used *black* only as an adjective paired with *white* ("black men as well as white men," for example). A survey of black and white college students in 1963 still showed a decided preference among both groups for *Negro* over *black*, and it would be another decade before *black* or *Black* was more widely accepted as a proper noun. As late as 1969 a Gallup poll of African Americans of all ages still showed a decided preference for *Negro* (38 percent) over *Black* (19 percent) and *Afro-American* (10 percent), with a surprising number (20 percent) still preferring *Colored*, no doubt owing to the continued preeminence of the NAACP among an older generation. Yet the change in nomenclature over the course of the 1960s clearly reflected the influence of SNCC, Malcolm X, the Black Panthers, and other militants among the younger generation.

The converse effect was a retrenchment among whites.

The classical phase of the civil rights movement, from 1954 through 1964, brought the demise of legalized segregation, argued Bayard Rustin, but it did comparatively little, especially outside the South, to address the tangled relationship between racial inequality and economic inequality. "What is the value of winning access to public accommodations for those who lack the money to use them?" asked Rustin. Because blacks were disproportionately poor, compensatory treatment based on economic status would have benefited them in significant numbers. If economic remediation would have been more just, however, remediation based on race was more urgent.

In this respect, too, 1963 may be seen as a watershed. When King hoped for the day when his four little children would be judged not "by the color of their skin but by the content of their character," he announced a colorblind ideal that was at once sincere and, as he soon argued, not yet possible. Although the legal decisions and policy directives that authorized affirmative action unfolded largely over the remainder of the decade, their principal touchstone, the Civil Rights Act of 1964, took shape in debates that spanned the Kennedy and Johnson administrations, and the question of *how* equality was to be achieved—the question of what, in King's words, "the fulfillment of equality" actually meant—loomed as large in those debates as it did in public consciousness. Like the "Negro Revolution" generally, the March on Washington and King's speech in particular placed a premium on "Freedom Now!" It was not only in the South that the demand was pertinent; neither was it only in the South that it would be met with resistance. In answer "to the Negro demand for 'now,' to which the Deep South replied 'never,'" observed Murray Friedman in 1963, "many liberal whites are increasingly responding 'later.'"

Of the 63 percent responding to a Gallup poll that they had an "unfavorable" view of the March just days before (22 percent had a "favorable" view), only 8 percent cited a fear of violence, but more than twice that number thought that the March would be ineffective and might make it appear, as George Gallup wrote, that Negroes were "pressing their case too hard." In October *Newsweek* published a poll of whites that was a companion piece to its July poll of blacks, which had expressed their newfound pride and optimism. The poll of whites was, in key respects, a close match, showing that whites strongly favored equal rights in job opportunities (80 percent), voting rights (95 percent), access to good housing (85 percent), access to transportation (91 percent), access to restaurant service (79 percent), and integrated schooling (75 percent). The same poll, however, showed that whites were strongly opposed to quotas (81 percent against) and preferential hiring (97 percent against), and although 76 percent believed that blacks suffered discrimination, 74 percent also thought they were "moving too fast" in seeking redress. No fluke, this discrepancy forecast the frequently volatile battle over affirmative action, both North and South, in decades to come.

It may go without saying that the very power of King's speech created grounds for disappointment. As Benjamin Mays, president of Morehouse College and King's former teacher, mused some years after the March on Washington, it was inevitable that black people should have felt that "this is the moment, and this is the time, and the things we've been struggling for, for centuries, are just about at hand now. Well, it's never so." Mays's tempered judgment reminds us that the Dream speech shined brilliantly because, like the Declaration of Independence, it was a "prophecy of pure hope," to recall Ralph Abernathy's words. Yet this subtracts nothing from what King could and did achieve—and not simply in symbolic terms.

King could not have acted effectively without the advent of desegregation in *Brown v. Board of Education*, as well as the many other heroic actions and brave measures that laid the groundwork for the civil rights revolution in the postwar decades. The sacrifices of many thousands— their deaths, their injuries, their hardships and humiliations—were necessary just to make Martin Luther King, Jr., and the March on Washington possible and, afterward, to make them meaningful. But the president of the United States would not have been pressured to submit a new civil rights bill, nor would he, his successor, and the Supreme Court itself have been so quickly vindicated, as they would be when that bill became law in 1964, without the advent of King. Joining what Ronald Garet has referred to as the "oral tradition in American constitutionalism," King made the civil rights movement integral to the process of constitutional and legislative transformation through which the states' rights doctrine that had protected segregation for nearly a century was finally subordinated to federal authority. Reviving both the spirit of the Emancipation Proclamation and the substance of the Fourteenth Amendment, he participated alongside the Congress and the Supreme Court in making African Americans true citizens of the United States.

Freedom Now!

King's criticism of the nation grew more radical, even somewhat bitter, over the course of the 1960s. Nevertheless, wrote Julius Lester, King believed in America "as if he were one of the signers of the Constitution. He loved America as if he had sewn the first flag. And he articulated a dream for America more forcefully than any man since Thomas Jefferson." Or, one might rather say, any man since Abraham Lincoln. King's dream that "one day this nation will rise up and live out the true meaning of its creed: 'We hold these truths to be self-evident, that all men are created equal,'" read the words of Jefferson through the mind of Lincoln, nowhere more clearly than in his extended metaphor of the "promissory note" on which the nation had defaulted:

> But one hundred years later, the Negro still is not free. One hundred years later, the life of the Negro is still sadly crippled by the manacles of segregation and the chains of discrimination. One hundred years later, the Negro lives on a lonely

island of poverty in the midst of a vast ocean of material prosperity. One hundred years later, the Negro is still languished in the corners of American society and finds himself an exile in his own land. And so we've come here today to dramatize a shameful condition.

In a sense we've come to our nation's capital to cash a check. When the architects of our republic wrote the magnificent words of the Constitution and the Declaration of Independence, they were signing a promissory note to which every American was to fall heir. This note was a promise that all men, yes, black men as well as white men, would be guaranteed the "unalienable Rights of Life, Liberty and the pursuit of Happiness." It is obvious today that America has defaulted on this promissory note insofar as her citizens of color are concerned. Instead of honoring this sacred obligation, America has given the Negro people a bad check, a check which has come back marked "insufficient funds."

But we refuse to believe that the bank of justice is bankrupt. We refuse to believe that there are insufficient funds in the great vaults of opportunity of this nation. And so, we've come to cash this check, a check that will give us upon demand the riches of freedom and the security of justice.

Brown v. Board of Education was a new promissory note, a belated renewal of the note issued in the Emancipation Proclamation of 1863, which renewed the one issued in 1776.

Conceptually, there is nothing complex about the idea of the promissory note. In essence, says King, it is the covenant of individual rights set forth in the Declaration of Independence and the Constitution. The note promised a kind of prosperity on which no price could be put, the riches of freedom stored in the bank of justice. It was a sacred obligation because it was entered into by men, the signers of the Declaration of Independence, who acted on the authority of "the Laws of Nature and of Nature's God." It guaranteed not wealth as such but the right, in a nation not of monarchs but of laws, to lay claim to the great vaults of opportunity through which every man (and woman) might enjoy the treasures of liberty and the pursuit of happiness. It was a note to which every American was to fall heir because, argued King, following Lincoln, the Jeffersonian promise was made not just to the native heirs of the Founding Fathers and to those immigrants who had adopted America as their home but also to those held in bondage. "A translation of the legacy of God," as King put it in one of the early drafts of the Dream speech, the Fathers' promissory note was "no restrictive covenant which specified brown men or black men or yellow men or white" but rather "a pledge to all who came after them, as Americans, inhabitants of a new and glorious land."

Insofar as slavery contradicted that promise, however, the Emancipation Proclamation was required before these "magnificent words" of "the architects of our republic" could be realized. And yet neither Lincoln's decree, nor the Civil War, nor the Civil War amendments, nor, nearly a century later, *Brown v. Board of Education*, nor the paltry steps taken in the wake of *Brown* had yet been sufficient to cash the check. King thus spoke in the shadow of Lincoln on August 28 to dramatize a figure of speech whose meaning was so self-evident as to have been the lead sentence in a *Newsweek* cover story, "The Negro in America," a few weeks earlier: "History would mark it: the summer of 1963 was a time of revolution, the season when 19 million U.S. Negroes demanded payment of the century-old promissory note called the Emancipation Proclamation."

Economic figures of speech indicating what is owed to emancipated black Americans stretch from Reconstruction ("forty acres and a mule") through the modern-day reparations movement ("Once we know how much damage has been done to us, and what is required to repair the damage," the National Coalition of Blacks for Reparations in America has maintained, "we will know how much is owed"). In King's day, the most common figure of speech was the overdue bill. After the miscarriage of racial justice at the center of Harper Lee's *To Kill a Mockingbird* (1960), set in the 1930s, Atticus Finch estimates a future in which his young children will live as adults by the 1950s: "Don't fool yourselves—it's all adding up and one of these days we're going to pay the bill for it." "A bill is coming due," echoed James Baldwin in *The Fire Next Time*, "that I fear America is not prepared to pay."

Other variants, some more threatening, were also in evidence. Throughout "his long, cruel history in this land, the Negro has been the most avid seeker of the American dream," wrote Julian Mayfield in 1959, but "just as an insurance company will not issue a policy without determining the life expectancy of the buyer, neither should the Negro . . . accept the policy before he determines that the company is solvent." "Segregation is an expensive commodity," wrote the ex-Marine Robert F. Williams the same year, and it may be that "the purchase check of democracy must be signed in blood." The Nation of Islam raised the stakes. "A bill is owed to us and must be collected," warned Malcolm X in the summer of 1963. Unless America truly repents of its sins against black people and shares its land and wealth, he said, "God will take this entire continent away from the white man."

King himself returned to the ideas of debt and payment in *Why We Can't Wait*, where he argued that the African American was being asked to "purchase something that already belongs to him by every concept of law, justice, and our Judeo-Christian heritage." Because the Founding Fathers did not intend liberty to be "doled out on a deferred-payment plan," he said in a metaphor harking back to the Montgomery bus boycott, mere tokenism—one or two blacks admitted to a school or hired by a firm—offered "the glitter of metal" in place of "the true coin," for whoever provides the token instead of the coin can always "command you to get off the bus before you have reached your destination."

What, however, would constitute a bill paid in full? The idea of a check not yet cashed, like other such monetary metaphors, indicated a debt—for work done, for property stolen, for wealth seized. It implied, in other words, that recompense had already been earned, something more than an equal chance to earn in the future. And yet King was constrained, as his focus on abstractions such as "the riches of freedom" and "the security of justice" showed, to walk a fine line between equality in the form of opportunity and equality in the form of compensatory treatment. Well beyond his death there would be anguished debate about whether the promissory note had been—or ever could be—fulfilled. The national holiday in King's honor, complains Jesse B. Semple, the folk raconteur created by Langston Hughes and later revived by Derrick Bell, is one more cheap concession to blacks made by a nation unwilling to pay the costs of true equality. "From the Emancipation Proclamation on, the Man has been handing us a bunch of bogus freedom checks he never intends to honor," observes Bell's version of Semple. "Before you can cash them in, the Man has called the bank and stopped payment or otherwise made them useless—except, of course, as symbols."

■

Those who demonstrated in Washington, as well as dozens of other cities in the summer of 1963, recalled the nation to the highest ideals of its own revolutionary tradition. Having turned to the streets when supplication and reasoned argument failed, said a New Orleans insurance executive, "we are writing our Declaration of Independence in shoe leather rather than ink," as did "the original thirteen colonies [when they] took up arms against George III." It was by no means only black moderates who claimed the words of the

Founding Fathers as their own. Consider the case of Robert F. Williams, one-time leader of the Monroe, North Carolina, branch of the NAACP and a proponent of armed self-reliance who had fled the country in 1961 following a confrontation with the Ku Klux Klan. After being granted asylum in Cuba, Williams spread his philosophy of resistance through broadcasts over "Radio Free Dixie," many of which were reprinted in a monthly newsletter, the *Crusader.* After excoriating the courts as "cesspools of racial injustice and persecution," Williams declared in a 1963 address that it would be "better to live just 30 seconds in [the] full and beautiful dignity of manhood than to live a thousand years crawling and dragging our chains at the feet of our brutal oppressors. In the spirit of Lexington and Concord, LET OUR BATTLE CRY BE HEARD AROUND THE WORLD, FREEDOM! FREEDOM! FREEDOM NOW OR DEATH!!!"

Such appropriations of the American Revolution to the purpose of black freedom date back at least to David Walker's *Appeal to the Coloured Citizens of the World* (1829), in which Walker quoted from the Declaration of Independence and asked white Americans whether their sufferings under Great Britain were "one hundredth part as cruel and tyrannical" as those inflicted on blacks, who "have never given your fathers or you the least provocation!" Virtually every black leader in the nation's history has argued, as did Du Bois, that there are "no truer exponents of the pure human spirit of the Declaration of Independence" than African Americans. In King's era, some let the words of the Declaration speak for themselves. The platform of the Black Panther Party, following its call for a United Nations–sponsored plebiscite in America's "black colonial" ghettos, simply quoted at length from the document, while the pop group the Fifth Dimension released a choral rendition of "The Declaration," likewise quoted verbatim, that was sugarcoated enough to be a modest hit but incendiary enough to be banned by Armed Forces Radio.

Others, however, dismissed the Founding Fathers as corrupt or mendacious. "Whose independence?" asked Elijah Muhammad in his millennialist *Fall of America* (1973). "Since 1776, you, Black man, have been worshipping" a white man's holiday, not realizing that "they wrote the Declaration of Independence for themselves." (Muhammad counseled that blacks should instead celebrate July 4, 1930, the day on which Fard Muhammad supposedly revealed to him the truths of the Nation.) "When I see some poor old brainwashed Negroes—you mention Thomas Jefferson and George Washington and Patrick Henry, they just swoon, you know, with patriotism," concurred Muhammad's most eminent disciple, Malcolm X. "But they don't realize that in the sight of George Washington, you were a sack of molasses, a sack of potatoes." The "Black Declaration of Independence," issued by the National Committee of Black Churchmen on July 4, 1970, began with a variation on the Declaration— "When in the course of Human Events, it becomes necessary for a People who were stolen from the lands of their Fathers, transported under the most ruthless and brutal circumstances 5,000 miles to a strange land"—and submitted a list of reasons to censure the United States for its "Racist Tyranny over this People" comparable to those leveled in 1776 against George III.

On the other side of the ledger, however, was an antithetical understanding of American liberty and the revolutionary tradition— namely, the segregationists' claim that it was *their* freedom that was at stake, that *Brown v. Board of Education* and other federal intrusions into the southern way of life were violations of the Constitution. Although it sanctioned segregation, as well as racial vigilantism, the states' rights argument was not inherently racist. Its philosophical core was perhaps nowhere more clearly stated than by the 1964 Republican presidential candidate Barry Goldwater. "The good Lord raised up this mighty Republic to be a home for the brave and to flourish as the land of the free," declared Goldwater, "not to stagnate in the swampland of collectivism—not to cringe before the bullying of Communism." Bewitched by false prophets, he asserted, Americans needed to return to the fundamental cause espoused by the Republican Party, whose "every action, every word, every breath, and every heartbeat" had a single purpose:

Freedom!

Freedom—made orderly for this nation by our Constitutional government.

Freedom—under a government limited by the laws of nature and nature's God.

Freedom—balanced so that order, lacking liberty, will not become the slavery of the prison cell; balanced so that liberty, lacking order, will not become the license of the mob and the jungle.

The key to racial tolerance lay not in laws alone—not even in the Declaration's "Laws of Nature and Nature's God"—but in the hearts of men, said Goldwater, a sentiment with which King would in principle have agreed. No racist himself, Goldwater condemned segregation but felt that racial equality had to be achieved by common consent and was dead set against governmental dictate taking the place of moral suasion.

Although they constituted a tiny minority, a handful of blacks shared Goldwater's view. Notwithstanding that it is "morally wrong, nonsensical, unfair, un-Christian and cruelly unjust," wrote the *Pittsburgh Courier* columnist George Schuyler, segregation "*remains* the majority attitude." The provisions of the 1964 Civil Rights Act, as he saw it, were just one more encroachment of the federal government on the rights of states, a blow to "individual liberty and preference" whose main consequence would be to create a mammoth enforcement bureaucracy. "Armed with this law enacted to improve the lot of a tenth of the population," charged Schuyler, "the way will be opened to enslave the rest of the populace. Is this far-fetched? I think not." As King was quick to reply to such arguments, however, "the law cannot make an employer love me, but it can keep him from refusing to hire me because of the color of my skin," and a century of moral suasion had so far failed to make more than token claims on equality.

A. Philip Randolph, the driving force behind the March on Washington, believed that the relationship between freedom and equality could be stated as a logical proposition: "Negroes must be free in order to be equal and they must be equal in order to be free. . . . Men cannot win freedom unless they win equality. They cannot win equality unless they win freedom." These are axioms as unquestionable as "two plus two equals four," said Randolph. Perhaps so, but many whites in the South, and not a few in the North, believed that freedom and equality, though not incompatible, were by no means equivalent. To the extent that they supported civil rights, they were more likely to share the view of William Faulkner. "To live anywhere in the world of A.D. 1955 and be against equality because of race and color, is like living in Alaska and being against snow," he said at a meeting of the Southern Historical Association that same year. Once upon a time the nonwhite, in the United States or abroad, accepted "his instinct for freedom as an unrealizable dream," Faulkner continued, but no more. Freedom for blacks was the nation's strongest weapon against communism, so long as Americans recognized—here Faulkner sounded like Lincoln—that "there is no such thing as equality *per se*, but only equality *to:* equal right and opportunity to make the best one can of one's life within one's capacity and capability, without fear of injustice or oppression or threat of violence."

Although Faulkner elsewhere defended states' rights more vehemently, his contention here constituted a preemptive dissent from the 1956 "Declaration of Constitutional Principles," a document known colloquially as the "Southern Manifesto," which was drafted by Senator Strom Thurmond of South Carolina and signed by more than 90 percent of southern senators and congressmen. Calling the decision in *Brown v. Board of Education* "contrary to the Constitution," Thurmond and his colleagues charged the Supreme Court with usurping rights reserved to the states and "destroying the amicable relations between the white and Negro races that have been created through ninety years of patient effort by the good people of both races." Casting back to James Madison's doctrine of interposition and especially to John C. Calhoun's doctrine of nullification, the manifesto laid the foundation for arguments that the state had a right to "interpose" itself between the federal government and a state's citizens in order to protect them from coercive power. Although such strategies had routinely been deemed unconstitutional by the Supreme Court—as when it rejected the argument of Arkansas governor Orval Faubus in 1957 that his defiance of court-ordered integration in Little Rock was meant to protect the citizenry—the Court's rebuke was red meat for southern politicians.

The language of racial outrage—striving to "out-nigger" one's opponent, as segregationist politicians were wont to say—was part and parcel of interposition, a surefire way to goad an audience. In his attempt to block James Meredith's registration at the University of Mississippi, for instance, Governor Ross Barnett first read the Constitution's Tenth Amendment: "The powers not delegated to the United States by the Constitution, nor prohibited by it to the states, are reserved to the states respectively, or to the people." After declaring that Mississippi would not "drink from the cup of genocide," he then invoked the doctrine: "Therefore, in obedience to legislative and constitutional sanction I do hereby interpose the rights of the Sovereign State of Mississippi to enforce its laws and to regulate its own internal affairs without interference on the part of the Federal government or its officers. With the help of Almighty God, we shall be invincible, and we shall keep the faith."

In his notorious "Segregation today, segregation tomorrow, segregation forever" inaugural speech—a point of view he would repudiate in later years—George Wallace likewise couched his states' rights argument in a rejection of the federal imposition of "amalgamation," a term which for Wallace combined the twin threats of racial degeneration and totalitarian enslavement. "This nation was never meant to be a unit of one," said Wallace, for "our freedom loving forefathers" divided rights and powers among the states so as to ensure that no central power could gain "master" control. "But if we amalgamate into the one unit as advocated by the communist philosophers," the American people will become "a mongrel unit of one under a single all powerful government," standing "for everything . . . and for nothing."

Drinking from the "cup of genocide," descending into the communist slough of "amalgamation"—this was the demagogic version of states' rights that King addressed on any number of occasions, as when, in his 1956 sermon "Paul's Letter to American Christians," he declared the doctrine of interposition to be un-American and un-Christian. It also led to one of the most vociferous passages of his Dream speech:

> I have a dream that one day down in Alabama, with its vicious racists, with its governor having his lips dripping with the words of "interposition" and "nullification," one day right there in Alabama little black boys and black girls will be able to join hands with little white boys and white girls as sisters and brothers.

King's rejoinder meant first of all that only an interracial coalition could end Jim Crow, but his vilification of Wallace as a kind of slobbering ogre—Wallace's visage is deformed before our eyes by King's alliterative but grammatically distorted participial construction, "having his lips dripping"—was shocking in a speech otherwise marked by high idealism.

■

The Dream speech is filled with invocations of interracial partnership, from King's proclamation that the destiny of white people "is tied up with our destiny . . . their freedom is inextricably bound to our freedom" to his glorious hope that "one day on the red hills of Georgia, the sons of former slaves and the sons of former slave owners will be able to sit down together at the table of brotherhood." If his image of white and black boys and girls joining hands was a cause of pride among his allies, however, it was more likely to stir apprehension, if not hysteria, among his opponents. Pointedly suffused with innocence, King's interracial image was calculated nonetheless to touch the very nerve that segregationists recurred to time and again—the danger posed by "social integration" to the innocent white children of the South. The popular Baptist minister W. A. Criswell, to take one example, nearly wept when he addressed a South Carolina church conference in 1956 about the calamity of *Brown v. Board of Education*. "Don't force me to cross over in those *intimate things* where I don't want to go," Criswell pleaded. "Let me have my home. Let me have my family. And what you give to me, give to every other man in America and keep it like our glorious forefathers made it—a land of the free and the home of the brave."

Anxiety about being forced to cross over in intimate areas could be arrayed along a spectrum. At one end was mere proximity—blacks and whites sitting side by side on a bus or at the dime-store lunch counter, a mundane example of the "table of brotherhood." Segregationists were fond of arguing that desegregation was an infringement of their constitutionally protected "freedom of association." (Not just then but later: King is the closest thing to "a secular saint" the United States has produced, the white nationalist Jared Taylor maintained in 1999, but his sanctification came at the cost of "destroying the right to freedom of association" for whites.) However commonsensical such arguments may have appeared in one setting or another, they studiously ignored the fact that many Jim Crow laws explicitly prohibited freedom of association, frequently encompassing the simplest forms of communal intercourse. The segregation ordinances of Birmingham, for example, not only mandated segregated service in theaters, restaurants, buses, and streetcars but also forbade other kinds of voluntary association in public places or establishments: "It shall be unlawful for a Negro and a white person to play together or in company with each other in any game of cards, dice, dominoes, checkers, baseball, softball, football, basketball, or similar games."

Seemingly innocuous racial proximity could arouse deep aversions. In a 1961 sermon King borrowed from E. Franklin Frazier's essay "The Pathology of Racial Prejudice" in telling the story of a white woman who, after discovering in horror that a light-skinned woman who had sat on her expensive sofa was not really white, immediately burned the sofa. "Segregation has its destructive effect upon the segregator also," reported Diane Nash in describing the sit-ins at Nashville lunch counters. "Here were Negro students, quiet, in good discipline, who were consciously attempting to show no ill will, even to the point of making sure that they had pleasant and calm facial expressions," said Nash. From the reaction of white employees and onlookers, however, one might think that "some dreadful monster . . . [was] about to devour them all. Waitresses dropped things. Store managers and personnel perspired. Several cashiers were led off in tears." The law might be able to mandate behavior, but it could do little in the short run to alter habitual repugnance. "We break every glass they drink out of," said a southern bar owner forced to serve blacks in the wake of the Civil Rights Act of 1964. "There ain't no law against that."

At the other end of the spectrum, toward which white fears of mere association with blacks continually tilted, lay the threat of sexual intimacy and intermarriage. Segregationists argued incessantly that unaccustomed proximity was the first step down the slippery slope identified by the Montgomery City Commission, which affirmed its intention during the bus boycott to "forever stand like a rock against social equality, intermarriage, and mixing of the races under God's creation and plan." During a televised debate with King in November 1960, *Richmond News Leader* editor James J. Kilpatrick asserted that the goal of sit-ins was miscegenation, which was bound to destroy the "racial characteristics that have contributed to Western civilization over the past two thousand years." In a 1963 *U.S. News and World Report* article entitled "Intermarriage and the Race Problem," Henry Garrett, a Virginia native but also a longtime Columbia University psychology professor, likewise declared that amalgamation would be "catastrophic," resulting in a "lowering of the cultural and intellectual level of the American people." When televised coverage of the voting rights march from Selma to Montgomery showed Mary Travers of the folk group Peter, Paul, and Mary kissing Harry Belafonte on the cheek, CBS headquarters was besieged with calls of protest.

Although King himself had to be persuaded to break off a relationship with a white girlfriend when he was in the seminary, he spoke for the vast majority of blacks in saying that "the Negro's primary aim is to be the white man's brother, not his brother-in-law." Blacks, of course, had far more reason to be fearful than whites. The southerner is saying "*he* won't integrate because black blood will *mongrelize* his race," scoffed Malcolm X, who, like King, like Frederick Douglass, like Booker T. Washington, like W. E. B. Du Bois, had at least one white ancestor. The white man had long since "*inte-*

grated" African Americans so that there were few left who were "the black color of our foreparents!" Integration, a light-skinned black man told James Baldwin, "has always worked very well in the South, after the sun goes down." It is not "miscegenation," he added, unless a black man is involved.

The legal enforcement of segregation in the decades following the Supreme Court decision in *Plessy v. Ferguson* (1896) brought much of the nation to a nearly total commitment to the "one-drop" rule, whereby virtually any admixture of "black blood" was sufficient to make a person "Negro," and stimulated a rabid popular literature about the dangers of miscegenation. Of the approximately five thousand blacks lynched between the Civil War and the March on Washington, according to an estimate contemporary with King's speech, those that involved men accused of raping or molesting white women were typically sanctioned by the defense offered on the floor of the United States Senate by Alabama's J. Thomas Heflin: "Whenever a negro crosses this dead line between the white and negro races and lays his black hand on a white woman he deserves to die."

No vigilante enforcement of this prohibition was more vivid in the mind of the public at the time of the March than the infamous 1955 murder of Emmett Till. A fourteen-year-old Chicago boy visiting relatives near Money, Mississippi, Till purportedly made lewd adolescent remarks or "wolf whistled" at a white woman tending a country store. Till's killers, the woman's husband and his half-brother, beat Till, shot him in the head, tied a cotton gin fan around his neck with barbed wire, and dumped his body in the Tallahatchie River. The swift acquittal of the self-confessed murderers was no less grotesque than the photos of Till's disfigured corpse that ran in *Jet* magazine and the *Chicago Defender.* Worse, however, was the *Look* magazine interview in which Till's murderers justified their actions by calling up the specter of miscegenation. When Till supposedly bragged about his white girlfriends in the North, said one, there was no alternative but to kill him: "I counted pictures o' three white gals in his pocketbook [wallet] before I burned it. What else could I do? No use lettin' him get no bigger!"

Calvin Hernton perceived that police at the March on Washington "constricted their eyes, tightened their faces, and fondled their [night] sticks" whenever they encountered an interracial couple. Although most would have chosen a more delicate term than *mongrelization*, few Americans, no matter where they lived, were ready to put aside their objections to interracial relationships. Gallup polling in 1958 showed that 92 percent of Americans nationwide, and 99 percent of those surveyed in the South, disapproved of interracial marriage, while 95 percent of whites polled by *Newsweek* in 1963 objected to their teenage daughter's dating a Negro. Objections to intermarriage remained so strong that it was not until 1967, when antimiscegenation laws were still on the books in twenty-two states, that the Supreme Court ruled them unconstitutional in *Loving v. Commonwealth of Virginia*. In doing so, the Court reversed the finding of the trial judge who, when he convicted Richard Loving and Mildred Jeter of violating Virginia's antimiscegenation law in 1958, proclaimed his belief in distinct races and their place in a divinely ordained order: "Almighty God created the races white, black, yellow, malay and red, and he placed them on separate continents . . . [showing] that he did not intend for the races to mix."* A year after

---

*Richard Loving was a white man and Mildred Jeter a "colored" woman. Though married in Washington, D.C., which had no antimiscegenation law, they were arrested in 1958 for living in Virginia, where their marriage violated the "Act to Preserve Racial Integrity," enacted in 1924. Their sentence was suspended on the condition that they leave the state, but after living in Washington for five years, they decided to appeal their conviction. Because the Virginia law prohibited only interracial marriages involving whites, it was evident to the Supreme Court that the law and its enforcement, regardless of claims that blacks and whites faced the same punishment, were "designed to maintain White Supremacy."

the decision in *Loving*, a new Gallup poll showed that 72 percent of Americans, whether or not they agreed with such specious reasoning, still disapproved of intermarriage, the highest percentage among thirteen Western nations surveyed. (By 2007 the figures were completely reversed. According to Gallup, 79 percent of Americans—including 75 percent of whites and 85 percent of blacks—now approved of intermarriage.)

"It is true," said the *New York Times* editorial lauding the decision in *Brown v. Board of Education* the day after it was handed down, "that the court is not talking of that sort of 'equality' which produces interracial marriages." Rather, said the editorial titled "All God's Chillun"—the allusion here was to the Eugene O'Neill's play *All God's Chillun Got Wings*—the highest court has affirmed its faith in the equality of "all children before the law." But the two issues were not separable. From the outset, the southern campaign against *Brown* portrayed it as the opening wedge in an assault on southern values, none more fundamental than the inviolable taboo against interracial intimacy. In Tom P. Brady's broadside *Black Monday*, so called for the day *Brown* was announced, the decision was thus ascribed to communism and the Court accused of facilitating the violation of "the loveliest and the purest of God's creatures . . . a well-bred, cultured Southern white woman or her blue-eyed, golden-haired little girl." Brady's subtitle, *Segregation or Amalgamation . . . America Has Its Choice*, echoed Theodore Bilbo's *Take Your Choice: Separation or Mongrelization* (1947), in which the longtime United States senator and governor of Mississippi declared that he would rather see "his race and civilization" annihilated by a nuclear bomb than "destroyed in the maelstrom of miscegenation, interbreeding, and mongrelization."

Insofar as Brady, a state circuit court judge and vice president of the Mississippi state bar association, charged that Black Monday ranked with July 4, 1776, in the nation's history—because in his view *Brown* reversed rather than affirmed the intentions of the Founding Fathers—it may seem surprising that his defense of the "God-given American way of life" against the Court's "moral leprosy" also sought support in a speech by Abraham Lincoln, with a portion of it marked in bold: "I am not nor ever have been in favor of making voters or jurors of negroes, nor of qualifying them to hold office, nor to intermarry with white people; and I will say in addition to this that there is a physical difference between the white and black races which I believe **will forever forbid the two races living together on terms of social and political equality.**" For more than half a century, however, southerners had appealed to such sentiments to make Lincoln a friend of segregation.*

Nor was fear that the dismantling of segregated schools would lead inexorably to the collapse of the sexual color line a sectional issue alone. Writing in the mainstream *Atlantic Monthly*, Herbert Ravenel Sass argued in 1956 that *Brown* flouted natural law and left

---

* Not least because of King's generally admiring citation of both Lincoln and Jefferson, it is important to recall that a central feature of southerners' apprehension about emancipation was writ large once again in debates over desegregation. After his return to political life in 1854, Lincoln gave little evidence that he did not share the racial prejudices of his day. "There is a natural disgust in the minds of nearly all white people at the idea of an indiscriminate amalgamation of the white and black races," he remarked in reply to charges by his senatorial opponent Stephen A. Douglas that his opposition to slavery amounted to an endorsement of racial mixing. Yet the fact that "I do not want a black woman for a *slave*," Lincoln argued, does not mean "I must necessarily want her for a *wife*." Although Lincoln's public disdain of intermarriage and his espousal of colonization were forms of "strategic racism" intended to silence race-baiting Democrats, as James Oakes argues, they also revealed trepidation about the results of emancipation that he shared, to a lesser degree, with Jefferson. ("Nothing is more certainly written in the book of fate, than that these people are to be free," states the misleadingly truncated quotation gracing the Jefferson Memorial. "Nor is it less certain," Jefferson went on to say, "that the two races equally free, cannot live in the same government. Nature, habit, [and] opinion have drawn indelible lines of distinction between them.") By the time of his

amalgamation "lurk[ing] in ambush." If the South failed to defend its young children, not yet capable of defending themselves, he contended, "if it permits their wholesale impregnation by a propaganda persuasive and by them unanswerable, the salutary instinct of race preference which keeps the races separate, as in Nature, will be destroyed before it develops and the barriers against racial amalgamation will go down." As Sass's unmistakable pun on "impregnation" implied, the doctrine announced in *Brown* was tantamount to the sexual violation of defenseless white schoolgirls. President Dwight Eisenhower made his own feelings clear as he grudgingly implemented *Brown:* "It's all very well to talk about school integration—if you remember that you may also be talking about social disintegration. Feelings are deep on this, especially where children are involved."

Gandhi renamed the untouchables *Harijans,* "children of God," taking them by the hand and leading them into the temples from which they had been excluded. To equal that, wrote King in 1959, Eisenhower would have to "take a Negro child by the hand and lead

---

presidency, Lincoln clearly distinguished natural rights (guaranteed by the Constitution) and citizenship rights (the privileges and immunities that would be included in the Fourteenth Amendment) from social and political rights (those pertaining to education, marriage, voting, jury service, and the like), which he considered the prerogative of the states, regardless of his personal views. Statements such as those made in his debates with Douglas led to Lincoln's later embrace by southern segregationists, from Thomas Dixon to Tom Brady, and later still to his condemnation by scholars determined to prove him a racist. In his own lifetime, however, Lincoln was frequently accused by political opponents of promoting interracial licentiousness. During the election of 1860 he was dubbed the "Black Republican," secretly a Negro, and lampooned in plays such as *The Royal Ape* and *King Linkum the First.* Others soon spoke of Lincoln's "Miscegenation Proclamation" and ridiculed him in the "Black Republican Prayer," a parody of the Lord's Prayer that beseeched Lincoln to "lay waste the Southern States, murder the inhabitants, confiscate their property, ravish their women, and burn their cities and towns," so that the United States may become "a regenerated nation of half-breeds, and mongrels."

her into Central High School in Little Rock." That, in effect, was what the Supreme Court did in *Brown v. Board of Education.* In federalizing oversight of education, while setting in motion the sequence of judicial and legislative actions that led eventually to affirmative action and the backlash against it, *Brown*, in the words of the unanimous opinion written by Chief Justice Earl Warren, assumed that education was "the very foundation of good citizenship . . . a principal instrument in awakening the child to cultural values, in preparing him for later professional training, and in helping him to adjust normally to his environment." It assumed, in other words, that the rights of children *as* children, not just as prospective adults, were deserving of protection.

By design, *Brown* was far-reaching not just because the school setting, standing for society at large, allowed children to stand for the nation's citizens, but also because of its unorthodox constitutional reasoning. The doctrine of "separate but equal," codified in *Plessy v. Ferguson*, wrote Warren, did devastating psychological damage, especially to children, creating in them "a lasting feeling of inferiority as to their status in the community that may affect their hearts and minds in a way unlikely ever to be undone." In formulating his opinion, Warren relied on the work of the African American psychologist Kenneth Clark, whose findings about the inculcation of racial self-hatred and inferiority derived from experiments in which black children, given black and white dolls, were presented with choices such as "Give me the doll that is the nice doll" and "Give me the doll that looks bad." Elaborated a few years later in *Prejudice and Your Child*, Clark's findings were issued in a 1950 report for a White House conference before Warren cited them in *Brown.* The Court's appeal to social science experiments, rather than judicial precedent, was immediately attacked, and Clark's conclusions were soon questioned—judged by his own assumptions, for example, Clark's data demonstrated that black children attending integrated schools in the North showed even lower self-esteem than blacks in segregated schools—but the role of children in *Brown* proved instrumental.

Hannah Arendt criticized *Brown* for not striking down laws against interracial marriage, but in addition to arguing that school segregation involved ambiguous private social spheres where "no human and no basic political right is at stake," she insisted that the Supreme Court had wrongly put children on the front lines in the battle for equal rights. Although Arendt had good reason to scrutinize *Brown*'s limits, neither the nation nor the Court itself was ready to confront the prospect of interracial marriage. In the opinion of the ruling's proponents, moreover, Arendt's objection to putting children at risk missed its fundamental point. "She has absolutely no conception of what goes on in the minds of Negro parents when they send their kids through those lines of hostile people," replied Ralph Ellison, and his reasoning was nearly identical to King's. "Our children and our families are maimed a little every day of their lives," said King. Not only are the risks acceptable, if blacks can end their children's pain by a single climactic confrontation, but fighting together as a family "will make us whole again."

King's repeated use of the phrase "all of God's children" in the Dream speech inscribed the voice of God into *Brown v. Board of Education* and reminded his audience that in the battle over desegregation, from the Supreme Court to the streets of Birmingham, it was children, black and white alike, who were at the eye of the storm. Indeed, the civil rights movement was predominantly a youth movement fueled by baby-boom demographics—in 1964 seventeen-year-olds were the largest age group in the country. When he wisecracked that King was "a boy on a man's errand," Thurgood Marshall meant not only that lawsuits could do more than nonviolent direct action to advance desegregation; he also drew a generational distinction between the wise elders of the NAACP and the impetuous "youth" of the SCLC and SNCC. At Central High School in Little Rock, at the University of Alabama and the University of Mississippi, in the sits-ins and Freedom Rides, and most powerfully in the Children's Crusade in Birmingham, young blacks and whites were the spearhead of desegregation. It was their constitutional rights, no less than those of their parents and grandparents, that were at stake.

King was given no more painful opportunity to make the case for the nation's youngest citizens than in his eulogy for the four girls killed in the Ku Klux Klan bombing of the Sixteenth Street Baptist Church. These "beautiful children of God," said King, these actors on the stage of history and holy martyrs, had something to say to every politician who has "fed his constituents with the stale bread of hatred and the spoiled meat of racism." The mother of one of the girls put it in more harrowing terms. She could not feel bad about her daughter's death, said Alice Collins, because "this is a great Christian movement. This is integration and this is God's way of getting it done."

The depravity confronted by parents such as Alice Collins was evident enough in the cheers that greeted the aptly named minister Charles Conley Lynch, a member of the white supremacist National States' Rights Party, when he addressed a Florida Klan rally soon after the bombing: "Children are little people, little human beings, and that means white people. There's little dogs and cats and apes and baboons and skunks and there's also little niggers. But they ain't children." Lynch then mocked King as "Martin Lucifer *Coon*," the Klan's biggest enemy, and turned his Dream speech into a prediction of his death: "I heard him on TV the other night saying, 'the *Neee*-gro is not satisfied.' Well, he never will be, because before they are satisfied they all will be six feet under the ground."

■

An alien visitor to Birmingham in the spring of 1963, observed
King, might conclude that it was a city trapped "in a Rip Van Winkle slumber." It was a city whose leaders had apparently never heard
of Lincoln and Jefferson, or the Preamble to the Constitution, or
the Bill of Rights, or the Thirteenth, Fourteenth, and Fifteenth
Amendments, or *Brown v. Board of Education*, he said, and where
even sympathetic white moderates, ministers no less, hid behind
"the anesthetizing security of stained-glass windows" and advised
the Negro to "wait until a 'more convenient season.'" The South,
indeed, was frozen in time, its penchant for "tradition" and its rev-
erence for the Lost Cause of the Confederacy having created a par-
alyzing retrospection. "Going slow" meant, in effect, going nowhere at all. Imagining a Jim Crow bus as though it were a spaceship
"caught in a time warp of history," Ralph Ellison portrayed the
Montgomery boycott in allegorical terms. Outside "the scenery
flashed and flickered, but [the black riders] themselves remained,
like Zeno's arrow, ever in the same old place," playing out their roles
"like figures in dreams" until at last "a single tired Negro woman refused to go on with what had now become an unbearable farce."

Integral to the conceit of the promissory note, as well as its seemingly endless deferral, was the sense of urgency animating nearly
every sentence of King's speech, beginning with his repeated charge
that the long century since the Emancipation Proclamation had left
blacks less than second-class citizens, continuing with his insistence
that the moment is urgent, that now is the time—

> We have also come to this hallowed spot to remind America
> of the fierce urgency of now. This is no time to engage in the
> luxury of cooling off or to take the tranquilizing drug of grad-
> ualism. Now is the time to make real the promises of democ-
> racy. Now is the time to rise from the dark and desolate valley
> of segregation to the sunlit path of racial justice. Now is the

time to lift our nation from the quicksands of racial injustice to the solid rock of brotherhood. Now is the time to make justice a reality for all of God's children.

It would be fatal for the nation to overlook the urgency of the moment

—and concluding with his exhortation to "speed up that day when all of God's children" will be "free at last!"

In a formulation that he applied repeatedly to other leaders, as well as to himself, King said of Rosa Parks that she "had been tracked down by the Zeitgeist—the spirit of the time." Already in 1951 Roy Wilkins had addressed the question of *when* with the answer that blacks "want their rights as Americans and they want them now, not next year, or in 1960. They don't believe in gradualism. They believe what the Declaration of Independence says, that their rights are God-given, and that no man or system has the right to bestow or withhold them." After the earthquake of its initial decision in *Brown*, however, the Supreme Court issued an ambiguous decree of implementation the following year, requiring that desegregation be undertaken "consistent with good faith compliance at the earliest practicable date" and "with all deliberate speed." Perhaps no one understood better the potential cruelty of "deliberate speed" than Thurgood Marshall, the NAACP's lead attorney in *Brown*. In the wake of the white rioting that accompanied Autherine Lucy's 1956 attempt to enroll at the University of Alabama, Marshall was asked whether he did not believe in gradualism, to which he laconically replied: "The Emancipation Proclamation was issued in 1863, ninety-odd years ago. I believe in gradualism, and I also believe that ninety-odd years is pretty gradual."

King, said Louis Lomax, was the "foremost interpreter of the Negro's tiredness"—a truth already evident, as we have seen, in his first speech as leader of the Montgomery Improvement Association:

"And you know, my friends, there comes a time when people get tired of being trampled over by the iron feet of oppression. There comes a time, my friends, when people get tired of being plunged across the abyss of humiliation. . . . There comes a time." Rhetorically, the high point of King's transformation of black weariness into triumph came at the end of the Selma to Montgomery voting rights march in 1965. In the shadow not of Lincoln but of Jefferson Davis, as George Wallace peered furtively through the drawn blinds of his office in the state capitol, King drove toward his concluding recitation of "The Battle Hymn of the Republic," the crusading song of Union soldiers a century earlier, by transforming the long march of African Americans into a call-and-response in which he was both speaker and audience:

> I come to say to you this afternoon, however difficult the moment, however frustrating the hour, it will not be long, because truth crushed to earth will rise again.
> How long? Not long, because no lie can live forever.
> How long? Not long, because ye shall reap what you sow. . . .
> How long? Not long, because the arc of the moral universe is long but it bends toward justice.
> How long? Not long, because "Mine eyes have seen the glory of the coming of the Lord . . . "

Some listening to King that day would have heard Langston Hughes addressing the question of freedom in "Ask Your Mama" (1961): "*TELL ME HOW LONG — / MUST I WAIT? CAN I GET IT NOW? . . . OR MUST I HESITATE?*" Others may have heard strains of Bob Dylan's hymn of disillusionment, "Blowin' in the Wind": "How many years can some people exist before they're allowed to be free?" King's black audience in particular would have heard an echo of Psalms 13:1–2: "How long wilt thou forget me, O LORD? for ever? . . . how long shall mine enemy be exalted over me?" The Psalmist's refrain was familiar among southern black ministers—so familiar that William H. Pipes, commenting on a Macon County, Georgia, sermon recorded in the 1940s, remarked that the black preacher's repetition of "How long?" was like a key unlocking "the door of frustration," like "placing a match to gasoline."

More of his audience, perhaps, would have recognized King's citation of an old slave spiritual, "Before This Time Another Year?"—

Before this time another year, I may be gone.
Out in some lonely graveyard, O Lord, how long? . . .
By the grace of God I'll follow on, O Lord, how long?

—just as they would have noticed echoes of the song Mahalia Jackson had sung at the March on Washington, "I Been 'Buked and I Been Scorned" (figure 13). It was at King's request that she chose this song, which she had also performed at the 1957 Prayer Pilgrimage for Freedom, the first occasion at which he spoke at the Lincoln Memorial. Weariness from waiting for freedom so long postponed, for justice so long delayed, was as integral to Jackson's performance as it was to King's. She recalled the sensation created in her audience in 1963:

At first I sang the words softly . . .

I been 'buked and I been scorned.
I'm gonna tell my Lord
    When I get home.
Just how *long* you've been treating me wrong.

As I sang the words I heard a great murmur come rolling back to me from the multitude below and I sensed I had reached out and touched a chord. . . .

Now I wanted to let the joy that was inside me about this day come pouring out. I was moved to shout for joy. I lifted up the beat of the rhythm to a gospel beat.

I found myself clapping my hands and swaying and the great crowd joined in with me with a great wave of singing and clapping. . . .

Flags were waving and people were shouting. It looked as if we had the whole city rocking. I hadn't planned to start a revival meeting but for the moment the joy overflowed throughout the great rally.

They later said my singing seemed to bounce off the golden dome of the Capitol far down the Mall and I've always hoped it reached inside to where some of those Congressmen were sitting!

Unlike King's "how long" in Montgomery, which drew out both words evenly, as a piercing question followed by an answering affirmation, "not long," Jackson's "how long" drew out the *long*—the italics are hers—with a sense of deep pain, one that King expressed in "Letter from Birmingham Jail" when he alluded to the same song: "Abused and scorned though we may be, our destiny is tied up with America's destiny."*

---

*Jackson's sense of time past and time to come, of justice served at long last on the Day of Judgment, if not on earth, bears comparison in its emotional tenor to the greatest movement song in rhythm and blues, Sam Cooke's "A Change Is Gonna Come" (1964). Inspired by "Blowin' in the Wind" and influenced by Cooke's arrest for trying to register at a segregated motel in Shreveport, Louisiana, "A Change Is Gonna Come" first appeared on a little-known album entitled *The Stars Salute Dr. Martin Luther King*, designed to raise money for the SCLC, before being released as a single in 1965, when its most overtly political lines were cut ("I go to the movies, and I go downtown, / Somebody keeps telling me not to hang around"). Rich with blues and gospel, its message of liberation rendered surreptitiously, the song nevertheless seemed a statement of faith born of suffering:

It's been too hard living, but I'm afraid to die,
Cause I don't know what's up there beyond the sky;
It's been a long, a long time coming,
But I know a change gonna come, oh yes it will.

For Jackson and King alike, salvation in God's time was more than real—it was the one abiding truth—but that in no way diminished the need for freedom in secular time. "There is never time in the future in which we will work out our salvation," as James Baldwin put it. "The challenge is in the moment, the time is always now."

By 1963 the urgency of the moment, the urgency of now, was on every black person's lips. "FREE IN '63" had become an NAACP rallying cry, "FREEDOM NOW" and "NOW" were among the principal slogans of CORE and SNCC, and buttons and signs with "NOW!" prominently featured, by official decree of the planning committee, were visible by the hundreds at the March. Although he cut it from his speech at the March, Joachim Prinz had originally intended to put to the nation the famous questions of Rabbi Hillel: "If I am not for myself, then for whom am I? If I am only for myself, then what am I? And if not now, when?" At a Carnegie Hall benefit for SNCC earlier in the year, Lena Horne premiered "Now!," written to the rousing melody of the Hebrew folk song "Hava Nagila." Horne's history lesson on black rights, punctuated by "Now is the time," "Now is the moment," and "Now, now, now, now" in repeated refrains, began:

> If those historic gentlemen came back today,
> Jefferson, Washington, and Lincoln,
> And Walter Cronkite put them on Channel Two
> To find out what they were thinking,
> I'm sure they'd say,
> Thanks for quoting us so much,
> But we don't want to take a bow,

His inspiration for lyrics such as "I don't know what's up there beyond the sky," Cooke explained, was "like somebody talking about I want to go to heaven, really, but then who knows what's up there? In other words, that's why you want justice on earth."

Enough with the quoting,
Put those words into action,
And we mean action now!

Called to the podium by the ecstatic crowd at the March on Washington, Horne shouted a simple declaration: "Freedom!" But some were less decorous. Such was the case of one man at the March who cried out in reply to King's dream cadences, "Fuck that dream, Martin! Now, now, goddamit, NOW!"

■

Whatever caused King to "tell about the dream," his deviation from his prepared text led him closer in spirit to Mahalia Jackson's performance, not simply in the music of his own voice, so powerful in its own right, but specifically in his concluding use of two songs in conjunction, one a black spiritual and the other a classic of American patriotism:

This will be the day, this will be the day when all of God's children will be able to sing with new meaning:

My country, 'tis of thee, sweet land of liberty, of thee I sing.
Land where my fathers died, land of the pilgrim's pride,
From every mountainside, let freedom ring!

And if America is to be a great nation, this must become true.
And so let freedom ring from the prodigious hilltops of New Hampshire.
Let freedom ring from the mighty mountains of New York.
Let freedom ring from the heightening Alleghenies of Pennsylvania.
Let freedom ring from the snowcapped Rockies of Colorado.

Let freedom ring from the curvaceous slopes of California.

But not only that: Let freedom ring from Stone Mountain of Georgia.

Let freedom ring from Lookout Mountain of Tennessee.

Let freedom ring from every hill and molehill of Mississippi.

From every mountainside, let freedom ring.

And when this happens, when we allow freedom [to] ring, when we let it ring from every village and every hamlet, from every state and every city, we will be able to speed up that day when all of God's children, black men and white men, Jews and Gentiles, Protestants and Catholics, will be able to join hands and sing in the words of the old Negro spiritual:

Free at last! Free at last!

Thank God Almighty, we are free at last!

When King deviated from his prepared text, as we have seen, his words were not a matter of unique inspiration. Similar versions of this peroration had appeared on earlier occasions, most recently at the "Walk for Freedom" in Detroit, where he included a version of the "I have a dream" sequence but excluded the lines from "America" before ending, "Free at last! Free at last! Thank God Almighty, we are free at last!" In two prior instances of the peroration, his prefatory phrase, "as I heard a powerful orator say not long ago," appeared to credit, without naming, Archibald J. Carey, Jr., an attorney, alderman, and pastor of the Quinn Chapel AME Church in Chicago, from whose address to the 1952 Republican National Convention King borrowed virtually the whole of his conclusion, from "My Country, 'Tis of Thee" through the incantation "Let freedom ring."*

* Readers first encountering Archibald Carey's speech in a collection of African American orations titled *Rhetoric of Racial Revolt*, published in 1964, might have noticed its similarities to King's speech, not least since the Dream speech was also in-

Carey's extrapolation from the lyrics of "America" may not have been original with him, but his unequivocal vision of black participation in the American Creed—"We, Negro-Americans, sing with all loyal Americans," he insisted—along with the geographic sweep of his vision, provided a template for King:

That's exactly what we mean—from every mountain side, let freedom ring. Not only from the Green Mountains and the White Mountains of Vermont and New Hampshire; not only from the Catskills of New York; but from the Ozarks in Arkansas, from the Stone Mountain in Georgia, from the Great Smokies of Tennessee and from the Blue Ridge Mountains of Virginia—let it ring, not only for the minorities of the United States, but for the persecuted of Europe, for the

---

cluded as the last entry in the volume, along with a brief commentary on it by the editor, Roy L. Hill. Yet this borrowing by King, along with a host of others in his speeches and sermons, was first analyzed only in 1992 by Keith D. Miller in *The Voice of Deliverance*. King's lifelong habit of appropriating material from other sources, now being carefully documented by the editors of the King Papers, has been the cause of much dismay and debate. Improvising upon familiar themes, King often took words and ideas from other preachers, from philosophers, from poets, and from essayists. Whether those borrowings he did not acknowledge constituted plagiarism is a more difficult question. Richard Lischer ascribes King's practice to the preacher's habit of approaching all knowledge and creative work as potential raw material for use in sermons, while Miller speaks of King's "voice-merging," whereby he exploited the expectations of his audience, derived from oral black folk culture, that they would hear familiar materials reworked in ingenious and exhilarating ways. Given the frequency and transparency with which he incorporated well-known and less-well-known sermonic or oratorical materials into his own work, transforming and making them his own, little is gained by charging King with plagiarism in his sermons and speeches, perhaps even in his books and essays, in that their purpose was not to enrich King but to make him a more effective leader and to advance the cause of the civil rights movement. There is no doubt, however, that King's undocumented borrowings in his academic work, including the dissertation he wrote at Boston University, constituted punishable plagiarism.

rejected of Asia, for the disfranchised of South Africa and for the disinherited of all the earth—may the Republican Party, under God, from every mountainside, LET FREEDOM RING!

Quotation of the lyrics from "America," as we will see, had a substantial tradition in African American culture, from its composition in the 1830s through King's own day. But the rest of Carey's 1952 speech merits brief consideration for what it can tell us about King's speech eleven years later.

After Dwight Eisenhower's eight years in office, African Americans would have reason to be frustrated by his lukewarm support of civil rights. On the eve of his nomination, however, Carey challenged the party of Lincoln—which at that time took a stronger stand on civil rights than did the Democrats and which the great majority of blacks still supported—not only to fight for democracy abroad but also to widen "freedom's borders" at home. In keeping with its occasion, Carey's speech contained a good deal of political boilerplate, but he was no apologist for prevailing racial norms and struck a number of chords resonant with King's later words. We cannot "compromise with righteousness," Carey insisted, nor can we temporize. Although some would say that "the time is not ripe," his rejoinder was to the point: "No man can enjoy his civil rights posthumously. Last Friday's anniversary of the Declaration of Independence reminds us that if we gave the disfranchised their every right to which they are entitled today, we'd still be one hundred seventy six years late." In other passages, indeed, Carey was more daring than King. "The string of promises dangled before my people like a glittering necklace," he said, employing a metaphoric version of the promissory note more provocative than any ventured by King, "has been fashioned into a tight-fitting noose about their throats, strangling their freedom . . . and sometimes even their hopes."

At the same time, Carey was careful to specify the limits of his demands. His answer to the question "What does the Negro-American want?" rejected any form of favoritism. All blacks want, he argued, is "the right to live and work and play, to vote and get an education and be promoted, to fight for our country and hope to be President, like everyone else. More than that we do not ask, but with less than that we shall never be content." Still, it would be a mistake to assume that Carey's espousal of colorblind equal opportunity was a partisan position. On this point and others his speech and King's had much in common. Few listening in 1963 to King's famous wish that one day his children "will not be judged by the color of their skin but by the content of their character," not to mention those listening to Carey in 1952, would have openly advocated racial favoritism. King's answer to the question "When will you be satisfied?" was more militant than Carey's answer to the question "What does the Negro want?" So, too, his warning to those who "hope that the Negro needed to blow off steam and will now be content" was somewhat more threatening than Carey's assertion that the Negro "shall never be content" with less than equal rights as citizens. The differences in tone help to explain why King sounded radical to many, but they must also be measured against the fact that King, no less than Carey, made the Declaration of Independence his principal touchstone, while Carey, just as emphatically as King, underscored the unredeemed promissory note held by black Americans.

If Carey's name and words may have been lost on them, many in King's black audience, if not so many in his white, would certainly have recognized the source of his final words in the slave spiritual "I Thank God I'm Free at Last," one of those songs whose religious meaning was overlaid, even before emancipation but most certainly afterward, with concrete political meaning:

Free at last, free at last, I thank God I'm free at last.
On-a my knees when the light pass'd by . . .
Thought my soul would rise and fly . . .
Some of these mornin's bright and fair . . .
I'm gonna meet my Jesus in the middle of the air . . .
Free at last, free at last, I thank God I'm free at last.

Beyond its adaptation in a powerful freedom movement song, the phrase "free at last" crops up often in the civil rights discourse of the postwar era. The theologian Howard Thurman, for example, employed it in his 1949 book *Jesus and the Disinherited* to illustrate the parable of Jesus and the adulteress in John 8:7 ("He that is without sin among you, let him first cast a stone at her"), who by virtue of Christ's forgiveness is liberated in grace: "Free at last, free at last. / Thank God Almighty, I'm free at last." The year before King's speech, the poet Robert Hayden had woven the phrase ingeniously into "The Ballad of Nat Turner," his meditation on Turner's apocalyptic slave revolt: "At last free / And purified, I rose and prayed . . . And bided my time." After the South's surrender at Appomattox, the slaves in Alex Haley's *Roots* break into great jubilation, "whooping, shouting, singing, preaching, praying 'Free, Lawd, free' . . . 'Thank Gawd A'mighty, free at las'!'" Not long after becoming president, even Lyndon Johnson told Roy Wilkins that he was "free at last" to act as president without the constraints placed upon him as a senator from Texas, while at the 1960 Democratic Convention, King himself declared simply, "We want to be free everywhere, free at last, free at last." The spiritual's concluding lines—Free at last. Free at last. Thank God Almighty I'm Free at Last—would supply the epitaph for his tomb in Atlanta.

In the conjunction of lyrics from "America" and those from "I Thank God I'm Free at Last," the white and black songs joining hands, as it were, King gave musical voice to a new proclamation of emancipation while calling to mind other lyrics of liberation. King's exhortation to "let freedom ring" encompassed the progressivist beliefs celebrated in "If I Had a Hammer" (1949), a Pete Seeger song whose words about "the hammer of justice" and "the bell of freedom" being heard "all over this land" had already entered the civil rights vocabulary before the Top Ten versions by Peter, Paul, and Mary in 1962 and Trini Lopez in 1963. No doubt King was also drawn back to the familiar lyrics of "America" because they were congruent with the pledge cards that were to be signed by March on Washington participants, according to which they vowed to work for justice and make sure that "my voice and those of my brothers ring clear and determined from every corner of our land."

More specifically, however, King alluded to the nation's preeminent symbol of freedom, the Liberty Bell, on which was inscribed a biblical injunction: "Proclaim liberty throughout *all* the land unto all the inhabitants thereof" (Leviticus 25:10). Only when it was adopted as an antislavery symbol in the abolitionist pamphlet *The Liberty Bell* in 1837, in fact, did the Old State House Bell, which had called Philadelphia residents to hear the first reading of the Declaration of Independence, become known by that name. Subsequent editions of the pamphlet and related poems made the Liberty Bell a patriotic emblem of black freedom. H. R. H. Moore's 1844 sonnet "The Liberty Bell," for example, sounded a clarion call toward the South later emulated by King: "Ring, ring the mighty Bell. . . . Ring it Southward, till its voice / For slavery toll, for slavery toll. . . . Ring it, till the slave be free." In "Lift Every Voice and Sing," written in 1900 for Lincoln's birthday and subsequently adapted with music as the Negro National Anthem, James Weldon Johnson likewise began with a vocal ringing of the Liberty Bell—"Lift every voice and sing / Till earth and heaven ring, / Ring with the harmonies of Liberty"—and ended by calling upon heaven to keep blacks "True to our God, / True to our native land."

Johnson wrote at a time when the Liberty Bell was traveling to a variety of cities and expositions across the country in a goodwill tour intended to symbolize the nation's post–Civil War unity. But his poem was meant to demonstrate that the bell's injunction from Leviticus remained unfulfilled—that the reunion of North and South had come at the cost of African American rights. In his own sweeping, repeated call to "let freedom ring" in 1963, King not only alluded to Johnson and to the abolitionist tradition associated with the Liberty Bell. He also, as we shall see, returned to 1863, the "year of jubilee," when the commandment of Leviticus to redeem indebted bondsmen and restore alienated land had suddenly been made real—or so it seemed. In joining his voice to the nation's transcendent values, at once scriptural and republican, King once again, a century later, proclaimed "liberty throughout *all* the land."

King was often charged with being an "outside" agitator. It was a charge he easily refuted in "Letter from Birmingham Jail" by pointing to the region-wide operations of the SCLC and its affiliation with the Birmingham-based Alabama Christian Movement for Human Rights. By the same token, he pled guilty to the charge by insisting that, like the Apostle Paul, he was compelled to carry the gospel beyond his home community. "Injustice anywhere is a threat to justice everywhere," as King frequently argued, for all people "are caught in an inescapable network of mutuality, tied in a single garment of destiny." This philosophical argument was also, at its core, King's most potent moral argument against the states' rights underpinnings of segregation. "A breakdown of law in Alabama weakens the very foundations of lawful government in the other forty-seven states," he wrote of the Montgomery boycott. "When a police dog buried his fangs in the ankle of a small child in Birmingham," he said of his Birmingham campaign, "he buried his fangs in the ankle of every American."

President Kennedy reiterated these sentiments, more blandly, in his June 11 speech—"the rights of every man are diminished when the rights of one man are threatened"—but the religious dimension of the contest between the authority of the nation and the authority of the states was better stated by Joachim Prinz in his speech at the March. "Neighbor is not a geographic term," Prinz declared, citing an idea vital to the history of both Jewish and Christian ethics. "It is a moral concept. It means our collective responsibility for the preservation of man's dignity and integrity." The states' rights argument, according to Prinz and King, set neighbor against neighbor—white against black, South against North—diminishing rather than enhancing the nation's security and moral authority. Only those who sat down together at "the table of brotherhood" and joined hands "as brothers and sisters" could be true neighbors—true citizens of one nation and one world.

In portraying the nation as a set of interconnected mountain ranges, King thus placed its destiny not only in a discourse of transcendence and redemption but also in one of constitutional significance. His blazing climactic lines made mountains both impediments to freedom and prospects from which freedom could be seen, as they were in his many sermons and speeches built upon the Exodus. The lines made for magnificent oratory—their cadences and alliteration were perfectly fitted to the booming tones of his voice—but their circumscription of the country from north to south and east to west was also significant for the way they expressed King's continuing insistence that, although his first aim was to transform the South, he spoke as a citizen of the *nation*. King called for national unity—but not the specious post–Civil War unity that required acquiescence in proliferating Jim Crow laws. He called instead for a new age in which Lookout Mountain in Tennessee (site of a Confederate stronghold during the Civil War, but one that fell to Union forces in the 1863 "Battle above the Clouds") and Stone Mountain in Georgia (site of the founding of the second Ku Klux Klan in

1915) would also be included in the grand panorama of American freedom.

The audacity of King's dream, in 1963, can be measured by simple reference to coverage of the March appearing in the *Atlanta Constitution* the day after the event. Writing in a front-page story, the paper's editor, Eugene Patterson, portrayed a majestic occasion and quoted extensively from King's speech, emphasizing its "powerful appeal founded on patriotism and peace." In the story's continuation deeper in the paper, however, Patterson's message of brotherhood, along with the paper's two other lead stories about the March, sat side by side with a two-column, six-inch advertisement:

**NATIONAL
KU KLUX KLAN RALLY**

**Prominent Speakers
Cross Burning**

**STONE MOUNTAIN, GA.
AUGUST 31, 1963
7:30 P.M.**

Largest Ever Held in the Country

Delegations from 46 States

Press Representatives from 5 Foreign Countries

PUBLIC INVITED

Klansmen and families urged to attend

FREE PARKING

Stone Mountain did not yet belong to the United States of America envisioned by King.

Soul Force

When news came that the Supreme Court had declared the segregation of Montgomery buses unconstitutional, King remembered, one bystander called out, "God Almighty has spoken from Washington, D.C." No one in King's circle would have been surprised by such a response, least of all King. In explaining the success of the boycott, against great odds, King attributed it not just to the impetus of *Brown v. Board of Education;* not just to the long-building frustration of fifty thousand blacks who, like Rosa Parks, were ready to "substitute tired feet for tired souls"; not just to the fresh leadership of the Montgomery Improvement Association and King himself. The true explanation—a "suprarational" explanation—could only be that God chose the Cradle of the Confederacy "as the proving ground for the struggle and triumph of freedom and justice in America."

King spoke somewhat differently from the pulpit than from the secular rostrum, of course, but only somewhat, and many of his most significant political speeches were made in churches or explicitly as sermons. Borrowing equally from theology and folk tradition,

King turned everyday faith into an instrument of racial justice. Andrew Young described the galvanizing effect:

> Nobody could have ever argued [simply about] segregation and integration and gotten people convinced to do anything about that. But when Martin would talk about leaving the slavery of Egypt and wandering in the wilderness of separate but equal and moving into a Promised Land, somehow that made sense to folks. . . . When they heard that language, they responded. You could go into Mississippi and tell people they needed to get themselves together and get organized. And that didn't make much sense. But if you started preaching to them about dry bones rising again, everybody had sung about dry bones. Everybody knew the language. . . . You had a ready framework around which you could organize people.

If people responded to King's biblical language because it was familiar, they also responded because it was King speaking—speaking in an alluring voice whose authority came from on high. When he began his ministry at Dexter Avenue Baptist Church in 1954, King set forth thirty-four specific recommendations to his congregation but prefaced his agenda with an unambiguous statement of his authority: "Inherent in the [minister's] call itself is the presupposition that God directed that such a call be made. This fact makes it crystal clear that the pastor's authority is not merely humanly conferred, but divinely sanctioned."

However much youthful brashness was at work in King's challenge to his congregation, the midnight visitation he experienced less than two years later confirmed him as a man who spoke if not with God's authority, at least with his blessing. Having listened to yet another hate-filled phone call from a white supremacist threatening him with death because of his leadership of the bus boycott, King prayed for strength and suddenly, as though by grace, received it: "At that moment I experienced the presence of the Divine as I had never experienced Him before. It seemed as though I could hear the quiet assurance of an inner voice saying: 'Stand up for righteousness, stand up for truth; and God will be at your side forever.' Almost at once my fears began to go. My uncertainty disappeared. I was ready to face anything." Although he had moments of exhausted despair and premonitions of death until they finally came true in Memphis, King never again lacked for courage or doubted the righteousness of the role he had been called to play, for his people and for his nation.

Telling the story of Birmingham and the March on Washington in *Why We Can't Wait*, King began with a simple declarative sentence: "It is the year of our Lord 1963." In his echo of the Emancipation Proclamation ("in the year of our Lord one thousand eight hundred and sixty-three"), as well as of Abraham Lincoln's penchant for dating his actions or events setting the course of the nation's history with reference to God's time, King's language cast back to the public rhetoric of an earlier era. Think of Lincoln's argument, just to take one example, that the central premise of the Declaration of Independence—"we hold these truths to be self-evident: that all men are created equal; that they are endowed by their Creator with certain unalienable rights; that among these are life, liberty, and the pursuit of happiness"—reflected the Founding Fathers' "understanding of the justice of the Creator to His creatures. Yes, gentlemen, to *all* His creatures." All of God's "creatures," all of those created in his image, in Lincoln's usage, were likewise God's "children," all of those born of divinity, in King's lifelong usage.

"If they ask you who you are, tell them you're a child of God," sang Odetta at the March on Washington, a locution less familiar in our day than in King's—when school prayer had not yet been declared unconstitutional, when the words "under God" had just been added to the Pledge of Allegiance in 1954, when two years later

Congress would make "In God We Trust" the national motto, and when it was in no way curious, but perfectly normal, for the narrator of *The Great Emancipation March on Washington*, one of the recordings released immediately after the event, to say: "Perhaps not since men turned their ears to the preachings of a mere carpenter, two thousand years ago, have the words of humble men reached so many with such force and meaning." King used the phrase "all of God's children" three times in the Dream speech:

> Now is the time to make justice a reality for all of God's children.

> This will be the day, this will be the day when all of God's children will be able to sing with new meaning:
>
>> My country, 'tis of thee, sweet land of liberty, of thee
>>   I sing.
>> Land where my fathers died, land of the pilgrim's pride,
>> From every mountainside, let freedom ring!

> And when this happens, when we allow freedom [to] ring, when we let it ring from every village and every hamlet, from every state and every city, we will be able to speed up that day when all of God's children, black men and white men, Jews and Gentiles, Protestants and Catholics, will be able to join hands and sing in the words of the old Negro spiritual:
>
>> Free at last! Free at last!
>> Thank God Almighty, we are free at last!

In each case, he announced that all Americans were God's children; all were heirs to the precepts of the Founding Fathers; all should be able to claim the "sweet land of liberty" as their own.

In King's usage, "God's children" were the "children of Israel," as in Exodus 6:5, where God speaks to Moses, promising deliverance from Pharaoh: "And I have also heard the groaning of the children of Israel, whom the Egyptians keep in bondage; and I have remembered my covenant." They were likewise the New Testament's "children of God," redeemed in Christ, as in Luke 20:36: "Neither can they die any more: for they are equal unto the angels; and are the children of God, being the children of the resurrection." Within the African American tradition, the children of God were specifically something other, something greater than the white man had tried to make them. In an assignment he prepared as a seminary student, King cited a story told by Howard Thurman, who heard it from his grandmother, who heard it in a slave preacher's secret worship service: "You—you are not niggers. You—you are not slaves. You are God's children," an affirmation, said Thurman, that established a "ground of personal dignity" strong enough to immunize them against degrading assault, whether physical or emotional.

In "the story of the children of Israel," wrote R. Nathaniel Dett, an early scholar of the slave spirituals, blacks found "much in the way of a text that was ready made." In African American practice, however, the sufferings of the Jews and the suffering of Christ were wedded, so that the slaves' Jesus frequently resembled an avenging Hebrew prophet, a warrior who promised physical emancipation as well as spiritual liberation, or a new incarnation of Moses, ready to lead them to the Promised Land. Several scenes of prophecy, as well as their implicit New Testament fulfillment in the saving power of Christ, provide the main biblical framework for the Dream speech. But the foundation for King's message, because it was also the foundation of African American political life expressed in religious terms, was the Exodus—God's promise to the children of Israel translated into the promise of equality articulated in the Declaration of Independence and subsequently renewed in the promissory note of the Emancipation Proclamation.

This rendition of the Exodus was ready made for African American use because it built upon a dominant analogy of colonial American life. Inscribed within a narrative of biblical redemption, the nation sprang from a deep identification with the Israelite experience—the belief that Americans, having fled religious persecution, were to liberate the world in fulfillment of scripture. Cotton Mather declared that William Bradford was the Moses of the Puritan migration, and on the eve of the American Revolution theologically conservative preachers portrayed corrupt England as a typological Egypt, a conception that endured metaphorically into the next century. "Escaped from the house of bondage," wrote Herman Melville of the nation's providential claim, America is "the Israel of our time . . . the peculiar, chosen people." Yet the persistence of slavery proved to Lincoln that the metaphor had failed, and he asked to be made a "humble instrument in the hands of the Almighty, and of this, his almost chosen people," for perpetuating the "great promise" made by the Founding Fathers "to all the people of the world [for] all time to come."

"Emancipation," W. E. B. Du Bois argued on the fortieth anniversary of Lincoln's order in 1903, "was the key to [a] promised land of sweeter beauty than ever stretched before the eyes of wearied Israelites." What once came "suddenly, fearfully, like a dream," however, remained just a dream forty years later—and then sixty years after that, when Du Bois's words might have been spoken by King. Each generation from slavery onward refashioned the Exodus to fit its needs, and the analogy stayed alive in countless forms because African Americans, to cite Langston Hughes, were left forever seeking a "dream deferred," left forever in pursuit of Canaan's mirage, a Promised Land that is "always just ahead." When they migrated north "on that long-overdue Judgment Day," wrote Claude Brown in *Manchild in the Promised Land* (1965), the "black chillun o' God" inherited not milk and honey but poverty and hopelessness:

"For where does one run to when he's already in the promised land?" The "manacles of segregation" were manacles still, as King stated in the Dream speech, because segregation extended "the long night of [the slaves'] captivity" into the present, where the African American still found "himself an exile in his own land."

As early as 1956, when he was featured on the cover of *Jet* magazine as "Alabama's Modern Moses," King was seen, and saw himself, as the one who might at long last lead his people to Canaan. The topic of his speech at the 1957 Prayer Pilgrimage for Freedom was voting rights—"give us the ballot," King repeated in his trademark incantatory style—but its thematic center was a variation on the Exodus: "It is always difficult to get out of Egypt, for the Red Sea always stands before you with discouraging dimensions. And even after you've crossed the Red Sea, you have to move through a wilderness with prodigious hilltops of evil and gigantic mountains of opposition." No figurative language was better suited than the Exodus to show King's binary presupposition that only those who have suffered enslavement and exile can know the true taste of freedom; only those who have scaled the "hilltops of evil" and the "mountains of opposition" will hear the true glory of freedom when it rings not just from the "heightening Alleghenies" but also from Stone Mountain.

King's exceptional command of the narrative structure of the biblical Exodus, which reached its oratorical climax in his "Promised Land" speech in Memphis, both reflected and heightened his own identity as a Mosaic figure called to a great but hazardous struggle for liberation. To achieve freedom, as he later put it, blacks had to maintain their unity and bear in mind a primary lesson of the Exodus: "You know, whenever Pharaoh wanted to prolong the period of slavery in Egypt, he had a favorite formula for doing it. . . . He kept the slaves fighting among themselves." Here, as elsewhere in his speeches and writings, King introduced a basic device of the Exodus—the halting, episodic delivery from bondage brought on by uprisings among those who doubt the leader's wisdom or envy his power. Dissent from his nonviolent strategy by members of SNCC or other militants illustrated to King that "every revolutionary movement has its peaks of united activity and its valleys of debate and internal confusion," with victory achieved only after periods of "inevitable counterrevolution."

As though revealing biblical typology in his own example, King identified not just with Moses and the prophets. He also wrapped himself in the garment of St. Paul, first in "Paul's Letter to American Christians"—"I was on fire with the words I was hearing," said John Lewis, who listened to the sermon on the radio—and most famously and self-consciously in "Letter from Birmingham Jail." Even before his death, moreover, King made himself one with the Passion of Christ, with whom Coretta Scott King felt he had "a mystical identity." When he went to jail in Birmingham, King said that he represented the millions of black Americans "who dreamed that someday they might be able to cross the Red Sea of injustice and find their way to the promised land of integration and freedom," but he chose Good Friday for the power of its symbolic message, stated repeatedly in his sermons, that to reach the resurrection of Easter, one must pass through the crucifixion of Good Friday. It was not just the newspaper editor James Gray of Albany, Georgia, who began to mark time past as "B.K."—that is, "Before King"— the era before the messianic rupture King created in the southern, as well as the American, way of life. "I was praying and hoping when they put him in [jail on] Good Friday," joked comedian Dick Gregory, that they would have "checked back there Easter morning and he would have been *gone*."

Like the biblical Moses, King did not live to enter Canaan—a fact poignantly presaged in the speech he delivered on the eve of his assassination: "I just want to do God's will. And He's allowed me to go up to the mountain. And I've looked over, and I've seen the Promised Land. I may not get there with you. But I want you to know tonight, that we, as a people, will get to the Promised Land." He did, however, find his Golgotha. "The cross is something that you bear and ultimately that you die on," he told an SCLC audience near the end of his life. "And that's the way I have decided to go." In his Memphis speech, King was the picture of exhaustion, desperation, and crucifixion combined. Having truly become the Man of Sorrows, his face contorted with weariness, King summoned up, for the last time, his vision of the Promised Land he would not reach and closed abruptly with the opening line of "The Battle Hymn of the Republic"—"Mine eyes have seen the glory of the coming of the Lord"—as he wheeled awkwardly back to his left and collapsed, before the sentence was finished, into the arms of Ralph Abernathy.

In juxtaposing the language of prophecy with that of patriotism, King drew upon a tradition with its roots in the antislavery movement. It was an argument he had been rehearsing for years. In a college paper on the prophet Jeremiah, for example, King dwelled on the fact that the covenant given at Mount Sinai had failed to accomplish its purpose. Because of the people's apostasy, a new covenant was needed, one in which the supersession of Old Testament law by New Testament faith had parallels in the higher law of racial justice that would supersede the unjust laws of segregation. "The law written upon stone is to be replaced by the law written in the heart," argued King, so that the children of God will be "no longer subject to external laws of the state, but ruled by impulses of good, acting upon the heart as a principle which grows from within." In political terms, this new covenant would restore the law of the Founding Fathers, subverted first by slavery and then by segregation, to its original purpose. It has been said that King, a latter-day Jeremiah, demythologized the American covenant, exposing its corruption and hypocrisy, but it is more accurate to say that he *re*mythologized the covenant, inhabiting and redeeming it in his own visionary language.

This was the new covenant envisioned by Margaret Walker in her poem "At the Lincoln Monument in Washington, August 28, 1963":

Write this word upon your hearts
And mark this message on the doors of your houses
See that you do not forget
How this day the Lord has set your faces toward Freedom
Teach these words to your children
And see that they do not forget them.
Recite them in your going out and your coming in
And speak them in the silence of the night.
Remember the covenant we have made together
Here in the eyes of our Liberator.

Spoken under the gaze of Lincoln, the words of King's Dream speech here merge with core elements of the Hebrew Bible. Walker ingeniously combines the commandment to celebrate the Passover —signifying the last of the ten plagues, when the Egyptian firstborn were slain by God, who "passed over" the houses of the Israelites because they had marked their doorposts with the blood of the Pascal lamb (Exodus 12:21–27)—with the commandment to remember God's words: "thou shalt teach them diligently unto thy children" and "thou shalt write them upon the posts of thy house" (Deuteronomy 6:7,9). Just as God's covenant with Moses required testing and renewal, so the American covenant, incompletely realized in the Declaration of Independence and then again in the Emancipation Proclamation and the Civil War amendments, required renewal. Not only that, but Walker made King's own words the new commandment, as though God himself were speaking "here in the eyes of our Liberator" and instructing that his words, the Dream speech, be marked "on the doors of your houses," taught "to your children" and spoken "in the silence of the night."

■

When at last the Israelites came into their Promised Land, led not by Moses but by Joshua, they came in fighting. Armed revolt would have gained nothing for African Americans in the 1960s, however, and King considered any resort to violence on the part of blacks both foolhardy and immoral. Still, it would be mistaken to say that King did not appreciate the instrumental power of violence.

When King moved back to Atlanta in 1960, Georgia Governor Ernest Vandiver said that he was not welcome, for wherever King had gone there followed in his wake "a wave of crimes including stabbing, bombings, and inciting of riots, barratry, destruction of property and many others." Vandiver was not alone in charging that King's nonviolence caused violence. The FBI harped on this idea, and both *Time* magazine, in its "Man of the Year" story, and *U.S. News and World Report*, in its story about his Nobel Prize, made the same point. Seeking to stop the demonstrations led by King and others, Alabama in 1962 enacted a law making it a criminal offense to commit any "acts or make any gestures or communications which are calculated to, or will probably so outrage the sense of decency and morals or so violate or transgress the customs, patterns of life and habits of the people of Alabama as to be likely to cause a riot or breach of the peace." In other words, civil rights demonstrators were responsible for the harm inflicted upon them by white mobs.

There is no better example than King's imprisonment on Good Friday, 1963, in the Birmingham city jail. The injunction that King defied that day came in response to the city's contention that the demonstrators' conduct was "calculated to provoke breaches of the peace" and constituted a threat to "the safety, peace and tranquility of the City." (The contempt convictions of those who violated the injunction were eventually upheld by the Supreme Court in *Walker v. City of Birmingham*, handed down in 1967.) Both the new Alabama statute and the injunction proved that King's tactics were effective. Nonviolent direct action was, indeed, calculated to provoke breaches of the peace, if not outright brutality, on the part of city and state law enforcement. It required discipline and courage, but, as King argued at two points in the Dream speech, the reward was social justice and personal redemption:

> But there is something I must say to my people, who stand on the warm threshold which leads into the palace of justice: In the process of gaining our rightful place, we must not be guilty of wrongful deeds. Let us not seek to satisfy our thirst for freedom by drinking from the cup of bitterness and hatred. We must forever conduct our struggle on the high plane of dignity and discipline. We must not allow our creative protest to degenerate into physical violence. Again and again, we must rise to the majestic heights of meeting physical force with soul force.

> I am not unmindful that some of you have come here out of great trials and tribulations. Some of you have come fresh from narrow jail cells. And some of you have come from areas where your quest for freedom left you battered by the storms of persecution and staggered by the winds of police brutality. You have been the veterans of creative suffering. Continue to work with the faith that unearned suffering is redemptive.

"Christ furnished the spirit and the motivation," King said of the Montgomery boycott, "and Gandhi furnished the method." The method was an American adaptation of Mohandas Gandhi's idea of a *shanti sena*, an army of peace volunteers, whose defining feature would be *Satyagraha*, a neologism meaning, in Gandhi's words, "holding on to the Truth," hence "truth force" or "soul force." Satyagraha excludes the use of violence, said Gandhi, because "man is not capable of knowing the absolute truth and, therefore, [is] not competent to punish." "Soul force" resembled the civil disobedience of Henry David Thoreau—so long as any state is complicit in slavery, wrote Thoreau, "the true place for a just man" is jail, where he will have God on his side—but it differed from "passive resistance" in that it was not "a weapon of the weak" but rather a weapon of strength by means of which the enemy could be "weaned from error by patience and sympathy."

King's frequently reiterated doctrine of *agape*—the selfless capacity to love the person who does an evil deed while hating the deed, to abhor the unjust system rather than individuals who are caught in that system—was a Christian form of Satyagraha whose aim was constantly to enlarge the "beloved community," a concept King borrowed from Josiah Royce. "The power that gives to the Christian convert the new loyalty is what Paul calls Grace," wrote Royce. "And the community to which, when grace saves him, the convert is thenceforth to be loyal, we may call . . . 'The Beloved Community.'" In its most expansive form, this was King's dream, to draw more and more converts into the beloved community of spiritual resistance to injustice, ultimately encompassing what he referred to as the "world house," the global family of black, brown, and yellow "brothers" moving "with a great sense of urgency toward the promised land of racial justice."

Well before King, Gandhi had shaped more than a generation of African American protest. As early as 1922 James Weldon Johnson wondered why the methods of Gandhi, already having a dramatic impact in colonial India, could not also be used to "bring the white man to his knees in the South." In an essay addressed "To the American Negro" seven years later, Gandhi himself counseled American blacks not to be "ashamed of the fact that they are the grandchildren of slaves." Dishonor belonged to the slaveholders, not the slaves, and the future lay with those who would be "truthful, pure and loving." A. Philip Randolph's March on Washington Movement was conceived as a Gandhian campaign of nonviolent direct action, and CORE itself grew out of a 1942 plan James Farmer submitted to the Fellowship of Reconciliation, headed by A. J. Muste, calling for the "creative" application of Gandhian tactics in a national campaign to extend over a period of up to ten years. Along with Bayard Rustin, the Fellowship's director of race relations and later, as we have seen, the logistical mastermind of the March on Washington, Farmer integrated public transportation facilities in some northern and border states through the 1947 Journey of Reconciliation, the first Freedom Ride.

The Gandhian philosophy of nonviolent direct action was promulgated among African Americans in the postwar radio sermons of William Holmes Borders and Kelly Miller Smith, among others. Having traveled to India, a number of leading black academics, including Benjamin Mays and Mordecai Johnson, likewise spread Gandhi's word to an African American audience. A commentary on Gandhi by Harris Wofford, an attorney for the United States Commission on Civil Rights, formed the foundation of King's chapter "The Pilgrimage to Nonviolence" in *Stride toward Freedom*, while Rustin and James Lawson, an SCLC staff member, deepened King's knowledge of the philosophy of nonviolence during and after the Montgomery campaign. (Rustin also convinced King that, even if he had no intention of using it, it was improper to keep a gun in his house.) Following his own trip to India 1959, King spoke of Gandhi, a Hindu, as "the greatest Christian of the twentieth century" and likened him to Lincoln. Both were assassinated, as King would be, for attempting to "heal the wounds of a divided nation."

King did not try to duplicate Gandhi's personal asceticism—his self-imposed poverty, his hunger strikes, his sexual abstinence. He also took as much from students of Gandhi as from Gandhi him-self—for example, Richard Gregg's argument that nonviolence is a kind of "moral jiu-jitsu" whose aim is not to injure one's opponent but to reestablish "his moral balance" on a higher plane. Nor did King wrestle strenuously with the limitations of Gandhian non-violence. Writing in 1961, Ved Mehta called Gandhi "a supreme political artist," whose boycotts, fasts, and marches were "symbolic, dramatic gestures" intended to embarrass and defeat the enemy, a description that applied equally well to King, who approvingly re-peated Gandhi's garish dictum, "rivers of blood may have to flow before we gain our freedom, but it must be our blood." As Mehta observed, however, such tactics would have been useless in Stalin's Soviet Union or Hitler's Germany.

The more radical claims of Black Power to the contrary, America was not a fascist state, and King was not required to follow nonvio-lence to its endgame. Because he calculated correctly that the fed-eral government, backed by the Supreme Court, would have to in-tervene and constrain the authority of southern states, Jim Crow laws and customs were the perfect target for nonviolent direct ac-tion. He also calculated correctly that even avowed racists, gradu-ally if not immediately, could be affected by Gandhian practices couched in the tenets of Christ. "These young people are about their Father's business," said King of the children protesting in Birmingham, thereby comparing them to the twelve-year-old Jesus, who alarmed his earthly parents when he tarried in Jerusalem after Passover, discussing theology with the rabbis. ("How is it that ye sought me?" replied Jesus to his worried mother when his parents returned to find him, according to Luke 2:49. "Wist ye not that I must be about my Father's business?") In doing the right thing, he frequently reminded his enemies, they would be doing both the constitutional thing and the Christian thing. The Birmingham Manifesto was thus a direct answer to the states' rights creed of the

Southern Manifesto: "We act today in full concert with our Hebraic-Christian tradition, the law of morality, and the Constitution of our nation. The absence of justice and progress in Birmingham demands that we make a moral witness to give our community a chance to survive." Where better than the South, in the aftermath of World War II and *Brown v. Board of Education*, to make "the blood of the martyr . . . the seed of the tabernacle of freedom?"

The concepts of creative protest and creative suffering to which King referred in the Dream speech, at first glance curious, carried several mutually reinforcing connotations. Nonviolent direct action was designed, in the simplest sense, to create a crisis in which public protest would become political theater, a clash between good and evil, ideally in the spotlight of international newspaper and television coverage. In a memo to Andrew Young during the Selma campaign, for example, King reminded him not to let a day go by without a demonstration: "In a crisis we must have a sense of drama."

Suffering in the cause of nonviolent direct action was creative because, as Gandhi taught, it was purifying and morally elevating—it re-created the self on a higher plane with a higher purpose. In this respect, Gandhi's philosophy was the opposite of that promulgated by Frantz Fanon in *The Wretched of the Earth*, which was translated into English in 1961 and soon became, as Eldridge Cleaver put it, "the Bible" of Black Power. It is not nonviolence but rather the violence of anticolonial revolt, declared Fanon, that cleanses the oppressed and forges "a new language and new humanity" born of the "bloodstained knives which emanate from it." Given the upsurge in protests during 1963, King, as if answering Fanon, wondered rhetorically why "the knife of violence" had not pierced the nation's aorta. (His metaphor was both visceral and personal. After King was stabbed by a deranged woman in Harlem in 1958, his doctor remarked chillingly that, had he sneezed, the blade of the knife would have punctured his aorta and he would have "drowned in his own blood.") More rampant violence had been averted in 1963, said King, because nonviolent direct action, the "triumphant tactic of the Negro Revolution," is a "sword that heals," one that "cuts without wounding and ennobles the man who wields it."

If nonviolent direct action was intended to be ennobling, it was also, in King's view, pragmatic. After the bombing of the Sixteenth Street Baptist Church, Anne Moody lost patience with nonviolence, telling God that if he was white, she rejected him, but if he was black, "I'll try my best to kill you when I get to heaven." Moody's anger notwithstanding, King preached the power of love in his eulogy for the girls, and he would have concurred with Christopher McNair, the father of one, who asked, "What good would Denise have done with a machine gun in her hand?" As King later remarked of calls by the Black Panthers and others for an urban guerrilla uprising, violence was not just sinful but futile: "The courageous efforts of our own insurrectionist brothers, such as Denmark Vesey and Nat Turner, should be eternal reminders to us that violent rebellion is doomed from the start." (Here King appeared to borrow from Du Bois in *The Souls of Black Folk*: "The death of Denmark Vesey and Nat Turner proved long since to the Negro the present hopelessness of physical defense.") Rejecting both the "Uncle Tomism" of Negro accommodationists and the "hot-headedness" of Black Power, King, as he put it, sought to reconcile "the truths of two opposites—acquiescence and violence—while avoiding the extremes and immoralities of both."

King's antagonists had ready rejoinders to his philosophy of love. Proponents of Black Theology such as Albert Cleage, Jr., and James Cone rejected his Pauline nonviolence as a falsification of scripture and espoused a Marxian liberation theology grounded in the politics of color. Because God chose the oppressed as his allies, wrote Cone, "Christianity is not alien to Black Power; it is Black Power." Even Kenneth Clark, no radical, worried that King's strategy, the antithesis of the damaging "doctrine of hatred and racism preached by the black nationalists," would produce pathological effects in those asked to suffer because of its seeming comportment with the "stereotype of the Negro as a meek, long-suffering creature who prays for deliverance but who rarely acts decisively against injustices." Malcolm X may have struck a comradely note in speaking with Coretta Scott King during an unpublicized visit to Selma—"If the white people realize what the alternative is," Malcolm confided, "perhaps they will be more willing to hear Dr. King"—but he owed much of his allure to cavalier insistence that nonviolence was no match for violence: "If [the white man's] language is with a shotgun, get a shotgun. . . . If he only understands the language of the rope, get a rope. But don't waste time talking the wrong language to a man if you want to really communicate with him."

Only once did King appear to concede such a point. "Maybe it's good to shed a little blood," he told an interviewer in February 1956, as the hardships endured by bus boycotters, as well as the danger to his own life, grew day by day. "What needs to be done is for a couple of those white men to lose some blood; then the Federal Government will step in." When his own home had been bombed just five days earlier, however, King dispersed an angry mob bent on revenge by insisting that they put away their weapons and love their white enemies. Rather than white blood, black blood was to be shed—not submissively, not uselessly, but in order to break the white man's spirit, disgrace him before God, and lead him to salvation. "If the oppressors bomb the home of one Negro for his courage," King maintained, they must be forced to recognize that they are "required to bomb the homes of fifty thousand more Negroes. This dynamic unity, this amazing self-respect, this willingness to suffer" will shame the oppressor and force him "to stand before the world and his God splattered with the blood and reeking with the stench of his Negro brother."

There will always be an audience for a powerful idea.

Before it's an event, it's an idea. For 90 years and counting,

The New Republic has been at the forefront of liberal thought.

And that's where you should join us.

Subscribe today at **tnr.com/subscribe** or call 800.827.1289.

Where opinions get started.

1. Advertisement in the *New Republic*, February 27, 2006. Created by The Ryan Group, courtesy of the *New Republic*. Photograph © Bettmann / CORBIS.

2. Police dog attacking civil rights demonstrator, Birmingham, Alabama, May 3, 1963. Associated Press photograph featured in the *New York Times* and *Newsweek*, among other publications. © AP Images / Bill Hudson.

3. Governor George Wallace, facing Brigadier General Henry Graham of the Alabama National Guard, blocks a doorway at the University of Alabama, June 11, 1963. © Shel Hershorn / Hulton Archive / Getty Images.

4. Martin Luther King, Jr., featured as "Man of the Year," *Time*
magazine cover, January 3, 1964. Illustration by Robert Vickery.
© Time Magazine / Time and Life Pictures / Getty Images.

POWDER KEG

5. Bill Mauldin, "Powder Keg," *Chicago Sun-Times*, August 24, 1963. Copyright © 1963 by Bill Mauldin. Courtesy of the William Mauldin Estate. Print from the Library of Congress.

6. (*opposite, top*) A. Philip Randolph at the Lincoln Memorial,
March on Washington, August 28, 1963. © Bettmann / CORBIS.

7. (*opposite, bottom*) Martin Luther King, Jr. (center, on the white line) and
other March on Washington leaders set forth along Constitution Avenue,
August 28, 1963. Others pictured include John Lewis (second from left),
Mathew Ahmann (third from left), A. Philip Randolph (far right),
Roy Wilkins (second from right), Whitney Young (third from right),
and Joachim Prinz (fifth from right). © Bettmann / CORBIS.

8. (*this page*) Martin Luther King, Jr., photographed and filmed greeting
the crowd at the March on Washington, August 28, 1963.
© AFP / Getty Images.

9. Crowd gathered on the steps of the Lincoln Memorial and around the
Reflecting Pool at the March on Washington, August 28, 1963.
© Flip Schulke / CORBIS.

10. Crowd facing the speakers' podium, with the Reflecting Pool and the
Washington Monument in the background, at the March on Washington,
August 28, 1963. © Flip Schulke / CORBIS.

11. (*opposite, top*) Martin Luther King, Jr., speaking at the March on Washington, August 28; 1963. © Bettmann / CORBIS.

12. (*opposite, bottom*) Martin Luther King, Jr., speaking at the March on Washington, August 28, 1963. © Flip Schulke / CORBIS.

13. (*this page*) Mahalia Jackson singing at the March on Washington, August 28, 1963. Martin Luther King, Jr., is seated at the lower right; seated to his right are Whitney Young and Coretta Scott King. © Bob Parent / Hulton Archive / Getty Images.

14. Marian Anderson presenting an Easter concert before the Lincoln
Memorial, April 1, 1939. © Thomas D. McAvoy /
Time and Life Pictures / Getty Images.

15. Medgar Evers is laid to rest at Arlington National Cemetery,
June 19, 1963. Myrlie B. Evers, accompanied by her children,
is seated in the front row at the right. © Bettmann / CORBIS.

16. "I Had a Dream," cover image for the *Nation*, January 29, 2001.
Illustration by Art Spiegelman. Reprinted by permission of the *Nation*.

In addition to creating and sustaining public drama at a moment of crisis, then, nonviolent direct action was meant, as King wrote in "Letter from Birmingham Jail," to establish "such creative tension" that a community is forced to negotiate; it was designed "so to dramatize the issue that it can no longer be ignored" and "help men rise from the dark depths of prejudice and racism to the majestic heights of understanding and brotherhood." By acting in opposition to the "negative peace" and "uncivil disobedience" practiced by segregationists, King explained in 1961 to an audience of southern white liberals anxious about civil rights protest, the person who disobeys an unjust law actually expresses "the very highest respect for law." Her suffering becomes a "most creative and powerful social force" that touches people "where the law cannot reach them." Even some of King's staunchest black antagonists came to respect what he achieved. Speaking at Morehouse College in 1970, Stokely Carmichael, the former chairman of SNCC and prime minister of the Black Panthers, rebuked those who mocked King's nonviolent tactics and said it was King, not Malcolm X, not the Panthers, who first mobilized the masses and taught blacks to confront injustice.

Striking evidence of the power of soul force came when Birmingham firemen, who had previously knocked young protestors to the ground with water cannons strong enough to rip off their clothes, defied Bull Connor's orders to stop a group headed for a prayer vigil at the city jail. Even if the story of "Miracle Sunday" is somewhat apocryphal, its immediate entry into civil rights lore epitomized the faith of King's followers in the supremacy of nonviolent protest. "Suddenly, in the face of genuine Christian witness," Ralph Abernathy later recalled, Connor "was powerless to make his own men obey him. It was a moment of revelation that might have epitomized the entire meaning of the civil rights movement." Bull Connor knew only the physics of the material world, one that "didn't relate to the trans-physics that we knew about," said King, reflecting on

Birmingham in his final speech. "And that was the fact that there was a certain kind of fire that no water could put out."

■

"We just went on before the [police] dogs . . . singing, 'Over my head, I see freedom in the air,'" King continued, describing the triumph of soul force over the time-honored laws of segregation. Even in jail, "we'd see the jailers looking through the windows being moved by our prayers and being moved by our words and songs." Words and songs—the freedom music of the freedom movement was Gandhian Satyagraha made vocal, "the gift of the people to themselves, a bottomless reservoir of spiritual power," in the words of Andrew Young. The collective fortitude instilled by the music, said SNCC worker Phyllis Martin, translated dread into courage: "The fear down [South] is tremendous. I didn't know whether I'd be shot at, or stoned, or what. But when the singing started, I forgot all that. I felt good within myself."

Like other forms of witness, the nonviolent direct action of freedom music could touch people where the law did not reach them. Charles Sherrod related a story about the power of a movement version of "I've Been 'Buked and I've Been Scorned" during the Albany movement in 1962. When the local sheriff swaggered into a church where blacks were conducting a strategy meeting and declared, "We don't wanta hear no talk 'bout registerin' to vote in this county. . . . There won't be no Freedom Riders around here," the crowd began to sing softly, then louder, one woman beginning to moan, then others—"We've been 'buked and we've been scorned, / We've been talked about sure's you're born, / But we'll never turn back"—until at last the sheriff and his deputies were drowned out and driven from the church.

Freedom music was not just a movement phenomenon. Exemplifying the rapid crossover between black and white markets in jazz,

folk, rhythm and blues, and rock, freedom titles permeated all gen-
res. Folk music converged with civil rights protest by the late 1950s,
with Joan Baez, Bob Dylan, Phil Ochs, and others taking the labor
organizing influence of Pete Seeger and Woody Guthrie in a new
direction confirmed by the March on Washington performances
of Baez ("We Shall Overcome"), Dylan ("Only a Pawn in Their
Game"), Odetta ("I'm on My Way"), and Peter, Paul, and Mary ("If
I Had a Hammer"). Marvin Gaye and Amiri Baraka thought the
pulsing, gospel-pop sound of Martha and the Vandellas—"Dancing
in the Street," "Nowhere to Run," and especially "Heat Wave," a
crossover hit in 1963—was eminently political. The airwaves pro-
pelled the desegregation of concert halls, sports facilities, restaurants, stores, and schools, offering the promise, writes Brian Ward,
of "a genuinely integrated, egalitarian America."

Jazz, in particular, addressed itself to the freedom movement.
"The student radicals," contended Ron Carter, citing the modal,
collective improvisation of Ornette Coleman's *Free Jazz* (1960) as
an example, "are like the freedom jazz players" who are moving beyond standard chord progressions and melodic forms. Sonny
Rollins, who argued that "jazz has always been a music of integration," a way of "talking about freedom," released *Freedom Suite*
in 1958. In one title after another—"Haitian Fight Song" (1955),
"Fables of Faubus" (1957), "Prayer for Passive Resistance" (1960),
"(Soul Fusion) Freewoman and Oh, This Freedom's Slave Cries"
(1963), "Meditations on Integration" (1964)—Charles Mingus
testified to the music's driving motivation: "I can't play it right unless I'm thinking about prejudice and hate and persecution. . . .
There's sadness and cries in it, but also determination."

If jazz is the most original American art, this musicological truth
must include the fact that jazz, black jazz in particular, is a language
of dissent in which the prevailing idea of America is torn apart and
remade in African American terms. The alto saxophonist Jackie

McLean recorded "Let Freedom Ring" in 1962, the year before King wrote the phrase into oratorical history, while John Coltrane reportedly modeled the searing soprano saxophone wails of "Alabama," a tribute to the four girls killed in the bombing of the Sixteenth Street Baptist Church, on the cadences of King's eulogy, rising from mourning to protest. Sponsored by CORE, drummer Max Roach's *We Insist! The Freedom Now Suite* (1961) was conceived as a work for the Emancipation Proclamation centennial, but with the advent of the sit-in movement—the album cover featured a photograph of a lunch counter sit-in—Roach turned it in a more militant direction, with Abbey Lincoln's vocals, marked by wrenching screams, telling the story of black freedom from Africa to slavery to the contemporary freedom movement. Inspired by Birmingham, Duke Ellington wrote "King Fit the Battle of Alabam," which he performed at the Newport Jazz Festival in 1963 and included in his musical *My People*, commissioned for the centennial of the Emancipation Proclamation presented at the Century of Negro Progress in Chicago:

> Bull turned the hoses on the church people,
> Church people, ol' church people,
> Bull turned the hoses on the church people,
> And the water came splashing, dashing, crashing.

All of this, however, was possible only because of the music that moved the freedom movement—its fusion of slave spirituals and gospel reborn as marching songs, going to jail songs, getting to vote songs. "Woke Up This Morning with My Mind Stayed on Jesus" became "Woke Up This Morning with My Mind Stayed on Freedom"; in "Go Tell It on the Mountain" the line "That Jesus Christ is born" became "To let my people go," taken from "Go Down, Moses"; in "I'm on My Way," "to Canaan Land" became the barely different "to Freedom Land"; the first line of "Some of These Days," "I'm gonna sit at the welcome table," was adapted to lunch counter protests; and "Wade in the Water" became an accompaniment to swim-ins at public beaches and pools. As such examples suggest, the transformation from spiritual to movement song was but an augmentation of the coded language of freedom that most every slave spiritual already contained.

"We Shall Not Be Moved," "Which Side Are You On?," and "We Shall Overcome," among others, were adaptations of union organizing songs of the 1930s—the last and most famous having spread from a civil rights workshop at the Highlander Folk School in Tennessee, where Pete Seeger performed it in King's presence in September 1957:

> We shall overcome,
> We shall overcome,
> We shall overcome some day.
> Oh, deep in my heart,
> I do believe, oh
> We shall overcome some day.

But this, too, was an adaptation of an antebellum song distilled once already in C. Albert Tindley's 1901 hymn "I'll Overcome Some Day." Published with the epigraph "Ye shall overcome if ye faint not" (derived from Galatians 6:9: "And let us not be weary in well doing: for in due season we shall reap, if we faint not"), the hymn's central metaphor—

> This world is one great battlefield,
> With forces all arrayed;
> If in my heart I do not yield,
> I'll overcome some day

—easily lent itself to the crusade for black liberty.

The same was true of another movement favorite, "Oh Freedom" (also known as "Before I'd Be a Slave"), which dates to the period immediately after emancipation, when African Americans were emboldened to sing their freedom songs more openly:

Oh, freedom, oh, freedom,
Oh, freedom over me
Before I'd be a slave, I'd be buried in my grave,
And go home to my Lord and be free.

Music was the vehicle of conversion—not to faith in Jesus but to faith in the black freedom movement, even to faith in retribution. After the Sixteenth Street Baptist Church bombing, said Nina Simone, "I sat struck dumb in my den like St. Paul on the road to Damascus: all the truths that I had denied to myself for so long rose up and slapped me in the face." After trying to make a zip gun and realizing she was not cut out for street violence, Simone sat down at the piano and wrote "Mississippi Goddam," with its blistering attack on gradualism (and pacifism):

But my country is full of lies,
We're all gonna die and die like flies,
'Cause I don't trust you any more,
They keep on saying go slow!

Do things gradually
Will bring more tragedy.

Along with the murder of Medgar Evers, the deaths of the four girls "were like the final pieces of a jigsaw puzzle," Simone recalled. "I suddenly realized what it was to be black in America in 1963. . . . It came as a rush of fury, hatred and determination. In church language, the Truth entered into me and I 'came through.'"

■

Just as Nina Simone found it perfectly natural to recount a moment of political awakening as though it were a moment of religious conversion, many in King's audience would have heard a sermonic undercurrent throughout his political oratory. There is hardly a sentence in the Dream speech that is untouched by "church language." God's covenant, the Exodus, Joseph's dream, the Passion of Christ, the teachings of Paul—all of these, we have seen, inform the Dream speech. Passages such as "Let us not wallow in the valley of despair," "Now is the time to rise from the dark and desolate valley of segregation to the sunlit path of racial justice," and "Now is the time to lift our nation from the quicksands of racial injustice to the solid rock of brotherhood" reverberate with allusions to such familiar scriptures as Psalms 23:4 ("Yea, though I walk through the valley of the shadow of death, I will fear no evil: for thou *art* with me") and Matthew 7:24–26 ("Therefore whosoever heareth these sayings of mine, and doeth them, I will liken him unto a wise man, which built his house upon a rock. . . . And every one that heareth these sayings of mine, and doeth them not, shall be likened unto a foolish man, which built his house upon the sand"). King's warnings to the nation likewise drew on the Bible's numerous prophetic admonitions. "The whirlwinds of revolt will continue to shake the foundations of our nation until the bright day of justice emerges" thus reminds us of Isaiah 40:24 ("Yea, their stock shall not take root in the earth: and he shall also blow upon them, and they shall wither, and the whirlwind shall take them away as stubble") and Hosea 8:7 ("For they have sown the wind, and they shall reap the whirlwind").

One need not recognize all such allusions in order to understand King's meaning, nor can we always be certain King intended to refer to a particular scripture. His numerous metaphoric contrasts—the dark valley / the sunlit path; quicksands / solid rock; joyous daybreak / long night; sweltering summer / invigorating autumn; jangling discord / beautiful symphony—are perfectly intelligible in secular terms. "Seared in the withering flames of injustice" likens slavery to martyrdom or the torments of hell, while at the same time it evokes more recent lynchings in which the victims were burned to death. "Sweltering with the heat of oppression" puts his listeners under the blistering sun not only of Egypt but of a Mississippi cotton field. When King says, "Now is the time to lift up our nation," or dreams that "one day this nation will rise up and live out the true meaning of its creed," he joins the idea of racial uplift, a stock conceit from Frederick Douglass through Booker T. Washington and Jesse Jackson, to the language of the church revival. The "hallowed spot" of the Lincoln Memorial is hallowed not only because it *is* the Lincoln Memorial or because it instantly calls to mind the Gettysburg Address ("we can not dedicate—we can not consecrate—we can not hallow—this ground"). It is hallowed, in King's usage, by its association with the Lord's Prayer: "After this manner therefore pray ye: Our Father which art in heaven, Hallowed be thy name" (Matthew 6:9).

Speaking in a religious vernacular recognizable to much of his audience, King sought a common language that would forge bonds between people of all races and all faiths—Christians and Jews, at the very least—while reminding them that the nation's political foundations, though hardly theocratic, nonetheless rested on "the Laws of Nature and Nature's God." Even devout secularists might be moved by knowing that they, too, were "God's children," and even they might feel that the Declaration of Independence gained authority when thought of as emerging from a biblical narrative. Without following an exactly linear rhetorical development over the course of his speech, King's use of scripture allowed him to move historically from slavery to post–*Brown v. Board of Education* liberation in both biblical and American terms; poetically from the archaic stories of the King James Bible to their illumination of the evils of Jim Crow; and prophetically from a fierce jeremiad calling down God's wrath upon a sinful nation to a radiant prophecy promising salvation at his hands. In short, it gave him some of the most vital words and images in which to realize the meaning of his dream.

In the case of his substantial quotations from the language of the prophets Isaiah and Amos, and from Daniel, an interpreter of dreams, King's intentions are unambiguous. In each instance the scripture's religious message bears directly on the political argument King is making at that point in the speech and elucidates the purpose of the speech in its totality. Each is important as an expression of the prophet's refusal to surrender God's truth to man's law, but Amos stands out for the fact that King included him, in a number of sermons and essays, among "the maladjusted" of history—those like Lincoln, who insisted that the nation could not survive half slave and half free; like Jefferson who cried out "in words lifted to cosmic proportions: 'All men are created equal and are endowed by their creator with certain inalienable Rights'"; and like Christ, who was so maladjusted as to say, "Love your enemies." In allying himself with these renegades, King joined a biblical tradition of prophetic dissent that meant not to undermine the authority of the nation but righteously to restore it.

Part of the dream catalogue he added extemporaneously, King's quotation from Isaiah is a well-known passage and one he used in many sermons:

> I have a dream that one day every valley shall be exalted, and
> every hill and mountain shall be made low; the rough places
> will be made plain, and the crooked places will be made
> straight; and the glory of the Lord shall be revealed, and all
> flesh shall see it together.

Understood to be the work of "Second Isaiah" (one or more authors living after the Isaiah responsible for the first half of the book), the scripture from which King quotes (40:1–5) is written in a celebratory voice, as though the Babylonian captivity has already occurred and is coming to an end. Punished and forgiven, the people of Israel will be restored by the edict of Cyrus of Persia after his conquest of Babylonia in 538 B.C. and returned to Jerusalem, where they will rebuild the Temple:

> Comfort ye, comfort ye my people, saith your God.
> Speak ye comfortably to Jerusalem, and cry unto her,
> That her warfare is accomplished,
> That her iniquity is pardoned:
> For she hath received of the LORD's hand double for all her
>   sins.
> The voice of him that crieth in the wilderness, Prepare ye the
>   way of the LORD,
> Make straight in the desert a highway for our God.
> Every valley shall be exalted,
> And every mountain and hill shall be made low:
> And the crooked shall be made straight,
> And the rough places plain:
> And the glory of the LORD shall be revealed,
> And all flesh shall see *it* together:
> For the mouth of the LORD hath spoken *it*.

Preparing "the way of the LORD" refers to the custom of sending workers or representatives ahead to prepare the way for a visiting king—more specifically, to removing obstacles on a road and smoothing rough areas, as on the way to Jerusalem. Having left the land of Israel along with the people, the "glory of the LORD" will now return with them, and all nations shall witness it ("all flesh shall see it together"), this deliverance from the "wilderness" of exile recapitulating the deliverance of the Exodus. For Christians, of course, the redemption of Israel is superseded by redemption through Christ. All three Synoptic Gospels quote this passage and identify John the Baptist as the "voice crying in the wilderness" and preparing the way for Christ, as in Luke 3:4–5: "As it is written in the book of the words of Esaias the prophet, saying, The voice of one crying in the wilderness, Prepare ye the way of the Lord, make his paths straight . . . and the rough ways *shall be* made smooth." God's salvation through Christ, says Luke's typological reading of the Hebrew scripture, will be made known to Jews and Gentiles alike ("And all flesh shall see the salvation of God"), and exile will end with the coming of Christ.

As it is taken by King into his own voice in the "I have a dream" catalogue, the prophecy of Isaiah, central to the millennial imagery that sustained his social message and allied King to the tradition of the black jeremiad, foretells the end of segregation and racial oppression, when the path to equality will be made straight and obstacles to justice removed, not only in the nation's laws but also in the people's hearts. It foresees a day of racial brotherhood in which "all of God's children, black men and white men, Jews and Gentiles, Protestants and Catholics, will be able to join hands"—in which, that is to say, the Lord's glory shall be revealed and "all flesh shall see *it* together." In the displacement of Old Testament by New, moreover, one may see King replacing the old covenant with the new and thus restoring the nation's law to its original intent—"the true meaning of its creed"—for in the new day of justice, according to Galatians 3:28–29, "There is neither Jew nor Greek, there is neither bond nor free, there is neither male nor female: for ye are all one in Christ Jesus. / And if ye *be* Christ's, then are ye Abraham's seed, and heirs according to the promise." The captivity, the long exile, of black Americans, will end, but so will the exile of the nation itself, a point to which we will return in looking at the relationship between King and Lincoln.

Absent its biblical framework, King's brief borrowing from the book of Daniel—"we will be able to hew out of the mountain of despair a stone of hope"—is more than a little enigmatic. The improvised passage of the Dream speech in which it is embedded allows one to assimilate it as an arresting, if peculiar, metaphor of soul force triumphant, comparable to the "jangling discord" of racial strife turned into "a beautiful symphony of brotherhood," an image of harmonious pluralism that descends from such figures as Horace Kallen and Judah Magnes earlier in the century:

> This is our hope. This is the faith that I go back to the South with. With this faith we will be able to hew out of the mountain of despair a stone of hope. With this faith we will be able to transform the jangling discords of our nation into a beautiful symphony of brotherhood. With this faith we will be able to work together, to pray together, to struggle together, to go to jail together, to stand up for freedom together, knowing that we will be free one day.

One may also read the passage in relation to the frequent appearance of mountains in the African American tradition. They may be obstacles to be overcome, as in Joshua 14:12—"Now therefore give me this mountain, whereof the LORD spake in that day"—in which Caleb, Joshua's loyal soldier, asks for strength to take Mount Hebron, or in *The Meeting*, a one-act play by Jeff Stetson dramatizing a fictive debate between King and Malcolm X that concludes in reconciliation, with Malcolm saying to Martin, "If you're around longer than I am, tell them we climbed one mountain, together." They may be symbols of salvation, as in "My Soul Is Anchored in the Lord," sung by Marian Anderson when she was barred from Constitution Hall and performed instead at the Lincoln Memorial in 1939: "I'm going to pray and never stop,/Until I reach the mountain top,/My soul's been anchored in the Lord." A staple in King's repertoire from the mid-1950s on, the mountain was most of all the glorious height, Mount Nebo or Pisgah, from which God shows Moses "the land of Canaan, which I give unto the children of

Israel for a possession" (Deuteronomy 32:49), but which Moses will never enter and which is now forever associated with King's uncanny premonition of imminent death in his final speech.

The mountain to which King alludes in the Dream speech, however, is altogether stranger. It derives from one of Nebuchadnezzar's dreams interpreted by Daniel. When the magicians and sorcerers cannot divine, let alone interpret, Nebuchadnezzar's dream, which he can no longer remember ("I have dreamed a dream, and my spirit was troubled to know the dream"), Daniel, having been given the secret by God, is brought before the king and interprets it (Daniel 2:31–38):

> Thou, O king, sawest, and behold a great image. This great image, whose brightness *was* excellent, stood before thee; and the form thereof *was* terrible.
>
> This image's head *was* of fine gold, his breast and his arms of silver, his belly and his thighs of brass,
>
> His legs of iron, his feet part of iron and part of clay.
>
> Thou sawest till that a stone was cut out without hands, which smote the image upon his feet *that were* of iron and clay, and brake them to pieces.
>
> Then was the iron, the clay, the brass, the silver, and the gold, broken to pieces together, and became like the chaff of the summer threshingfloors; and the wind carried them away, that no place was found for them: and the stone that smote the image became a great mountain, and filled the whole earth.

A book of dreams in which man's rule is consistently destroyed by God's rule, the book of Daniel was probably composed in the second century B.C., but its point of view dates from immediately after the Babylonian captivity ended, when Nebuchadnezzar was conquered and Israel's exile ended, as told in Isaiah. In Nebuchadnezzar's dream, the stone uncut by hands stands for God or the people of God, who crush the idolatrous statue before becoming a mountain and filling the whole earth. Daniel interprets the dream to mean, moreover, that successive kingdoms of man, from the Babylonian through the Greek, will fall, ultimately to be superseded by a messianic era, the kingdom of God: "And in the days of these kings shall the God of heaven set up a kingdom, which shall never be destroyed: and the kingdom shall not be left to other people, *but* it shall break in pieces and consume all these kingdoms, and it shall stand for ever" (Daniel 2:44).

Despite its enigmatic quality, or perhaps because of it, Nebuchadnezzar's peculiar dream is something of a fixture in African American culture. It is the subject of "Daniel Saw the Stone," a slave spiritual included in James Weldon Johnson's *Book of American Negro Spirituals:*

> Daniel saw the stone,
> Rollin', rollin',
> Daniel saw the stone,
> Cut out the mountain without hands,
> Never saw such a man before,
> Cut out the mountain without hands
> Preachin' gospels to the poor.

John Jasper, a popular black preacher of the late nineteenth century whose sermons were frequently rendered in heavy black dialect—his most popular was "The Sun Do Move," based on the idea that the sun revolves around the earth—published "The Stone Cut Out of the Mountain," not in dialect, in 1884. In King's own day, James Baldwin wrote admiringly in *The Fire Next Time* that "the Negro boys and girls who are facing mobs today" are "hewing out of the mountain of white supremacy the stone of their individuality." Ten years after the Dream speech, Alice Walker found that "the mountain of despair has dwindled, and the stone of hope has size and shape, and can be fondled by the eyes and by the hand"—but she also thought King would be dismayed to know that the majority of those helped by the civil rights movement had turned instead to "the pursuit of cars, expensive furniture, large houses, and the finest Scotch."

In addition to identifying with Daniel as an interpreter of dreams, King would have seen the strange dream he interprets in two lights. Certainly, King believed that God's kingdom would prevail over the kingdoms of man, the American kingdom included; and he believed that the soul force of the movement would prove more powerful than the unjust laws of the segregated South.* At the same time, the tautological form of Nebuchadnezzar's memory—"I have dreamed a dream"—resembles King's own characterization, as we saw earlier, of "the founding fathers of our nation [who] dreamed this dream." In this respect, the dream Nebuchad-

---

* A related episode from Daniel appeared often in King's sermons and speeches. After hearing his interpretation of the image of the mountain and the stone, Nebuchadnezzar elevates Daniel and three young men, Shadrach, Meshach, and Abednego, to positions of prominence. When the three subsequently refuse to worship Nebuchadnezzar's golden idol, they are cast into a fiery furnace but emerge unscathed because of God's protection. Once again Nebuchadnezzar is chastened and transformed. Portrayed as exemplars of civil disobedience in "Letter from Birmingham Jail," Shadrach, Meshach, and Abednego appeared in one of King's earliest sermons, preached just months after *Brown v. Board of Education*, when he spoke of the "courage of three Hebrew boys," three "nonconformists" who refused to bow down to Nebuchadnezzar's idol. Preaching in an Albany church in 1962, King used the fiery furnace as a way to characterize the people "askin' God to get us ready, askin' Him to purge us with His discipline and burn us with his fire and cleanse us and make us holy and ready to stand." God went into the furnace with Shadrach, Meshach, and Abednego, said King, for "there can be *no* injunction against God." Not only that, but Albany did not belong to the Democratic Party of the state of Georgia, or to the Republican Party, or to the governor of Georgia, or to the state's white people. "All-*benny*," exclaimed King, in the local pronunciation, "belongs to God."

nezzar has forgotten may be understood as the dream of equality and racial justice "deeply rooted in the American dream" but lost to memory and in need of restoration.

The restoration of justice is also the key message of the scripture from Amos, which King included in his prepared speech and used numerous times throughout his career:

> We can never be satisfied as long as our children are stripped
> of their selfhood and robbed of their dignity by signs stating
> "For Whites Only." We cannot be satisfied as long as a
> Negro in Mississippi cannot vote and a Negro in New York
> believes he has nothing for which to vote. No, no, we are not
> satisfied, and we will not be satisfied until justice rolls down
> like waters and righteousness like a mighty stream.

Referring to one of the most vivid and demeaning reminders of Jim Crow—the ubiquitous signs dividing public space between "White" and "Colored"—King drew an analogy between political disfranchisement and the psychological scarring of black children at a young age. No less than the equal right to be represented through one's vote, the equal right to use communal spaces and facilities is the essence of citizenship in a democracy. Both are matters of justice before the law, but they are also matters of justice in the eyes of God, the foremost concern of the prophet Amos.

Among the notecards made by King during his graduate study in the fall of 1952 was a comment on the scripture: "This passage might be called the key passage of the entire book. It reveals the deep ethical nature of God. God is a God that demands justice rather than sacrifice; righteousness rather than ritual." Just so, the words quoted by King appear in verses expressing God's rejection of Israel's indulgent worship, in which the trappings of piety have crowded out obedience to the covenant (Amos 5:21–24):

I hate, I despise your feast *days,* and I will not smell in your solemn assemblies.

Though ye offer me burnt offerings and your meat offerings, I will not accept *them:* neither will I regard the peace offerings of your fat beasts.

Take thou away from me the noise of thy songs; for I will not hear the melody of thy viols.

But let judgment run down as waters, and righteousness as a mighty stream.

Because God's judgment was the judgment of justice, variations in translation of the passage from Amos are self-reinforcing. "Until *justice* rolls down like waters," said King in the Dream speech, opting here not for the King James translation, his usual source, but for a variation that is comparable to those in the Revised Standard Version ("But let justice roll down like waters, and righteousness like an everlasting stream"), which he sometimes used, and the Jewish Publication Society translation of the Tanakh ("But let justice well up like water, / Righteousness like an unfailing stream"). King had used this formulation of the passage from Amos as early as his first speech to the Montgomery Improvement Association in 1955 (although on that occasion he said, "until justice *runs* down like water"), and, whether or not he was inspired by King, Abraham Joshua Heschel offered a nearly identical variation in his 1962 book *The Prophets:* "Let justice roll down like waters, and righteousness like a mighty stream." Both King and Heschel found in Amos inspiration for the dangerous but indispensable acts of protest required of the true prophet.

Accused of sedition when he prophesied prior to the Assyrian captivity of Israel, in the eighth century B.C., Amos dwelled on social and political injustice rather than religious ritual. Having fallen into idolatry and dissipation, Israel is doomed to suffer God's wrath, and Amos's judgment takes the form of a lamentation, as though Israel were already dead ("Hear ye this word which I take up against you, *even* a lamentation, O house of Israel"). Israel has prospered, says Amos, but at the expense of those less fortunate ("For I know your manifold transgressions and your mighty sins: they afflict the just, they take a bribe, and they turn aside the poor in the gate *from their right*"). Its laws and the courts are corrupt ("Ye who turn judgment to wormwood, and leave off righteousness in the earth"), and whoever seeks justice is spurned and condemned ("They hate him that rebuketh in the gate, and they abhor him that speaketh uprightly"). Whereas in later chapters of Amos chastisement is certain—the last, which proposes the return of a remnant from exile to rebuild cities and replant vineyards, is typically thought to have been added by a later writer—in Amos 5 there is still time for repentance. Although only God can decide, by becoming just and seeking redemption, Israel may yet save herself. So, too, might America save itself, said King, but only by recognizing "the fierce urgency of now" and acting to quiet "the whirlwinds of revolt."

In answer to the claim that laws could not dictate morality, King took from Walter Rauschenbusch, the century's leading proponent of the Social Gospel, an insight derived from Amos. Because religion and morality form the inseparable root of organic national life, argued Rauschenbusch, the Christian preacher must have "the prophetic insight which discerns and champions the right before others see it." And because its embodiment in law is the last stage of realized moral authority, the work of the prophet precedes and provides the foundation for the law: "Laws do not create moral convictions; they merely recognize and enforce them." No doubt King also found congenial the interpretation offered by Heschel, with whom he participated in the National Conference on Race and Religion in 1963, where both referred to Amos, and Heschel called specifically upon the clergy to give voice to God in the historical present: "A mighty stream, expressive of the vehemence of a never-ending, surging, fighting movement—as if obstacles had to be washed away for justice to be done. No rock is so hard that water cannot pierce it."

The scripture from Amos is carved on Maya Lin's Civil Rights Memorial at the Southern Poverty Law Center in Montgomery—but ascribed to King alone, with no attribution to the Bible, as if to say King's words had themselves become holy scripture. Along with the passages from Daniel and Isaiah, as well as other quotations from King, it will also be featured on the Martin Luther King, Jr., National Memorial in Washington, D.C. In the Dream speech, Stone Mountain stood for states' rights and segregation, but the granite portals forming the entrance to the Memorial, like a mountain split in two, will embody physically the power of King's language, inscribed on each side, with his visage, as though hewn from this mountain, emerging from a "stone of hope" to face the Jefferson Memorial across the Tidal Basin. No less than his belief in nonviolence, King's immersion in prophetic scripture is evident in virtually all of his writings and speeches, but none of them stated as urgently as the Dream speech the Bible's admonitory lessons for the nation. Like Isaiah, who announced the liberation of captive peoples, like Daniel, who divined the ascendancy of God's kingdom, and most of all like Amos, who called for righteousness to roll down like a mighty stream, King became a prophetic figure whose moral vision surpassed the laws of man and drew them, in his wake, closer to the laws of God.

Lincoln's Shadow

When the great contralto Marian Anderson rose to make her contribution to the March on Washington, where she sang "He's Got the Whole World in His Hands," not only African Americans but virtually all Americans with any knowledge of the civil rights struggle had in their mind's eye the image of her performance on Easter 1939. Although she did not feel that she was made for "hand-to-hand combat," Anderson became a civil rights heroine after she was barred from performing in Constitution Hall by its proprietors, the Daughters of the American Revolution (DAR), who cited a "whites only" clause in their contracts. Rather than seek another venue, Anderson's sponsor, Howard University, decided to fight the DAR, which in recent decades had begun to blacklist organizations and individuals considered subversive or unpatriotic. In doing so, Howard officials were able to call upon their good relations with Franklin Roosevelt's administration, in particular with Harold Ickes, secretary of the interior. Unexpectedly, they also got the support of Eleanor Roosevelt, whose resignation from the DAR in protest of their snub of Anderson, although it did not persuade them to change course, gained the issue national attention.

But for the DAR's obduracy, what might otherwise have been a routine concert became a riveting spectacle. When the concert promoter, Sol Hurok, fixed on the nearby Lincoln Memorial as an alternative venue, a *Washington Times-Herald* editorial captured its symbolic aptness in ascribing the words of the Thirteenth Amendment to Lincoln: "They [the DAR] stand almost in the shadow of the Lincoln Memorial, but the Great Emancipator's sentiments about 'race, creed, or previous condition of servitude,' are not shared by the Daughters." The performance was broadcast live on national radio; programs handed out by Boy Scouts, both white and black, had the Gettysburg Address printed on the cover; and extensive publicity for the event, attended by some seventy-five thousand persons, including cabinet members, Supreme Court justices, and congressmen, belabored the point of Anderson's singing on Easter at the feet of Abraham Lincoln (figure 14). Raising black music to an exalted plane that highlighted its contribution to American freedom, her program included "The Star-Spangled Banner," "America," two classical selections, and three spirituals. As would be the case again in 1963, and breaking a traditional rule, photos of Anderson were taken from behind, within the Memorial itself, as though to demonstrate that Lincoln himself looked out approvingly as Anderson faced the crowd.

Inside Henry Bacon's marble temple, whose thirty-six Doric columns stand for the number of states preserved in the Union, rests Daniel Chester French's massive sculpture of a seated Lincoln, brooding and wise. Above the statue is a simple tribute:

IN THIS TEMPLE
AS IN THE HEARTS OF THE PEOPLE
FOR WHOM HE SAVED THE UNION

THE MEMORY OF ABRAHAM LINCOLN

IS ENSHRINED FOREVER

In the south recess, beneath Jules Guérin's mural *Emancipation of a Race*, is inscribed the Gettysburg Address, in the north recess Lincoln's Second Inaugural, the two speeches that most movingly expressed his hopes for the nation's salvation. With Anderson's performance, the Lincoln Memorial became the principal site to which African Americans could bring their grievances and their dreams—a site at once common and sacred, like Lincoln himself. Although A. Philip Randolph's threatened mass march to the Memorial in 1941 was averted by Roosevelt's executive order, Paul Robeson led a crowd in singing "Go Down, Moses," at the Memorial in 1943 and returned in 1946, as chairman of the American Crusade to End Lynching, to mark the anniversary of the Preliminary Emancipation Proclamation. Even those proposing revolution have found Lincoln's symbolic power irresistible. Marking another emancipation anniversary in 1970, Black Panthers spoke at the Memorial, in the "Capital of Babylon, World Racism, and Imperialism," calling for a black constitutional convention, to be followed by armed rebellion.

In these and the many other instances in which the Memorial has been the setting for protest or commemoration, Abraham Lincoln has been a living presence, not only a witness to later history but, in effect, a participant in it. Lincoln's symbolic role in the March on Washington was especially evident in media coverage, whether in television or newsreels that frequently panned to his statue, in magazine cover stories—*Newsweek* had a shot of the Lincoln Memorial on the cover, while *Life* used a photo of Randolph and Bayard Rustin against the backdrop of the Memorial—or in numerous newspaper photos and stories. James Reston spoke of Lincoln's presiding "in his stone temple today above the children of the slaves he emancipated," while the lead editorial in the *Washington Post* made him a conduit between the black troops of the Civil War and the civil rights soldiers of the present:

> At the end of the Mall, inside the great memorial erected to his memory, the gaunt, grave, silent figure of the Great Emancipator sat and listened, remembering, perhaps, the words of other marchers for freedom long, long ago: "We are coming Father Abraham, three hundred thousand strong." Surely Abraham Lincoln yesterday heard the voices singing "Glory, Hallelujah," demanding fulfillment at last of the promise for which he lived and died.

As though its talismanic power could be conferred by proximity, Lincoln's promise has been revived by everyone who has stood and spoken in his shadow. In introductory remarks at Marian Anderson's concert, which had the effect of making her the truer "daughter" of the American Revolution, Harold Ickes proclaimed that by Lincoln's acts, the freedom envisioned by the Founding Fathers had been bequeathed as much to Anderson as to anyone. "Genius, like justice, is blind," he insisted. If it had "not been for the great mind of Jefferson, if it had not been for the great heart of Lincoln," Anderson would not be able "to stand among us a free individual today in a free land." Ickes may be forgiven his presumption of Anderson's freedom, for the logic of his connection between Lincoln's heart and Jefferson's mind—between the order of emancipation and the declaration of American liberty it strove to complete—was exactly the logic followed by King in 1963.

■

In the words "Fivescore years ago," so antique and magical, King evoked Lincoln before not quite naming him in the remainder of his sentence: "a great American, in whose symbolic shadow we stand today, signed the Emancipation Proclamation." Had King stopped speaking after the first few words, his audience would still have thought of Lincoln, the opening of the Gettysburg Address, "Four score and seven years ago," being among the most famous words in American history—more widely recognized, it may be, than "When in the Course of human events" or "We the People of the United States." Insofar as King's purpose, as he immediately stated, was to address the meaning of the Emancipation Proclamation in its centennial year, his allusion to Lincoln's best-known speech might at first have seemed a rhetorical trick. How many people, after all, would have recognized "Whereas on the twentysecond day of September," the Proclamation's opening words?

Perhaps any mention of Lincoln would have been sufficient to bring to mind the Emancipation Proclamation. From the moment it was issued, the order sanctified Lincoln for African Americans. Tall tales grew up among slaves and free blacks alike that the president himself had appeared at southern plantations to announce freedom, and all skepticism about his temporizing on the issue of emancipation was swept away. One administration official, touring Philadelphia's black churches on New Year's Day 1863 wrote to the president that in thirty years of antislavery activism he had seen nothing to rival the esteem in which Lincoln was now held by blacks, who "thought there must be some design of God in having your name 'Abraham,'" for if you are not truly their biblical patriarch, "you are the 'Liberator' of a People." Not doubting that black attitudes toward the "Great Emancipator" were "tinged by wish-fulfillment," Benjamin Quarles maintained a century later that Lincoln's motives and even the actual words of the Proclamation were immaterial to most blacks, who "loved him first and have loved him longest," making their "authorized version of the Lincoln Testament" a simple one. Like Moses, he had led them "out of the house of bondage"—but not quite.

Without condescension or false humility, both Lincoln and King couched the language of political argumentation in familiar religious cadences while advocating divisive policies. Both courted the wrath of white southerners who thought their principles mad, if not treasonous, as well as northern whites, many of whom who thought them rash. Without once naming Lincoln in a speech that might more fittingly be called "The Lincoln Memorial Address," as Neil Schmitz has suggested, King effectively recast Lincoln's words and made them his own, so that his petition to President Kennedy, the Congress, and the American people appropriated the authority of the nation's most esteemed president.

What King shared with Lincoln stands in greater relief if we turn briefly to his sermon "The Death of Evil upon the Seashore," in which King developed an extended allegory of contemporary liberation, with the forces of colonialism and segregation finally overcome as the Red Sea opens and enslaved peoples, both those abroad and those in America, win their freedom. King first preached the sermon at a service commemorating the second anniversary of *Brown v. Board of Education* at the Cathedral Church of St. John the Divine in New York in 1956, and then revised it for inclusion in his 1963 sermon collection *Strength to Love*. In each case King drew on traditional sermonic materials—he borrowed significantly from "Egyptians Dead upon the Seashore," a sermon by the nineteenth-century minister Phillips Brooks, among other sources—in order to depict the hard, halting journey to Canaan and the evanescence of freedom's dream, but the ideological tributaries and metaphoric structure of the 1963 sermon reflected a maturation of thought also evident in the Dream speech. By adding citations of Jefferson and Lincoln to the second version of the sermon, King anchored his modern adaptation of the Exodus more explicitly in its American historical equivalent—not simply the end of slavery but rather the ensuing century-long struggle to make real the promises of the Emancipation Proclamation and the Civil War amendments.

"We cannot turn back the clock to 1868 when the [Fourteenth] Amendment was adopted, or even to 1896 when *Plessy v. Ferguson* was written," said the Supreme Court in *Brown v. Board of Education*. That may be true in terms of legal precedent, King appeared to reason, but taking account of the lost years of opportunity for blacks—in fact, the nation—to enter the Promised Land entailed returning to Lincoln's equally bold point of departure. No doubt Emancipation had failed, insofar as the "new form of slavery" enshrined in *Plessy* permitted the South's latter-day pharaohs to employ legal maneuvers, economic reprisal, and physical violence to "hold the Negro in the Egypt of segregation." With the "world-shaking decree" of 1954, however, a new "Red Sea passage in history" was at hand. *Brown*, King argued, returned the nation to January 1, 1863, when Lincoln had resolved the ambiguity of the Constitution and laid the groundwork for those Civil War amendments, the Fourteenth and the Fifteenth, subsequently eviscerated by the Supreme Court in the string of decisions that culminated in *Plessy*.

Quoting Jefferson's well-known lament that the question of slavery, "like a fire-bell in the night," filled him with terror that the sacrifice of "the generation of 1776, to acquire self-government and happiness to their country, is to be thrown away," King portrayed the author of the Declaration of Independence as a man of principle at war with himself, as well as with his time and place. King likewise took note of Lincoln's "torments and vacillations," but in accurately referring to Lincoln's proclamation as an "executive order," he called attention to the power available to contemporary presidents—first to Eisenhower, then to Kennedy, and soon to Johnson—should they overcome their own vacillations on the matter of racial justice.

More important, King located the "moral foundation" of the Emancipation Proclamation in the explanation Lincoln addressed to Congress on December 1, 1862: "In giving freedom to the slave, we assure freedom to the free,—honorable alike in what we give and what we preserve." (Spoken in the midst of a "fiery trial" whose outcome was far from certain, Lincoln's words following those quoted by King aligned him even more exactly with Jefferson: "We shall nobly save, or meanly lose, the last, best hope of earth." By the same token, Lincoln at this point was still inclined to regard voluntary black colonization as a desirable adjunct to emancipation.) King's use of Lincoln thus comported with his contention, shared by nineteenth-century abolitionists, that the moral injury done to whites by racial prejudice might be worse than the physical injury done to blacks. In underscoring a sentiment he would restate in the Dream speech—"our white brothers . . . have come to realize that their destiny is tied up with our destiny . . . that their freedom is inextricably bound to our freedom"—King joined himself as well to Lincoln's belief that in giving "freedom to the free" lay the essence of Union, without whose preservation the Declaration of Independence would be stripped of its transcendental purpose.

It is especially significant, therefore, that the genealogy of political fathers to which King made himself heir in the revised version of the sermon included, in addition to Jefferson and Lincoln, that other "great American," Frederick Douglass, and that the particular passage from Douglass he cited was his astute assessment of the Emancipation Proclamation on the eve of its issuance:

> Unquestionably the first of January, 1863, is to be the most memorable day in American Annals. The Fourth of July was great, but the First of January, when we consider it in all its relationships and bearings, is incomparably greater. The one had respect to the mere political birth of a nation, the last concerns the national life and character, and is to determine whether that life and character shall be radiantly glorious

with all high and noble virtues, or infamously blackened, forevermore.

With the nation torn apart by fratricidal conflict, the "Angel of Liberty has one ear of the nation and the demon of Slavery the other," Douglass went on to say, echoing Lincoln's House Divided speech. "One or the other must prevail on the first of January."

When King revised his "Death of Evil" materials yet again for inclusion in *Where Do We Go from Here?*, published in 1967, he was despondent about the retreat of white liberals, close to impotent in responding to the violence of the urban North, and under heightened attack by Black Power radicals. In a darker mood, King regretted that neither Jefferson nor Lincoln, nor any of the Founding Fathers, "had a strong, unequivocal belief in the equality of the black man," and he took note of Jefferson's acquiescence in prevailing scientific theories later deemed racist. Yet even now, the sequence of his argument—from Jefferson to Lincoln to Douglass—was intended less to tear down the Founding Fathers than to add a black man to their pantheon. In examining Douglass's anger and frustration over the betrayal of Reconstruction, moreover, King made explicit an aspect of his argument less evident in 1963.

Despite the "luminous rhetoric" of emancipation, King pointed out, the post–Civil War nation turned over millions of acres of land to white settlers in the West and gave generations of European peasants a new beginning, while its "oldest peasantry, the Negro, was denied everything but a legal status he could not use, could not consolidate, and could not even defend." The inscription on the Statue of Liberty proclaims the nation the "mother of exiles," said King. Whereas the nation did nourish her white exiles, however, "she evinced no motherly concern or love for her exiles from Africa," and the sorrow song of old was still applicable: "Sometimes I feel like a motherless child, a long ways from home." Or, to recall

the potent phrase of the Dream speech, the African American remained an "exile in his own land."

Rather than dwell on the subordination of the rights of blacks to
those of white ethnic immigrants, however, King turned the metaphor of exile in a revealing direction. Here he cast back to a 1958
sermon in which he had likened the nation to the New Testament's
prodigal son, wandering in "the far country of segregation" but
ready for the favor of a patient and loving God: "I will bring you
back to your true home." Lamenting in the new sermon that the nation's "sojourn in the far country of racism" had brought about
moral and spiritual famine, King proceeded to argue that the nation
itself was in exile, that "national suicide" could be avoided only if
America returned to "her true home, 'one nation, indivisible, with
liberty and justice for all.'"

What did it mean for the nation to return to itself, to return to its
true home? This was the question King posed in Washington, D.C.,
in 1963. It was also the question Lincoln had posed in Washington,
D.C., in 1863—and had been posing for more than a decade. We
find a cogent expression of it in one of his 1858 debates with Stephen
Douglas. Who in America, Lincoln asked, belongs to the posterity
of the Revolutionary generation? In refuting the Supreme Court's
decision in *Dred Scott v. Sandford* (1857)—which denied citizenship
rights to blacks and declared that, insofar as slaveholders could not
be deprived of their property without due process, slavery in the
new territories could not be prohibited by Congress—Lincoln
posited that the Jeffersonian promise, "we hold these truths to be
self-evident, that all men are created equal," was made not just to
the native heirs of the Founding Fathers but to all who have, in the
meantime, adopted America as their new home. By virtue of that
choice, they too were bound by "the electric cord in [the] Declaration that links the hearts of patriotic and liberty-loving men together." If this promise defined the Union and constituted its

grounds for perpetuity, for native-born and immigrant alike, it also, argued Lincoln, applied to those held in bondage.

■

In its patently scriptural call for a "new birth of freedom," the Gettysburg Address cast the Civil War as an act of purification and redemption—specifically, a baptismal rebirth that echoed the command of Christ, "Ye must be born again" (John 3:7). Not only would the Union be reborn in its preservation, Lincoln asserted. The first principles of the Declaration would also be reborn—but only if slavery were ended as well. Although the few words he spoke in November 1863 were destined to achieve far greater renown, Lincoln once remarked that his emancipation order—his "momentous decree," as King called it in the Dream speech—was "the central act of my administration, and the greatest event of the nineteenth century." For several decades to come, Lincoln's forecast proved correct. In poetry, in prints and paintings, and most of all in commemorations of his life and death, it was emancipation, close behind the preservation of the Union, for which Lincoln was revered, at least in the North and certainly among African Americans, and only later did the Gettysburg Address become emblematic of his wisdom and moral stature. As Frederick Douglass recognized, and King after him, Lincoln's battlefield elegy, notwithstanding its stunning verbal beauty, depended for its significance on the proclamation that preceded it.

Although Lincoln's opposition to slavery was ardent and long-standing—"I am naturally anti-slavery," he wrote to Albert Hodges in 1864. "If slavery is not wrong, nothing is wrong. I can not remember when I did not so think, and feel"—this gave him, as he noted in the same letter, no authority simply to dictate emancipation. When Lincoln, upon his first inauguration as president, disclaimed any power to interfere with slavery, Douglass, among others, assumed that he had forsaken his antislavery views, while Lincoln meant only to announce that he would not to overstep his constitutional authority. The secession of southern states afforded him war powers that led inexorably, if slowly, to the Emancipation Proclamation. Nevertheless, the terms of Lincoln's Preliminary Emancipation Proclamation, which was issued on September 22, 1862, and gave the South one hundred days to lay down its arms and thus forestall emancipation, struck many abolitionists as parsimonious. When he issued the final proclamation on January 1, moreover, Lincoln cited "military necessity" and obfuscated its significance by a staged endorsement of black colonization, hardly the noble expressions of self-evident truth some might have preferred.

Lincoln's prudence and gradualism would be held against him in later generations by those attuned to his supposed racism. In Lincoln's view, however, an order more sweeping or issued earlier would have been either unconstitutional or useless or both. As Douglass appreciated far better than Lincoln's critics a century later, moreover, Lincoln's appeal to "military necessity" was the expression, albeit legalistic, of a pronounced egalitarian position. Racial justice depended on the survival of the nation, not the reverse, a fact that Douglass underscored when he spoke at the 1876 dedication of the Freedman's Memorial Monument to Lincoln: "Viewed from the genuine abolition ground, Mr. Lincoln seemed tardy, cold, dull, and indifferent; but measuring him by the sentiment of his country, a sentiment he was bound as a statesman to consult, he was swift, zealous, radical, and determined." (Shading somewhat both the negative and the positive, King might have said something similar about Kennedy.)

Even though the Emancipation Proclamation was limited in scope, applying neither to border states fighting on the Union side nor to southern areas already under Union control, it precipitated a surge in runaways and provoked fear among slaveholders of race wars led by new Nat Turners, new John Browns. Presuming that slaves in other parts of the South were "commodities" used in support of insurrection, the Proclamation extended the logic of the Confiscation Acts, which held that runaway slaves could be seized and held as contraband of war. (Of legal claims made by affected slaveholders, Lincoln argued that, by rebelling against the Union, the South had forfeited the labor of its slaves, who were "thus liberated.") Amid its dry, bureaucratic language there is but one sentence—proposed by Salmon Chase, Lincoln's secretary of the treasury—hinting at his usual eloquence: "And upon this act, sincerely believed to be an act of justice, warranted by the Constitution upon military necessity, I invoke the considerate judgment of mankind, and the gracious favor of Almighty God."

When taken in concert with the Gettysburg Address, as well as Lincoln's earlier speeches, the sentence is telling. "The considerate judgment of mankind," as Allen Guelzo points out, echoed Jefferson's "decent Respect to the Opinions of Mankind," while "the gracious favor of Almighty God" called up "Nature and Nature's God," making the proclamation "virtually a Second Declaration [of Independence]." In signing the Declaration "four score and seven years ago," said Lincoln at Gettysburg, "our fathers brought forth on this continent, a new nation, conceived in Liberty, and dedicated to the proposition that all men are created equal." Through his order of emancipation, however, Lincoln had already initiated what the Address refers to as the "unfinished work" of the Founding Fathers, transforming the proposition that all men are created equal into a bequest that applied not only to both sections of the country but also, in principle, to both races.

Seen from this perspective, Douglass's claim that Emancipation Day would be greater than the Fourth of July, which was concerned with "the mere political birth of the nation," was in no way eccentric—beginning with the simple reason that for African Americans the Fourth of July was at best a paradoxical holiday. Even if they escaped the racist violence that sometimes erupted during the festivities, the persistence of slavery gave credence to the slaveholding minister who declared that the Fourth of July belonged exclusively to whites, the American Revolution being a "quarrel among equals" with which Negroes had no more concern "than with the landing of the Pilgrims on the rock in Plymouth." No wonder blacks ignored Independence Day or, in a common practice, moved their celebrations to July 5 as an act of protest.

Such was the case when Peter Osborne announced at the New Haven African Church on July 5, 1832, that only "when the Declaration of Independence is fully executed . . . [may we] have our Fourth of July on the fourth." It was likewise the case when Nathaniel Paul, pastor of the First African Baptist Society of Albany, in a July 5, 1827, sermon celebrating the abolition of slavery in New York, looked forward to the appearance of a black Moses who would lead his brethren "from worse than Egyptian bondage, to the happy Canaan of civil and religious liberty." Paul chastised America for being "the first in the profession of the love of liberty, and loudest in proclaiming liberal sentiments towards all other nations," while nonetheless permitting slavery to make America's name "a byword, even among despotic nations." Anticipating Lincoln, as well as post–World War II civil rights activists, Paul argued that America's claim to lead the free world rang hollow so long as slavery had the protection of law, and he found divine provenance for the natural rights theory of the Founding Fathers. "If in this case I err," said Paul,

> the error is not peculiar to myself; if I wander, I wander in a region of light from whose political hemisphere the sun of liberty pours forth his refulgent rays, around which dazzle the starlike countenances of . . . Washington, Adams, Jefferson, Hancock and Franklin; if I err, it is their sentiments that have

caused me to stray . . . nor can we reasonably expect that since they have entered the unbounded space of eternity, and have learned more familiarly the perfections of that God who governs all things, that their sentiments have altered.

Paul's rhetorical gambit also foreshadowed the speech at Holt Street Baptist Church that launched King on the road to national leadership in 1955. Less ornately but no less powerfully, as we have seen, King called upon the same authorities: "If we are wrong, the Supreme Court of this nation is wrong. If we are wrong, the Constitution of the United States is wrong. If we are wrong, God Almighty is wrong."

Easily the most celebrated July 5 speech, however, was Frederick Douglass's "What to the Slave is the Fourth of July?" in which he declared the holiday "a thin veil to cover up crimes which would disgrace a nation of savages." He reproached his audience for celebrating a holiday of political freedom, likened to "what the Passover was to the emancipated people of God," when their "jubilee shouts" were countered by the "mournful wail of millions." Quoting the abolitionist William Lloyd Garrison ("God speed the year of jubilee / The wide world o'er!") and Psalm 137 ("By the rivers of Babylon, there we sat down. Yea! we wept when we remembered Zion. . . . How can we sing the Lord's song in a strange land?"), Douglass argued that not just blacks but the nation itself was in exile. Speaking "in the name of the constitution and the Bible, which are disregarded and trampled upon," Douglass sought to reclaim his own national patrimony and place black and white Founding Fathers on the same footing—slave rebels such as Madison Washington and Joseph Cinque standing side by side with George Washington and Patrick Henry—as one may see in the 1855 version of his autobiography, *My Bondage and My Freedom*, in which he averred that the slave who kills his master "imitates only the heroes of the revolution."

When he delivered a Fourth of July oration in 1862—this time on the fourth, not the fifth, and this time joining black Founding Fathers with white—Douglass, like Lincoln, placed the "slaveholders' rebellion" in opposition to the legacy of 1776. The Civil War continued the "tremendous struggle, which your fathers and my fathers began eighty-six years ago," he contended, and it aimed to fulfill the "principles in the Declaration of Independence, which would release every slave in the world." Two months hence Lincoln would issue the preliminary version of the emancipation order for which Douglass had long been pressing.

Much like King a century later, Douglass appreciated that the Emancipation Proclamation sought to redeem the promissory note of the nation's foundational documents. Because they shared Jefferson's view that the Declaration of Independence was "the fundamental Act of Union of these States," both Douglass and Lincoln believed that the Preamble to the Constitution, with its stated intention "to form a more perfect union," reiterated the Declaration and therefore that the idea of the Union preceded the Constitution. Speaking in Scotland in 1860, Douglass first quoted the Preamble and then parsed its defining phrase:

> Its language is "we the people"; not we the white people, not even we the citizens, not we the privileged class, not we the high, not we the low, but we the people; not we the horses, sheep, and swine, and wheel-barrows, but we the people, we the human inhabitants; and if Negroes are people, they are included in the benefits for which the Constitution of America was ordained and established.

Having renounced Garrison's view that the Constitution was a proslavery document—Garrison once burned a copy of the document, condemning it as a "covenant with death, an agreement with hell" before grinding its ashes under his heel—Douglass had also, like Lincoln, come to believe adamantly that the end of slavery, explicit in the Declaration, was implicit in the Constitution. The Founding Fathers, he argued, "carefully excluded from the Constitution any and every word which could lead to the belief that they meant it for persons of only one complexion." Lincoln, as we have already seen, likewise found that the Jeffersonian creed reflected the Founding Fathers' "understanding of the justice of the Creator to His creatures. Yes, gentlemen, to *all* His creatures." By making no explicit mention of slavery in the Constitution, Lincoln determined, the Founders purposely employed "covert language" so that when the Constitution was read in the future "by intelligent and patriotic men," there should be "nothing on the face of this great charter of liberty suggesting that such a thing as negro slavery had ever existed among us."

It may be that Douglass and Lincoln both strained to minimize the degree to which the Constitution compromised on the question of slavery. Given the concessions made to slaveholders to ensure the support of southern states—the fugitive slave clause meant that escape from bondage did not guarantee freedom; the three-fifths clause gave slave states far more power than was warranted by their free population; and permitting the slave trade to continue to 1808 resulted in a substantial increase in the slave population and with it the political power of the South—the evidence cited by Douglass and Lincoln might be deemed a sign of disingenuous political calculation rather than idealism. Without those concessions, however, there might have been no limit on slave imports, slaves might have counted for five-fifths in determining the South's representation, and there might not have been a Constitution at all. More to the point, if the citizenship rights of blacks came clearly, though briefly, under federal protection only with the Civil War amendments, this in no way impugned the high ideals of Douglass and Lincoln themselves. And it was these ideals to which King laid claim when he included the Constitution alongside the Declaration as a guarantor of black freedom.

In making the Union antedate the Constitution and concluding that the Declaration's rights apply to "*all* His creatures"—to "all of God's children," as King would put it in the Dream speech—Lincoln found grounds both to denounce secession as an act of rebellion and to justify emancipation. One of his most trenchant arguments about the priority of the Union, and one that was to reverberate a century later in the conflict between federal law and the rights of southern states to set their own racial codes, appeared in his rejection of the right of secession in his 1861 Fourth of July message to a special session of Congress: "Having never been States, either in substance, or in name, *outside* of the Union, whence this magical omnipotence of 'State rights,' asserting a claim of power to lawfully destroy the Union itself?" Only a more, not a less, "perfect union" could be perpetual; and only a Constitution that embodied the principles of the Declaration, which preceded it not only in time but also in the realm of the spirit in which the nation itself was first conceived, could guarantee the integrity of the Union. Taken in conjunction with the Emancipation Proclamation, Lincoln's eulogy at Gettysburg, as Garry Wills has argued, strove to make union "not a mystical hope but a constitutional reality," thereby "correcting the Constitution without overthrowing it." Secession could no more be unilateral on the part of the South than emancipation could be unilateral on the part of Lincoln, but once the former made possible the latter, Lincoln's belief that the Declaration applied to both sections and thus to all men—"yes, black men as well as white men," King would say in the Dream speech—could be vindicated.

Preservation of the Union was Lincoln's first priority, and neither he nor Douglass, nor King a century later, overlooked the constraints of the Emancipation Proclamation as a limited military order. In its presupposition of fundamental human equality, however, the Proclamation laid a strong foundation for the Civil War amendments. Both the proclamation and the amendments recognized, moreover, that the Union would be rightly preserved only with the end of slavery; only then might the nation be returned "home" to itself, its exile ended. Here we may think of the Union soldier who asserted that the Emancipation Proclamation would count "more than all the victories we can win in the field." All the same, he mused that the Moses in Washington needed soldiers like him to liberate the black Israelites. The only way out of "this horror blinding the nation," he continued, "is by the door of Justice to the oppressed. We must 'let the people go,' at any rate. If it be through the Red Sea, still they must go."

■

On January 1, 1863, cannon were fired, church bells were rung, parades were held, and orators great and small let loose at public observances throughout the North, as well as Union-held areas of the South. Formerly known among slaves as "Heartbreak Day," owing to the custom of holding large slave auctions on that day, January 1 would be known henceforth as a day of deliverance and jubilation, far surpassing the other holidays observed by blacks as occasions of thanksgiving and protest. Like the holiday named for King more than a century later, the Day of Jubilee took its place in a long, mostly unofficial tradition of celebrating the goal of black freedom and, finally, its provisional achievement in the Emancipation Proclamation and the Thirteenth Amendment to the Constitution. King's birthday on January 15 made it possible, fortuitously, to fold a history of Emancipation Day celebrations into the federal holiday signed into law by President Reagan in 1983 and initially celebrated in 1986.

The first such celebrations date to January 1, 1808, when the foreign slave trade to the United States was abolished. In a sermon commemorating the occasion, the African Episcopal minister Absalom Jones, another of King's oratorical ancestors, took his text from Exodus—"the deliverance of the children of Israel from their bondage is not the only instance in which it has pleased God to appear in behalf of oppressed and distressed nations"—before asking that the day be remembered as the beginning of African and black redemption. "Let the first of January, the day of the abolition of the slave trade in our country, be set apart in every year, as a day of publick thanksgiving," proclaimed Jones, so that our children and their children shall know that on this day the Lord "abolished the trade which dragged [their] fathers from their native country, and sold them as bondsmen in the United States of America."

Before January 1 was sanctified as the foremost Day of Jubilee, other days competed for the honor. Some communities commemorated the abolition of slavery in New York, the West Indies, the District of Columbia, or elsewhere. Still others preferred to recognize the black Revolutionary War hero Crispus Attucks, the slave rebel Nat Turner, or Toussaint L'Ouverture, leader of the Haitian Revolution, or to invent idiosyncratic local festivals such as "Jerry Rescue Day," begun in Syracuse on October 1, 1851, when a group of whites freed a slave named Jerry and sent him to Canada. In later years, September 22, in honor of the Preliminary Emancipation Proclamation, gained favor, as did February 1, known to some as National Freedom Day, when Lincoln signed the Thirteenth Amendment. In a folk tradition still widely observed, many African Americans came to celebrate "Juneteenth" in honor of June 19, 1865, the day news of emancipation finally reached slaves in Texas. By the early twentieth century, Emancipation Day was superseded by Negro History Week—later Black History Month—whose originator, Carter G. Woodson, chose the second week of February so as to encompass the birthdays of both Lincoln and Douglass.

Ever since 1863, however, January 1 has always been more than

New Year's Day to African Americans. "A time of times, nothing like it will ever be seen again in this life," proclaimed Henry M. Turner, pastor of Israel Bethel Church in Washington, D.C., on the Day of Jubilee. "Our entrance into Heaven itself will only form a counterpart." The celebration at Boston's Music Hall included such luminaries as John Greenleaf Whittier and Ralph Waldo Emerson, whose "Boston Hymn," written for the occasion, traced the nation's growth from colony to republic and made the Word of the Lord one with the word delivered by the angel "Freedom." In his concluding stanzas Emerson not only sounded the familiar abolitionist theme that emancipation would free the master as well as the slave ("To-day unbind the captive / So only are ye unbound") but also, like Du Bois and others to follow, posited a theory of reparations:

> But, lay hands on another
> To coin his labor and sweat,
> He goes in pawn for his victim
> For eternal years of debt.

Northern newspapers, at least those supporting the Republican Party, were ecstatic, the Washington *Morning Chronicle* declaring the proclamation "a shrine at which future visionaries will renew their vows, a pillar of fire which shall yet guide other nations out of the night of their bondage." The first claim proved more accurate than the second—though not without irony, since the renewal of vows, including King's in 1963, implied a promise not yet fulfilled—but the writer's allusion to the "pillar of fire," by which God led the Israelites toward Canaan (Exodus 13:21), underscored the scriptural significance attached to the Proclamation and to Lincoln himself.

Recalling the evening celebration at Boston's Tremont Temple, attended predominantly by blacks, Frederick Douglass later described the clamor greeting the telegraphed news that the proclamation had been issued:

Nor shall I ever forget the outburst of joy and thanksgiving that rent the air when the lightning brought to us the emancipation proclamation. In that happy hour we forgot all delay, and forgot all tardiness, forgot that the President had bribed the rebels to lay down their arms by a promise to withhold the bolt which would smite the slave-system with destruction; and we were thenceforward willing to allow the President all the latitude of time, phraseology, and every honorable device that statesmanship might require for the achievement of a great and beneficent measure of liberty and progress.

After the audience cheered for Lincoln, shouting at the tops of their voices and throwing their hats in the air, they prayed and sang songs of jubilee, including "Glory, Hallelujah," "Marching On," and Charles Wesley's hymn "Blow Ye the Trumpet, Blow," in which the biblical Exodus, American liberty, and black emancipation found common expression:

Blow ye the trumpet, blow!
The gladly solemn sound
Let all the nations know,
To earth's remotest bound:
   The year of jubilee is come!
   The year of jubilee is come!
   Return, ye ransomed sinners, home.
. . . .
Extol the Lamb of God,
The sin atoning Lamb;
Redemption by His blood
Throughout the lands proclaim:
   The year of jubilee is come!
   The year of jubilee is come!
   Return, ye ransomed sinners, home.

Ye slaves of sin and hell,
Your liberty receive.

Referring to Leviticus 25:9–13,* in which the Israelites, remembering their own delivery from bondage, incur obligations to redeem indebted bondsmen and restore alienated land, Wesley portrayed the redemption of "slaves of sin" through Christ's sacrifice. As it was sung on Emancipation Day, however, "Blow Ye the Trumpet, Blow" turned the commandment to "proclaim liberty throughout *all* the land" into a promise of literal, not just spiritual, liberty. As we saw earlier, moreover, the inscription of the passage from Leviticus on the Liberty Bell made it integral to King's magnificent call, at the conclusion of the Dream speech, to "let freedom ring" throughout the nation, even from Lookout Mountain in Tennessee and Stone Mountain in Georgia. The passage must also be understood in relation to King's earlier quotation from the prophet Isaiah ("I have a dream that one day every valley shall be exalted . . . and the glory of the Lord shall be revealed and all flesh shall see it together"), one of the three instances in which he specifically buttressed his own sermon on freedom with biblical authority. Seen within King's matrix of quotations and allusions at once biblical and republican, the Day of Jubilee consolidated his argument that political instruments such as the Declaration of Independence, the

---

* "Then shalt thou cause the trumpet of the jubile to sound on the tenth *day* of the seventh month, in the day of atonement shall ye make the trumpet sound throughout all your land.

"And ye shall hallow the fiftieth year, and proclaim liberty throughout *all* the land unto all the inhabitants thereof: it shall be a jubile unto you; and ye shall return every man unto his possession, and ye shall return every man unto his family.

"A jubile shall that fiftieth year be unto you: ye shall not sow, neither reap that which groweth of itself in it, nor gather *the grapes* in it of thy vine undressed.

"For it *is* the jubile; it shall be holy unto you: ye shall eat the increase thereof out of the field.

"In the year of this jubile ye shall return every man unto his possession."

Emancipation Proclamation, and the Civil War amendments were, in effect, instruments of God's will.

When Leviticus's proclamation of liberty reappears in Isaiah 61:1—"The Spirit of the Lord GOD . . . hath sent me to bind up the brokenhearted, to proclaim liberty to the captives, and the opening of the prison to *them that are* bound"—it recasts the promise of freedom to indentured servants as a broader promise to the nation Israel that it shall be restored after the Babylonian exile and, by implication, as the still broader promise of final messianic deliverance. When the scripture of Isaiah is repeated by Jesus, teaching in a Nazareth synagogue in Luke 4:18—"The Spirit of the Lord . . . hath sent me to heal the brokenhearted, to preach deliverance to the captives, and recovering of sight to the blind, to set at liberty them that are bruised"—the prophecy has *become* the messianic deliverance, for all those who accept salvation in Christ. As David Brion Davis and Ronald Garet have demonstrated, Charles Wesley wrote this same typological progression into "Blow Ye the Trumpet, Blow" in a way that King would have recognized, whether or not he had it consciously in mind while he was speaking. Insofar as the commandments given Moses on Mount Sinai called for observance of the Day of Atonement—that is, Yom Kippur—the Christian trumpet of Wesley's hymn derived from the shofar, the ram's horn, and made Christ, the "atoning Lamb," the vehicle of salvation. To this we may add that King, in ringing the Liberty Bell across the nation in centennial recognition of the Day of Jubilee and thus proclaiming "liberty throughout *all* the land unto all the inhabitants thereof," called for an act of atonement that would, in the motto of the SCLC, "redeem the soul of America."

Assassinated on Good Friday, Abraham Lincoln was instantly seen in terms of Christ's crucifixion. "If there were one day on which one could rejoice to echo the martyrdom of Christ," Phillips Brooks told his Philadelphia congregation, "it would be that on which the martyrdom was perfected." For King, too, the progression from Moses to Christ would be completed by his assassination. In 1963, however, he occupied the intermediate role of prophet and dreamer. King's challenge was to restore President Lincoln's promise on the Day of Jubilee—the "great beacon light of hope" shown "to millions of Negro slaves who had been seared in the flames of withering injustice" that came to them "as a joyous daybreak to end the long night of their captivity." He did so, as President Kennedy had declined to do, by issuing a Second Emancipation Proclamation.

■

In his book on the Emancipation Proclamation, written for its centennial, John Hope Franklin regretted that this "great American document of freedom" had been unjustly neglected. To judge from official conduct at the time, little was going to change in 1963. Despite the fact that the commission overseeing the events of the Civil War centennial strove to maintain balance between North and South—the formal opening on January 8, 1961, took place simultaneously at Grant's Tomb in New York City and Lee's Tomb in Lexington, Virginia—celebrations were marked by ongoing conflict over what could and could not be said, as well as the efforts of some southern states to form their own organization so that black rights need not be mentioned at all.

The centennial commemoration of the Preliminary Emancipation Proclamation, held at the Lincoln Memorial on September 22, 1962, was no less contentious. Thurgood Marshall played a minor part, and Mahalia Jackson sang, though she had nothing to say about the event in her autobiography. Apprehensive about alienating southern Democrats, Kennedy provided a prerecorded address memorable only for its banality. "One hundred years ago today Abraham Lincoln signed the Emancipation Proclamation," said the president. It "was not an end" but "a beginning"—all words that would be echoed to much greater rhetorical purpose by King a year later—and he congratulated the Negro for "his loyalty to the United States and to democratic institutions," despite humiliation and deprivation, and for working tirelessly "for his own salvation." After remarking the "spectacular quickening of the pace of full emancipation" over the previous twenty-five years, Kennedy closed by gingerly paraphrasing Lincoln's 1862 message to Congress: "In giving rights to others which belong to them, we give rights to ourselves and to our country."

More impressive, not least for its deep resonance with King's later speech, was Archibald MacLeish's poem "At the Lincoln Memorial," composed for the occasion. As though it were the sculpture of Lincoln himself, "the image of a man / Staring at stillness on a marble floor," MacLeish's poem broods with melancholy intensity on a simple question: "Is this our destiny—defeated dream?" Peeling away the hypocrisy that hovered over the Civil War centennial, MacLeish's poem mingles antebellum time with contemporary and depicts the "tarnished water" of the Potomac River, like the waters of history, pouring into the sea of eternity but bearing the refuse

> Of long injustice, of the mastered man,
> Of man (far worse! far worse!) made master—
> Hatred, the dry bitter thong
> That binds these two together at the last;
> Fear that feeds the hatred with its stale imposture;
> Spoiled, corrupted tramplings of the grapes of wrath . . .
>
> We bring the past down with us, the shame gathers
> And the dream is lost.

In portraying past and present, South and North, black and white bound together not by forgiveness and justice but by the "dry bitter thong" of racial hatred, MacLeish took a searching look at the price paid for reunion, no less great in its way than that paid for Union. Quoting from Lincoln's 1861 remarks at Independence Hall, in the presence of the Liberty Bell, MacLeish was true to the president who divined transcendental liberty in the Declaration of Independence:

> What made the Union—held it in its origins together?
> "I have often inquired of myself
> what great principle or idea it was . . .
> It was not the mere matter of the separation from the
>   motherland
> but something in the Declaration giving liberty
> not alone to the people of this country
> but hope to the world . . .
> It was that which gave promise
> that in due time
> the weights would be lifted from the shoulders of all men."

By underlining Lincoln's intention "To save the Union: / To renew / That promise and that hope again," however, MacLeish was also true to the president for whom black freedom, because it conflicted with his constitutional powers, had initially to be couched in an act of military necessity. The marble Lincoln, like the president at war, "sits there in his doubt alone," conceiving of the authority for an act that frees the nation itself from a terrible burden. MacLeish's Lincoln

> Discerns the Principle,
> The guns begin,
> Emancipates—but not the slaves,
> The Union—not from servitude but shame:
> Emancipates the Union from the monstrous name
> Whose infamy dishonored
> Even the Founders in their graves . . .

> He saves the Union and the dream goes on.

By this point in the poem it is clear enough that the "dream" remains equivocal, embracing both Lincoln's salvation of the nation and the lingering "shame" of the "promise" unfulfilled, and in concluding the poem MacLeish pleads with the river to "Think of our destiny, the place / Named in our covenant where we began," and with Lincoln "To scour the hate clean and the rusted blood" so as to "Renew the holy dream we were meant to be!"

MacLeish's poem and the ceremony for which it was written were little noticed at the time and are less remembered today. But for the March on Washington, observance of the centennial of the Emancipation Proclamation might almost have escaped notice, except by African Americans, amid the festive commemorations at Gettysburg and elsewhere. Whereas Lincoln's dream of Union, of *re*union, had been formally fulfilled, the "holy dream" of emancipation about which King soon spoke in more memorable words—that dream "goes on" in 1963, yet to be fulfilled. Where MacLeish dwelled on the "corrupted tramplings of the grapes of wrath," however, King believed, and spoke as though he believed, that the "covenant where we began" could still be redeemed.

Plainly not an observable fact, dogma such as "all men are created equal," as H. Richard Niebuhr once remarked, must be seen as a "faith statement," the basis for a pledge, a promise, a commitment that must be reenacted and renewed in successive acts and decisions. Taken together, the Emancipation Proclamation and the Gettysburg Address constituted such a promise, one in which the meaning of Jefferson's self-evident truth was given a "new birth of freedom." King, as he remarked a few days before the March on Washington, wanted to make "sort of a Gettysburg Address." He did more. In issuing a new Emancipation Proclamation on a new Day of Jubilee, King stood out from Lincoln's shadow and set his faded aspirations on their way to being living truths for all Americans.

FIVE

Whose Country 'Tis of Thee?

On June 11, 1963, against the backdrop of two months of dogged, violent resistance to King's protests in Birmingham, George Wallace capitulated to federal authority and permitted two black students to enroll at the University of Alabama. In his televised speech that evening, President Kennedy delivered his strongest statement to date on civil rights. He spoke forcefully, if belatedly, of a moral issue "as old as the scriptures and as dear as the American Constitution," and presented the issue of black rights in a simple question: "If an American, because his skin is dark, cannot eat lunch in a restaurant open to the public, if he cannot send his children to the best public school available, if he cannot vote for the public officials who represent him, if, in short, he cannot enjoy the full and free life which all of us want, then who among us would be content to have the color of his skin changed and stand in his place?"

Late that night, as he returned home from his work as Mississippi field secretary for the NAACP, Medgar Evers was shot from ambush and killed by Byron De La Beckwith, an avowed white supremacist who would not be brought to justice until 1994. At a memorial rally held the day after her husband's murder, Myrlie Evers addressed an angry audience who had every reason to seek vengeance, but she pleaded with them to persist in the path of nonviolence—to love, not to hate. Once she finished speaking, recalled National Urban League President Whitney Young, the crowd stood and spontaneously sang "America." In Young's view, the singing expressed "deeply felt faith in a country by a people who have had so little reason to keep alive such a belief. They said to America, 'We believe in you.'"

Young's account was published in 1964, and it is very likely that his memory of this mournful tribute to Medgar Evers, heard by few, was strongly colored by his memory of the words heard by millions that launched the peroration of King's Dream speech:

> With this faith we will be able to work together, to pray together, to struggle together, to go to jail together, to stand up for freedom together . . . this will be the day when all of God's children will be able to sing with new meaning:
>
>> My country, 'tis of thee, sweet land of liberty, of thee
>> I sing.
>> Land where my fathers died, land of the pilgrim's pride,
>> From every mountainside, let freedom ring!

Notwithstanding King's triumphs in Birmingham and Washington, as well as the civil rights legislation of 1964 and 1965 soon to follow, faith in the "sweet land of liberty" was by no means shared by all African Americans. Reacting to what he considered Young's delusion, Addison Gayle, Jr., ranked him high among latter-day Booker T. Washingtons and looked for inspiration instead to the slave rebel Nat Turner, in whose messianic uprising he found an antidote to "the absurd and nonsensical philosophy of Martin Luther King" that, as he saw it, had cost Evers his life.

Whether or not in explicit mockery of King's speech, and despite the favor the song had long enjoyed among civil rights activists, there was no shortage of counterexamples to his apparent endorsement of the patriotic sentiments of "America," also known to many simply by its first line. "You have to be able to laugh to stand up and sing, 'My country 'tis of thee, sweet land of liberty,'" Malcolm X insisted. "*That's* a joke. And if you don't laugh at it, it'll crack you up." Amiri Baraka inserted the lyrics into his 1964 play *The Slave* at a moment of cross-racial violence, accompanied by the stage direction: "*Screams off key like drunken opera singer,*" while Charles Mingus donned an oversized sombrero to sing a satiric version in which its second line became "sweet land of slavery." As recently as 2007, the musician Mos Def, performing a program of jazz, standards, and hip-hop at Lincoln Center, riffed on "America" by emphatically repeating the line "Land where my fathers died," before drifting into "The Star-Spangled Banner," the implication being that *his* fathers died not as patriots but as slaves.

King, of course, was nobody's fool, and he spoke not of present-day realities but of a day still to come when "all of God's children will be able to sing . . . 'My country, 'tis of thee.'" King knew as well as anyone the pain and sorrow that underlay any African American's faith in such words. One need only recall an incident that had already brought him and his family close to the fate of Medgar Evers. While King was waiting to address a meeting of the Montgomery Improvement Association during the 1956 bus boycott, his home was bombed, and his wife and infant daughter barely escaped injury. By the time King arrived, a menacing crowd of supporters, some of them armed, had gathered on his lawn to confront the mayor and police commissioner. Coretta Scott King remembered that even little boys carried broken bottles and that one man squared off with a white policeman, saying, "You got your thirty-eight, I got mine. Let's shoot it out." Their anger in all likelihood would have boiled over in retaliatory violence had King not begged the crowd to "love our white brothers" and go home peacefully. Rising out of tensions so strong that the least incident might have triggered "the most awful race riot in our history," as Coretta recalled, she heard the strains of "My Country, 'Tis of Thee," as though the song itself, like the pacifying effect of King's words, acted as an insecure brake on the simmering violence.

King may or may not have noticed the words of "America" amid the night's pandemonium, just as Myrlie Evers may or may not have noticed them amid her grief seven years later. These peculiar instances of the song's spontaneous performance, haunting and counterintuitive, remind us that it has held a special, if bittersweet, place in the hearts of African Americans.* It tells us, too, that King's use of it in 1963 was not a matter of sudden or unique inspiration—and not simply because he had already included the lyrics in a number of earlier speeches.

---

*The song even played a role in the landmark Supreme Court case *New York Times v. Sullivan* (1964), which grew from a 1960 advertisement placed in the *Times* by Bayard Rustin, Harry Belafonte, and others. In an effort to raise money to defend King against an indictment in Alabama, the ad charged unnamed "Southern violators of the Constitution" with trampling on the right to protest against segregation. Although he was not named in the ad, Montgomery police commissioner L. B. Sullivan brought suit for defamation. Hanging their decision on errors in the ad, an Alabama jury awarded Sullivan five hundred thousand dollars in damages. Among the portions of the ad said to be erroneous and thus libelous by Sullivan was this: "In Montgomery, Alabama, after students sang 'My Country, 'Tis of Thee' on the State Capitol steps, their leaders were expelled from school, and truckloads of police armed with shotguns and tear-gas ringed the Alabama State College Campus." The students, in fact, had sung "The Star-Spangled Banner." Other details of the ad were likewise in error, though not by design. When the Supreme Court reversed the lower court, it said such errors were extraneous, not substantial, and it determined, moreover, that even deliberately malicious and erroneous statements made against a public official must be protected, citing "a profound national commitment to the principle that debate on public issues should be uninhibited, robust, and wide-open, and that it may well include vehement, caustic, and sometimes unpleasantly sharp attacks on government and public officials."

■

Because he is "a man without a country," said the black writer Julian Mayfield in 1959, the Negro "sings the national anthem *sotto voce*," and the same could have been said of "America." Why, indeed, did African Americans care at all to sing a song that seemed at best an ironic commentary on the nation's failure to make them full and equal citizens? Part of the answer lies in the song's early history.

"America" was composed in 1831 when Samuel F. Smith, a student at Andover Theological Seminary commissioned to translate German songbooks into English, adapted the melody of "God Save the King" to a new set of lyrics. Colonial Americans had already appropriated the British lyrics—"God save great George our King, / Long live our noble King"—to their own purposes, whether rejecting the depredations of George III in 1776 ("Tell George in vain his Hand / Is raised 'gainst FREEDOM's Band, / When call'd to arms") or saluting George Washington's inauguration in 1789 ("Hail thou auspicious day! / Far let America / Thy praise resound"). Smith's adaptation did far more, overthrowing monarchical rule in favor of a new nation, conceived in liberty:

My country! 'tis of thee,
Sweet land of liberty,
  Of thee I sing:
Land, where my fathers died;
Land of the pilgrim's pride;
From every mountain-side,
  Let freedom ring!

My native country! Thee,
Land of the noble free;
  Thy name I love:
I love thy rocks and rills,
Thy woods and templed hills;

My heart with rapture thrills,
  Like that above.

No more shall tyrants here
With haughty steps appear
  And soldier-bands;
No more shall tyrants tread
Above the patriot dead;
No more our blood be shed
  By alien hands.

Let music swell the breeze,
And ring from all the trees
  Sweet freedom's song:
Let mortal tongues awake;
Let all that breathes partake;
Let rocks their silence break,
  The sound prolong.

Our fathers' God! To thee,
Author of liberty!
  To thee we sing:
Long may our land be bright
With freedom's holy light;
Protect us by thy might,
  Great God, our King!

Unlike the vocally demanding "Star-Spangled Banner," whose message of valor reflected Francis Scott Key's inspiration by the defense of Fort McHenry during the War of 1812, or the lush "America the Beautiful" (1893), periodically championed as a preferable national anthem, "America" is a brisk, catchy tune that was soon thought of as the "national hymn." Affirming that the "author of liberty," the true source of "sweet freedom's song," was no tyrannical monarch, Smith's adaptation expressed the postrevolutionary generation's declaration of faith in the Founding Fathers and "our fathers' God." But whose nation, whose country?

During the Civil War "America" was the first entry in *The Soldier's Companion,* a songbook carried into battle by Union troops, while those in Confederate uniform likewise had it in their *Soldier's Hymn Book,* just as they created their own variations ("Then, 'mid the cannon's roar, / Let us sing evermore: / God save the South!") in answer to northern variations ("Run up the Stripes and Stars, / Borne in our fathers' wars, / Victor through all"). The song would be put to a host of social and political uses in years to come, but satiric versions of "America"—more than a century before Charles Mingus and Mos Def—had long since become a staple of antislavery activism. In 1839, for example, William Lloyd Garrison's magazine *Liberator* carried "America—A Parody," which began:

> My country! 'tis of thee,
> Stronghold of Slavery—
>   Of thee I sing:
> Land, where my fathers died;
> Where men *man's* rights *deride;*
> From every mountain side,
>   Thy deeds shall ring.

"Fourth of July in Alabama," an 1854 ballad by the the black writer Joshua McCarter Simpson, dwelled on the paradox of slavery's being sanctioned in the land of liberty:

> While e'er four million slaves
> Remain in living graves,
>   Can I rejoice,
> And join the jubilee
> Which set the white man free,

And fetters brought to me?
   'Tis not my choice.

Alluding to the ultimate authority cited in the Declaration of Independence, "Nature's God," and demanding to know whether the "patriot blood" of the revolutionary generation, black alongside white, was shed only so that a new tyranny, worse than Babylonian exile, might be inflicted upon slaves, the African American poet James Monroe Whitfield borrowed the title "America" while satirizing its lyrics in his 1853 jeremiad:

> America, it is to thee,
> Thou boasted land of liberty,—
> It is to thee I raise my song,
> Thou land of blood, and crime, and wrong.
> It is to thee, my native land,
> From whence has issued many a band
> To tear the black man from his soil,
> And force him here to delve and toil.

Especially for those in bondage, however, the song's promise was real enough, as we find in the war journal of Colonel Thomas Wentworth Higginson, a Massachusetts minister and antislavery activist who commanded the black Union troops at Port Royal, South Carolina. (King had the 1962 edition of Higginson's journal, *Army Life in a Black Regiment*, in his personal library.) On January 1, 1863, the Day of Jubilee on which the Emancipation Proclamation took effect, as Higginson waited to receive the colors, there occurred a spontaneous demonstration among the black soldiers and those gathered to celebrate with them:

> Just as I took and waved the flag, which now for the first time
> meant anything to these poor people, there suddenly arose,
> close beside the platform, a strong male voice (but rather

cracked and elderly), into which two women's voices instantly blended, singing, as if by an impulse that could no more be repressed than the morning note of the song-sparrow—

> "My Country, 'tis of thee,
> Sweet land of liberty,
> Of thee I sing!"

. . . Firmly and irrepressibly the quavering voices sang on, verse after verse; others of the colored people joined in; some whites on the platform began, but I motioned them to silence. I never saw anything so electric; it made all other words cheap; it seemed the choked voice of a race at last unloosed. . . . Just think of it!—the first day they had ever had a country, the first flag they had ever seen which promised anything to their people. . . . When they stopped, there was nothing to do for it but to speak, and I went on; but the life of the whole day was in those unknown people's song.

Seen from our vantage point, Higginson's account may seem sentimental and the hopes of the newly freed slaves naïve. It should not be surprising, however, that for those closer to slavery—in contrast to their descendants, who exchanged the manacles of slavery, in King's words, for the "manacles of segregation"—the "choked voice of a race" would be released in the words of "America" and the flag of Union would offer a promise. On January 1, 1863, a people formerly enslaved—at least a portion of them—became, or so it was intended, Americans. Following emancipation, the song became a primer in love of country, included in the curriculum of schools established for freed slave children in the South. (In the 1989 film *Glory*, the black troops of the Fifty-Fourth Massachusetts Infantry, upon arriving in Union-held Beaufort, South Carolina, are greeted by black schoolchildren singing "My Country, 'Tis of Thee.") Yet even informally it held a powerful significance for those who had escaped slavery or been freed.

One former slave recalled that Abraham Lincoln himself stopped at her Washington, D.C., contraband camp on several occasions, sometimes mingling with the older freed persons rather than sitting on the platform reserved for distinguished guests. One day, after the opening prayer delivered by an elder, all of those gathered, black and white together, Lincoln included, stood up and sang "America." Other songs performed that day included "Nobody Knows the Trouble I've Seen," "Every Time I Feel the Spirit," "John Brown's Body," and, most notably, "I Thank God I'm Free at Last," during which, it was said, many of the "old folks forgot about the President being present and began to shout and yell," while Lincoln stood "like a stone and bowed his head," as though "the Holy Ghost was working on him."

It is not likely that Martin Luther King had this scene in mind when he ended his Dream speech with the powerhouse words of the "old Negro spiritual," "Free at last! Free at last! Thank God Almighty, we are free at last!" Between his own renditions of the "national hymn" and the slave spiritual, however, King in effect restaged this day of Lincoln's communion with those to whom emancipation promised their first flag, their first country. Like his engagement with Lincoln, King's engagement with "My Country, 'Tis of Thee" was primarily redemptive. Still, his recitation of its lyrics carried an undercurrent of dissent that appeared generation after generation, from emancipation through the March on Washington and beyond.

As the Civil War amendments were stripped of their power and the reunion of North and South ushered in the age of Jim Crow, the importance of emancipation faded among white Americans, while what Gabor Boritt has deemed the "Gettysburg gospel," with its vision of a common national sacrifice, became ascendant. On the fiftieth anniversary of both the Emancipation Proclamation and the

Gettysburg Address, celebrations of emancipation received no official governmental support, whereas Congress, the War Department, and several states funded a festival of reconciliation at Gettysburg, where more than fifty thousand veterans—Union and Confederate alike, but excluding black veterans—attended the "Peace Jubilee" over which Woodrow Wilson presided as the first southerner elected president since the Civil War. As Lincoln was reclaimed as a friend of the South, even by radical segregationists such as Thomas Dixon, whose novel *The Clansman* (1905) was the basis for D. W. Griffith's pro–Ku Klux Klan film *The Birth of a Nation* (1915), his iconic meaning likewise fractured along racial lines, nowhere more visibly than at the memorial constructed to honor him.

Initiated by an 1867 act of Congress for the purpose of erecting a monument "commemorative of the great charter of emancipation and universal liberty in America," work on the Lincoln Memorial did not begin for more than forty years. When it was dedicated in 1922, the Memorial celebrated sectional reconciliation at the expense of black rights, with Lincoln's egalitarianism diminished and his likely compassion for the defeated South, had he lived, magnified. In the words of the volume produced for the occasion, the Memorial represented "the restoration of the brotherly love of the two sections" in the marble image of a man "as dear to the hearts of the South as to those of the North." Aged Union and Confederate veterans were photographed side by side, and black guests, accordingly, were seated in a segregated section. As much in memory as in fact, reunion trumped emancipation. William Howard Taft, chief justice of the Supreme Court and chairman of the Lincoln Memorial Commission, said nothing about slavery in his remarks, while President Warren G. Harding assured the audience that Lincoln would not have resorted to force to abolish slavery. Edwin Markham read a version of his poem "Lincoln, the Man of the People," which idealized emancipation as an extension of Lincoln's prairie values: "The grip that swung the ax in Illinois / Was on the pen that set a people free."

Of greatest interest as a precursor to King's Dream speech, however, was that offered by Robert Russa Moton, successor to Booker T. Washington as president of Tuskegee Institute. Following Moton's address, the United States Marine Band played "America," the audience standing to sing, and it was therefore fitting that Moton, without quoting directly from the song, had summoned up its spirit in his opening words: "When the Pilgrim Fathers set foot upon the shores of America, in 1620, they laid the foundations of our national existence upon the bed-rock of liberty. . . . When the charter of the nation's birth was assailed [by southern secession], the sons of liberty declared anew the principles of their fathers and liberty became co-extensive with the Union." After drawing a sharp, but brief, contrast between the *Mayflower*, which bore the "pioneers of freedom," and the slave ships that had arrived earlier at Jamestown, bearing the "pioneers of bondage," Moton continued largely in a conciliatory vein and concluded by pledging the "unreserved cooperation" of twelve million black Americans to the project of sectional reunion.

This is the speech that appeared in the official commemorative volume, as well as in Carter Woodson's *Negro Orators and Their Orations*, first published in 1925 and reprinted in 1969. But it is not the speech that Moton wrote for the occasion. Not unlike John Lewis forty years later, as Adam Fairclough has shown, Moton had his speech censored and rewritten by those anxious to protect the politics of reunion and erase any elements of protest. Whereas the spirit of Lewis's speech was preserved, however, Moton's was gutted in the rewriting carried out by the Lincoln Memorial Commission. Missing was his assertion that the Lincoln Memorial was "but a hollow mockery, a symbol of hypocrisy, unless we can make real in our national life, in every state and every section, the things for which he died." Missing was his condemnation of mob violence within "our own borders." Missing was his contention that, until America learned to apply the Constitution to all its citizens, its professions of equal rights would be "as sounding brass and a tinkling cymbal before the nations of the earth."

Moton's allusion to the apostle Paul's lesson on charity in 1 Corinthians 13:1—"Though I speak with the tongues of men and of angels, and have not charity, I am become *as* sounding brass, or a tinkling cymbal"—may have been his own device, but it could also have been borrowed from Ida B. Wells's address "Lynch Law in All Its Phases," an address delivered at Boston's Tremont Temple in 1893, thirty years after the emancipation celebration attended by Frederick Douglass and other leading abolitionists. Reflecting on the post-Reconstruction dismantling of black rights and the retrenchment of the Republican Party, which had stood for thirty years as "the champion of human liberty and human rights," and addressing her own confrontation with southern terror when her newspaper, the *Memphis Free Speech*, was put out of business and she threatened with death after she condemned a spate of lynchings, Wells longed for a revival of the crusading spirit of abolitionism, so that

> mob rule shall be put down and equal and exact justice be accorded to every citizen of whatever race, who finds a home within the borders of the land of the free and the home of the brave.
>
> Then no longer will our national hymn be sounding brass and a tinkling cymbal . . . and all can honestly and gladly join in singing:

> My country! 'tis of thee,
> Sweet land of liberty
>   Of thee I sing.

Every member of this "great composite nation," argued Wells, should be able to sing the "national hymn," be it "The Star-Spangled Banner" or "America."

Her cunning use of scripture makes this point in stark terms. Greater than faith or hope, counsels Paul in the conclusion to this much-loved scripture, is charity, by which he means the selfless love of Jesus—which is to say, the kind of love that King advocated in the face of racial discrimination and violence. Even if it were spoken in the language of angels, said Paul, his message would have no meaning—no "soul force," as King, following Gandhi, might have said— unless it be given in the spirit of love. This alone would draw an important line from Wells, through Moton, to King, but her allusion to Paul's epistle carries with it a further subtext at once commanding and forbidding, namely, his offer of the exemplary love of the Christian martyr: "Though I give my body to be burned, and have not charity, it profiteth me nothing." In associating the lynched black martyrs of the South with Paul's doctrine, Wells effectively sanctified their sacrifice while making her invocation of the "sweet land of liberty" all the more searching and painful.

Wells's panegyric at the end of "Lynch Law" was not just decorative, nor was it falsely sentimental or foolishly hopeful. Rather, in calling for a reinvigoration of the moral authority of "this Christian nation, the flower of . . . nineteenth century civilization," whose sons had once marched into battle singing "Glory Hallelujah," she made her audience look directly at gruesome instances of modern-day martyrdom, such as that of Henry Smith. After being paraded on a float through the streets of Paris, Texas, Smith was bound on a ten-foot scaffold. He was branded the length of his body and had red-hot irons run down his throat and his eyes burned out before being slowly roasted alive as a mob of twenty thousand "howled with delight," then gathered up buttons and ashes for souvenirs once the remains had cooled. In confronting a national audience with such ghastly evidence, Wells wrote in the face of the politics of reunion and obeisance to states' rights, which let many in the North turn a blind eye to the brutalities of the South. "The general government is willingly powerless to send troops to protect the lives of its black citizens," she protested, "but the state governments are free to use state troops to shoot them down like cattle, when in desperation the black men attempt to defend themselves, and then tell the world that it was necessary to put down a 'race war.'"

Little in Wells's indictment would need to be changed for it to have been leveled seventy years later when King spoke at the March on Washington. The vigilante justice of "judge lynch" was in its last chapter, but this could not confidently have been predicted at the time—not when those who killed Emmett Till walked free and bragged about it, not when the murders of Medgar Evers and other civil rights workers, both black and white, went "unsolved," not when white supremacist bombings were a common answer to civil rights protest, and not when state law enforcement pursued such crimes lackadaisically and federal agencies seemed impassive. This was the protest version of "America" stressed in Wells's speech and stricken from Moton's, and we would be right to hear it, warring with contrary strains as Higginson heard them and as Lincoln sang them in the contraband camp, in every subsequent use of the song by African Americans.

■

Although Mahalia Jackson did not sing "America" at the March on Washington, she did perform it at the 1957 Prayer Pilgrimage for Freedom before King spoke from the steps of the Lincoln Memorial. More important is the story Jackson tells in connection with her inclusion of the song in a 1961 concert at Constitution Hall, where Marian Anderson had been forbidden to perform in 1939, leading to the first deliberate use of the Lincoln Memorial for a civil rights protest—not counting Moton's suppressed attempt—and where, of course, she too included "My Country, 'Tis of Thee" in her program.

After the concert, "pack-jammed with colored folks" who clapped and sang, as Jackson recounted, she was confronted in her dressing room by a sobbing sixteen-year-old girl who asked, "Miss Jackson, how can you sing 'My country, 'tis of thee, sweet land of liberty' as if you believed it when you know the white people in America don't want us here? It's not our country." Except for the barriers overcome between the time of Anderson's exclusion from Constitution Hall and Jackson's own performance, her reply might have seemed just as deluded to the girl as her repertoire. "Yes, honey, it is our country, too!" she said. "We colored folks were brought here long ago and we've been born here and raised our families here. We're Americans as much as anybody else."

Jackson's eloquence lay in her singing voice rather than her pat words of reassurance, but in her own way she was paraphrasing *The Souls of Black Folk*, in which Du Bois concluded his meditation on the sorrow songs—"the voice of exile," he called them—with a set of challenging questions:

> Your country? How came it [to be] yours? Before the Pilgrims landed we were here.... Actively we have woven ourselves with the very warp and woof of this nation,—we fought their battles, shared their sorrow, mingled our blood with theirs, and generation after generation have pleaded with a headstrong, careless people to despise not Justice, Mercy, and Truth, lest the nation be smitten with a curse. Our song, our toil, our cheer, and warning have been given to this nation in blood-brotherhood.... Would America have been America without her Negro people?

Black "pride," Du Bois insinuated, preceded "Pilgrims' pride." Sown for three hundred years with the blood and toil of Africans, the "land where [our] fathers died," in this account, carried a claim to freedom prior to the Constitution, prior even to the Declaration of Independence—a claim to freedom nowhere better expressed than in the slave spirituals themselves and later in the songs of the freedom movement.

Although Du Bois was not ready to signify upon the American promise so stingingly as would Malcolm X—"we didn't land on Plymouth Rock, Plymouth Rock landed on us," Malcolm once quipped, borrowing from Cole Porter—he understood the moral and economic claim African Americans had on the "sweet land of liberty." When sung in the voices of slaves and their descendants such as Marian Anderson and Mahalia Jackson, the lyrics of "America," as Du Bois understood, were both a sorrow song and an unfulfilled promissory note. They spoke of a nation to which African Americans did not yet fully belong but which did belong to them—a nation in which they were exiles but also, therefore, a nation in exile from itself.

All these strains of "America," which reached their apotheosis at the March on Washington, were already present in the speech prepared by a fifteen-year-old Atlanta student for a statewide oratorical contest sponsored by the Negro Elks Club in 1944. Speaking on the subject of "The Negro and the Constitution," and taking his cue from the Emancipation Proclamation as it might be interpreted within a framework provided by the Declaration of Independence, "The Star-Spangled Banner," "The Battle Hymn of the Republic," and the Gettysburg Address, as well as "Lift Every Voice and Sing," the young man hoped that his people, "inspired by the example of Lincoln, [and] imbued with the spirit of Christ," would soon "cast down the last barrier to perfect freedom." In relating the story of Marian Anderson's electrifying performance at the Lincoln Memorial, he, too, melded the language of black religion with the language of American liberty: "When the words of 'America' and 'Nobody Knows De Trouble I Seen' rang out over that great gathering, there was a hush on the sea of uplifted faces, black and white, and a new baptism of liberty, equality and fraternity." Like Du Bois, the student declared that the destiny of the nation was dependent upon the destiny of African Americans: "Before the Pilgrims landed at Plymouth we were here. Before the pen of Jefferson etched across the pages of history the majestic words of the Declaration of Independence, we were here."

Traveling home from the contest by bus, the student and his teacher, after being denounced as "black sons of bitches" when they failed to give up their seats to white passengers quickly enough, were forced to stand in the aisle for the ninety-mile trip. "That night will never leave my memory," Martin Luther King would later recall. "It was the angriest I have ever been in my life." And yet, in the speech he had just given, King had preemptively transcended that anger. Whether or not the speech was entirely his own composition,* he had already, at age fifteen, articulated the promise of emancipation for a new age—the promise of a *new* "new birth of

---

*The substance of the speech, as well as its style, when compared to King's contemporaneous letters, suggests that it is not entirely his own work. For example, his reference to freedom having been pledged "seventy-five years ago," since it can refer, in 1944, neither to the Emancipation Proclamation (1863) nor to the Thirteenth Amendment (1865)—conceivably, it referred to the Fourteenth Amendment (1868), rounding off by a year—may mean King was borrowing from someone's earlier text. If it reflected the editorial assistance of his father or one of his teachers at Booker T. Washington High School, or if parts of it were cribbed from other sources, or both, this would only make it the more exact prototype for the mature King's sermons and speeches. In spite of its occasionally confusing argument, "The Negro and the Constitution" is remarkable for the fact that King quickly established many of the ideas, historical points of reference, and metaphoric structures that would typify his vision the rest of his life. Indeed, a number of the speech's key phrases—for example, "Before the Pilgrims landed at Plymouth we were here. Before the pen of Jefferson etched across the pages of history the majestic words of the Declaration of Independence, we were here"—would reappear in "Letter from Birmingham Jail" and other works. King likewise referred to Marian Anderson in many later speeches, quoting from her autobiography and comparing himself to her as an expression of the Zeitgeist—a common person called to great things by the forces of history.

freedom"—and had tested the Lincolnian role he would assume on August 28, 1963, and relinquish on April 4, 1968.

■

"This is my country," said Ralph Bunche, speaking in honor of United Nations Day at Tougaloo College in the fall of 1963. "My ancestors and I helped to build it." Undertaking a road trip sponsored by *Holiday* magazine (modeled on John Steinbeck's *Travels with Charley*) about the same time, John A. Williams published the results of his encounter with America, not always segregated but never colorblind, in a book presumptively entitled *This Is My Country, Too*. In their 1968 single "This Is My Country," Curtis Mayfield and the Impressions embraced a moderate Black Power political stance even as their gospel message of brotherhood and love was meant as a rejoinder to the fact that "some people don't think we have the right to say it's my country." By then, however, King's increased militancy, specifically his outspoken opposition to the Vietnam War, left him vulnerable to the charge that he himself actively discouraged black allegiance to America. When Billy Graham spoke at Honor America Day, a rally in support of Richard Nixon and the Vietnam War held at the Lincoln Memorial on July 4, 1970, his purpose was to let the world know that "the vast majority of us still proudly sing: 'My country 'tis of thee, sweet land of liberty.'" Dismayed by King's antiwar speeches, the black journalist Carl Rowan found it tragically ironic that doubt about black loyalty should be created by a man who had done as much as anyone "to make America truly the Negro's country, too."

"This is your home, my friend, do not be driven from it," wrote James Baldwin in *The Fire Next Time*, which opened with a public letter to his nephew on the occasion of the Emancipation Proclamation centennial, for "great men have done great things here, and will again, and we can make America what America must become." African American history has been marked throughout by searches for a country, a nation, a home of one's own. The slave spirituals spoke of an ancestral land to which one could "fly away home" and more often of a home in which heaven and freedom were synonymous. "And before I'd be a slave / I'd be buried in my grave / And go home to my Lord and be free," says "Oh Freedom," a spiritual frequently reprised in the civil rights era. So, too, the gospel tradition. "Precious Lord, take my hand," sang Mahalia Jackson at King's funeral, "and lead me home." Whether through migration or emigration, or through the achievement of liberty here and now, however, post-emancipation blacks have more often sought literal Promised Lands.

Those less confident than Bunche, Williams, and Mayfield about their eventual inclusion in the nation sometimes longed for a home in Africa. Despite the modest success of nineteenth-century resettlements in Liberia and Sierra Leone, however, Marcus Garvey's "Back-to-Africa" movement—emboldened by his promise to "give back to Africa that liberty that she once enjoyed hundreds of years ago . . . when Ethiopia was in her glory," as he said in his Emancipation Day speech of 1922—succeeded only in establishing a rhetorical template for future black nationalists and Afrocentrists. Still others expressed their longing for a homeland in demands not for repatriation but rather for territorial sovereignty within the United States. Cyril V. Briggs, founder of the African Blood Brotherhood, called in his inaugural address of 1920 for a "colored autonomous state" in the American West, while Elijah Muhammad insisted in a 1959 speech that if whites refused to grant equal rights, they instead had to provide sufficient land to establish a Black Republic, "a home on this earth we can call our own." (The following year Malcolm X met in the Atlanta home of a Nation of Islam minister with members of the Ku Klux Klan who were trying to make a deal with Muhammad to provide a county-sized tract of land where the Nation could establish its own segregated state.) No less grandly, the National Black Government Conference called in 1968 for the creation of the "Republic of New Africa," which was to comprise five southern states ceded by the government, along with four hundred billion dollars in "back pay."

Whether plausible or fanciful, such searches for "my country" were encompassed in Chester Himes's somber observation about black migration in his 1965 novel *Cotton Comes to Harlem:*

> These people were seeking a home—just the same as the Pilgrim Fathers. . . . [They] had deserted the South because it could never be considered their home. Many had been sent north by the white southerners in revenge for the desegregation ruling. Others had fled, thinking the North was better. But they had not found a home in the North. They had not found a home in America. So they looked across the sea to Africa . . . a big free land which they could proudly call home, for there were buried the bones of their ancestors, there lay the roots of their families. . . . Everyone has to believe in something; and the white people of America had left them nothing to believe in.

"My 'old country' is Mississippi," wrote Roger Wilkins in 1974, "and I can trace the trail only three generations back, to Holly Springs, where it seems to peter out. Slavery broke the link with Africa. Our first American experience was to be de-Africanized and made into chattel." Given the profound flourishing of African diasporic culture in the modern era, Wilkins's assessment was myopic, but it captured well both the relative dead end of African repatriation and, what is more important, the right blacks have to claim the nation at large, and the South specifically, as their true home.

Two contemporary responses to King's Dream speech make this point clearly.

Living in Ghana with a group of fellow black American expatriates at the time of the March on Washington, Maya Angelou was disillusioned with King's tactics (we were "brave revolutionaries, not pussyfooting nonviolent cowards") and his showmanship ("who is he going to pray to this time, the statue of Abe Lincoln?"). But the group decided, nevertheless, to stage their own parallel march, if only to honor Du Bois, *their* hero, the news of whose death they received just as they set out. A mix of American émigrés, Peace Corps workers, and Ghanaian friends marched to the American embassy, where they taunted the black American soldiers who were raising the flag at dawn. "That flag won't cover you in Alabama," they jeered, but their anger, Angelou realized, was deeply tempered by the poignant realization that this was "our flag and our only flag"—that it was in the United States, not in Africa, that their ancestors had labored and died, where they had "worked and dreamed of 'a better by and by.'" The same doubleness of emotion expressed in every black rendition of "My Country, 'Tis of Thee" flooded through Angelou: "I shuddered to think that while we wanted that flag dragged in the mud and sullied beyond repair, we also wanted it pristine, its white stripes, summer cloud white. Watching it wave in the breeze . . . made us nearly choke with emotion. It lifted us up with its promise and broke our hearts with its denial."

Back home, Alice Walker joined the throng marching in Washington. Too far away to see well, she could still hear King clearly, "a man who truly had his tongue wrapped around the roots of Southern black religious consciousness." In King's challenge to "go back to Mississippi, go back to Alabama, go back to South Carolina, go back to Georgia, go back to Louisiana," Walker heard a black man demanding that blacks go to the South, not leave it, demanding that we fight "where we were born and raised and destroy the forces that sought to disinherit us." Born and raised in Eatonton, Georgia, Walker wrote, "I was an exile in my own town," but in King's powerful cadenza "let freedom ring" Walker heard a startling affirmation of her own rights: "I, in fact, had claim to the land of my birth. Those red hills of Georgia were mine, and nobody was going to force me away from them until I myself was good and ready to go." So it was that Frederick Douglass, in his 1848 "Letter to My Old Master," said that "we want to live in the land of our birth, and to lay our bones by the side of our fathers'; and nothing short of an intense love of personal freedom keeps us from the South."

■

The Lincoln Memorial marks a symbolic junction between North and South. The Washington Monument and the Capitol rise up to the east; behind the Memorial to the west, across the Potomac River, lies Arlington National Cemetery, established in 1864 on the site where Robert E. Lee and his wife lived at the time Virginia seceded from the Union. Freedman's Village, where former slaves lived and farmed, preceded the cemetery by a year and survived for another two decades. Among those recently buried in Arlington when King spoke in 1963 was Medgar Evers, a veteran of World War II (figure 15). Although she had planned to bury him in Jackson, Myrlie Evers realized that, as a member of the national board of the American Veterans Committee, Medgar could make a more lasting statement of his commitment to American freedom by being laid to rest in Arlington. Here, as she understood upon passing the Lincoln Memorial on the way to the cemetery, he would be "a great American" among "other American heroes." It was, after all, his country, too.

Following the funeral service, featured in a *Life* magazine cover story, Myrlie and her children met with President Kennedy at the White House for condolences, photographs, and souvenirs. But only after she returned home and received Medgar's personal effects, collected at the time of his murder, did the cost of freedom, from one century to another, sink in. In his wallet she found a five-dollar bill. "On the bill was Lincoln's face," she remembered, "and on Lincoln's face was Medgar's blood. One had freed the Negroes from slavery. . . . The other had worked to finish the job. Both were assassinated." So, too, would Kennedy be assassinated; and so, too, would King. In what way America had become Martin Luther King's country would remain a matter of dispute for years to come, but few had a greater claim to sing "My Country, 'Tis of Thee," and no one since Lincoln had done more to return the nation to "her true home."

Not by the Color of Their Skin

Even though it does not provide the Dream speech's most famous phrase, one sentence stands alone for the philosophy it appeared to announce and the contentious use to which it has since been put: "I have a dream that my four little children will one day live in a nation where they will not be judged by the color of their skin but by the content of their character." If King's dream began to be realized with passage of the Civil Rights Act of 1964, his apparently clear elevation of character over color proved central in subsequent arguments about the reach and consequences of that landmark legislation. Those thirty-five spontaneous words have done more than any politician's polemic, any sociologist's theory, or any court's ruling to frame public discussion of affirmative action over the past four decades.

Simply by alluding to his words, Shelby Steele was able to enlist King's implied support for a critique of affirmative action in his best-selling 1990 book *The Content of Our Character.* Other opponents of affirmative action—or, rather, of racial preferences and compensatory practices that evolved under that amorphous label—have likewise used King's words to prove that he stood for colorblind justice. Thus the Heritage Foundation sponsored a seminar in 1994 on the topic of "The Conservative Virtues of Martin Luther King," while Dinesh D'Souza wrote a year later that rejection of King's colorblind view had become "a virtual job qualification for leadership in the civil rights movement." What started as King's journey toward the ideal of colorblindness, remarked William Bradford Reynolds, the assistant attorney general for civil rights under President Ronald Reagan, deteriorated into a squabble over "the affirmative action pie, not by reason of merit but solely on the basis of racial or ethnic entitlement." Even King's niece Alveda King had by 1998 founded King for America, an organization whose conservative agenda included opposition to affirmative action. It was once "a bridge that was necessary and brought many of us across," she said, but it is nonetheless demeaning to be judged by the color of one's skin.

Such views reiterated those expressed by Ronald Reagan himself. When he signed into law the federal holiday in King's honor, despite reservations based on his lingering belief in King's ties to communism, Reagan invoked the colorblind ideal he more fully attributed to King in a radio address of 1985: "Twenty-two years ago Martin Luther King proclaimed his dream of a society rid of discrimination and prejudice, a society where people would be judged on the content of their character, not the color of their skin. That's the vision our entire administration is committed to—a society that keeps faith with the promise of our Declaration of Independence, a proud society in which all men and women truly are free and equal under God." Reagan intended to cite King again in revising a prevailing executive order that mandated goals and timetables for minority hiring in federal contracting, so as to eliminate preferential treatment, but in the face of opposition in Congress, including members of the Republican Party, he abandoned his plan, thus, like

Richard Nixon before him, extending the life of programs he had hoped to dismantle.

Nowhere was contention over King's legacy more evident than in the debate over California's Proposition 209, whose passage in 1995 banned the use of racial criteria in state hiring, contracting, and education. Like later such efforts, including those in Washington and Michigan, successful in 1998 and 2006, respectively, the California Civil Rights Initiative (as Proposition 209 was officially known) was written so as to mirror the Civil Rights Act of 1964: "The state shall not discriminate against, or grant preferential treatment to, any individual or group on the basis of race, sex, color, ethnicity, or national origin in the operation of public employment, public education, or public contracting." As Senator Robert Dole observed: "Both measures stand for the simple proposition that Americans should be judged as individuals, on the basis of their own unique talents and abilities and not on the basis of skin color or gender."

The initiative's foremost advocate, the black conservative and University of California Board of Regents member Ward Connerly, saw King as his "patron saint" in the fight against preferences. He also knew, however, that King's views were more nuanced than those depicted in an ill-conceived television ad that, had it run, might well have derailed the initiative altogether. "We should be judged on merit, not by gender or the color of our skin," began the ad's voice-over. Following a few particulars about the initiative, the ad then cut to film footage of King speaking his lines about "the content of their character" at the March on Washington, and concluded with the narrator saying, "Martin Luther King was right. . . . Let's get rid of all preferences." After an explosion of opposition, from both proponents and opponents of the initiative, including the King family, the ad was scrapped. (Opponents, for their part, ran an inflammatory television spot featuring the white supremacist David

Duke, as well as the mainstream conservatives Pat Buchanan and Newt Gingrich, portrayed against the backdrop of a burning cross, as a means of characterizing the measure's supporters. Radio commercials were generally more restrained, though one had the actress Candice Bergen saying of Proposition 209, "That's like the Ku Klux Klan calling itself 'The Martin Luther King Society.'")

Enlisting King in support of the California Civil Rights Initiative was risky not only because his own views on race-based compensatory treatment could be used in rebuttal but also because it went so strongly against the grain of his image among liberals in contemporary culture. A later example makes the point. When George W. Bush, following his first election as president, named Colin Powell as his secretary of state and Condoleezza Rice as his national security adviser, the *Nation* ran a cover, with the tagline "I Had a Dream," depicting a sleeping King as though he were in the throes of a nightmare comprising Bush, Powell, and Rice (figure 16). The implication, of course, was that King would be appalled not only by Bush's election but also, and specifically, by his appointment of conservative blacks to his cabinet. Indeed, the very existence of blacks like Powell and Rice appeared here to contradict the expectation that race—at least if one is African American—will determine one's beliefs and political views. According to this version of King's dream, ideological diversity within the race was impermissible, and character was radically subordinated to the color of one's skin. In colloquial parlance, Powell and Rice were "not really black."

During the flare-up over the Proposition 209 television ad, Coretta Scott King commented that those claiming that King opposed affirmative action were "misrepresenting his beliefs, and indeed, his life's work." Part of Ward Connerly's objection to the ad lay, in fact, in his realization that King had moved over the course of the 1960s toward support of race-conscious affirmative action and would eventually, as Connerly phrased it, have "wilted under the pressure from the preference cartel." Where Coretta Scott King's view pointed to an ideal of equal treatment realized through evolving law and public policy, Connerly's pointed to an ideal of equal treatment subverted through evolving law and public policy. This double view of King was succinctly encompassed in the syndicated columnist Jonah Goldberg's more recent remark that what makes King "an American icon, as opposed to purely a liberal one, is his vision for a colorblind nation."

Which of these views best represents the content of King's *own* character is a vexed question. One may begin by asking what, in fact, *is* the content of one's character, and in what way, if any, it is related to the color of one's skin.

■

If someone had to be arrested for refusing to move to the back of the bus, said King in the Holt Street Baptist Church address in which he assumed leadership of the Montgomery Improvement Association in 1955, he was happy it was Rosa Parks, "for nobody can doubt the boundless outreach of her integrity. Nobody can doubt the height of her character, nobody can doubt the depth of her Christian commitment and devotion to the teachings of Jesus." Rosa Parks's character, in King's approbation, was effectively defined by the other qualities he attributed to her. For those seeking to challenge Montgomery's segregated buses, Parks proved to be a better choice than Claudette Colvin, whose arrest sparked an initial effort that was abandoned when the young woman proved to be pregnant but unmarried. To be effective, the icon of the bus boycott had to be above reproach.

For a people liable at every turn to be subjected to demeaning racist insult or worse, good personal conduct, at least in public, was a prerequisite to negotiating the world of Jim Crow. Along with overcoming literacy tests, grandfather clauses, property ownership qualifications, and the like, any African American wishing to vote in much of the South before the Voting Rights Act of 1965 might have had to pass a "good character" test, just as likely to be rigged as the other criteria. Any leader of the black community might likewise have felt compelled to display the credentials of his cultivation. In the first paragraph of *Stride toward Freedom*, which described his drive from Atlanta to Montgomery, where he was to assume his new pastorate, King thus told readers that he enjoyed on the radio the Metropolitan Opera's performance of Donizetti's *Lucia de Lammermoor*, one of his favorites.

As the son and grandson of respected ministers and community leaders, an erudite man with a doctorate from a prestigious northern university, King was decidedly a member of the black bourgeoisie. When he spoke specifically to black people in the Dream speech—"there is something I must say to my people"—King was therefore not simply warning against the temptations of bitterness and retaliatory violence. He was also implicitly raising the question of character. The phrase "my people" could have very positive connotations, as when Marian Anderson spoke of being "a symbol, representing my people," in her Easter concert at the Lincoln Memorial, or when Duke Ellington, in his jazz operetta *My People*, proclaimed that the United States rests on "the sweat of my people." It could also, however, connote scolding or lament in response to the bad behavior of other blacks—chagrin "forced outward by pity, scorn and hopeless resignation," as Zora Neale Hurston wrote of the phrase—so that when King spoke to "my people" he was also preaching, as he did on a number of occasions, about the black community's obligation to attend to matters of criminality, illegitimacy, hygiene, and thrift. "We must not let the fact that we are victims of injustice," he argued in *Stride toward Freedom*, "lull us into abrogating responsibility for our own lives."

King in this respect belonged to a clearly delineated tradition. "Men and women who want to be of use to themselves and humanity must have good character," wrote Marcus Garvey in a lesson on the topic of "Character," composed in the late 1930s. Not so different from "the gospel of the tooth-brush" promoted by Booker T. Washington, Garvey's regime entailed the "kind of behaviour and demonstration of it that will meet with the moral precepts of a civilization," a combination of honesty, responsibility, cleanliness, and monogamy. "When I was a young man, we talked much of character," wrote W. E. B. Du Bois in a chapter of his *Autobiography* called "My Character." "At Fisk University character was discussed and emphasized more than scholarship."

The personal virtues and etiquette of which character consisted were by no means only an African American preoccupation. Before it was displaced by the now familiar culture of personality, organized around traits of self-gratification, self-expression, and celebrity, the culture of character, typified by books such as Harry Emerson Fosdick's *Twelve Tests of Character* (1923), was organized around an amalgam of citizenship, duty, honor, reputation, and integrity. Ralph Waldo Emerson's aphorism was widely quoted: "Character is [the] moral order seen through the medium of an individual nature." Not surprisingly, Abraham Lincoln was often featured in discussions of character, not least among blacks. The ideals on which America was founded had "their fullest fruition and greatest presentation in the life and character of Abraham Lincoln," said Du Bois, while for King the "Kentucky rail splitter" became "one of the greatest characters in the great drama of history," by which he meant not a personality, an actor, but a man of conviction, determination, and courage. What C. T. Vivian said of King would have been equally applicable to Lincoln: "Martin *was* what he talked about. People saw in Martin a person who, in fact, loved them. . . . You see, his character came through. They knew he was what he said."*

Seen from the minister's perspective, the essence of character was transcendental. Because every human being bears "the indelible stamp of the Creator," King would write in *Where Do We Go from Here?*, a person's worth lies not in his "intellect, his racial origin or his social position" but rather in his "relatedness to God." Whereas segregation reduced humans "to things rather than persons," the purpose of soul force was to return men and women to the divine relatedness of the beloved community. It was this "content" of human character to which King referred in his eulogy for the girls killed in the bombing of the Sixteenth Street Baptist Church—the antithesis of the moral degeneracy exhibited by the Klansmen who planted the dynamite—when he prayed that their tragic deaths might lead the nation "to substitute an aristocracy of character for an aristocracy of color."

In his frequent recurrence to an "aristocracy of character," King recalled merit-based ideals articulated by Frederick Douglass at the end of the Civil War and Booker T. Washington before the full flowering of Jim Crow, both of whom asked only that no impediments be put in their way, that their integrity and talents, regardless

---

*Although few people, other than his inner circle and government officials, knew about it during his lifetime, King's philandering, like his plagiarism, once it came to light, diminished estimates of his character, and many supporters were taken aback when Ralph Abernathy, no less, wrote openly about the matter in his autobiography. King's extramarital affairs played no small role in the FBI's efforts to harass and discredit him, the most reprehensible being the tape of King's trysts that the FBI sent anonymously to his SCLC office. Opened unknowingly by Coretta Scott King, the tape was accompanied by a letter, purporting to be from a fellow African American, telling King that his only recourse to national shame was suicide: "You better take it now before your filthy, abnormal fraudulent self is bared to the nation."

of their color, be allowed to speak for themselves.* History crushed their hopes, but in the early 1960s another such moment was at hand. Like *Brown v. Board of Education*, the Civil Rights Act of 1964 "induced no sudden transformation of character," observed Ralph Ellison, but "it provided the stage upon which [blacks] could reveal themselves for what their experiences have made them and for what they have made of their experiences."

Definitions of character are inherently fraught with tension between behavior or beliefs that spring from one's natal identity (who one "is") and behavior or beliefs acquired through nurture, choices, and actions (who one has "become"). Both can be construed in terms of race, but since the late twentieth century, notwithstanding widespread agreement that race is a cultural construction lacking credible scientific or genetic meaning, definitions grounded in natal identity have frequently held sway. For King, as for Ellison, however, race, while it no doubt circumscribed experience and thus shaped character in particular ways, no more determined character

---

* To the question "What shall we do with the Negro?" Douglass answered in a speech of April 1865: "Do nothing with us! . . . If the apples will not remain on the tree of their own strength, if they are worm-eaten at the core, if they are early ripe and disposed to fall, let them fall! I am not for tying or fastening them on the tree in any way, except by nature's plan. . . . And if the negro cannot stand on his own legs, let him fall also. All I ask is, give him a chance to stand on his own legs! If you see him on his way to school, let him alone, don't disturb him! If you see him going to a dinner-table at a hotel, let him go! If you see him going to the ballot-box, let him alone, don't disturb him! If you see him going into a work-shop, just let him alone!" In *Up from Slavery*, Washington disdained the idea of white superiority in advocating colorblind meritocracy: "Mere connection with what is known as a superior race will not permanently carry an individual forward unless he has individual worth, and mere connection with what is regarded as an inferior race will not finally hold an individual back if he possesses intrinsic, individual merit. Every persecuted individual and race should get much consolation out of the great human law, which is universal and eternal, that merit, no matter under what skin found, is, in the long run, recognized and rewarded."

than did being born in Georgia or Oklahoma. Abjuring the color chauvinism of Black Power, King later argued that the factor determining the best political candidate should be "not his color but his integrity," and in the 1965 version of his American Dream speech, presented as a Fourth of July sermon at Ebenezer Baptist Church, he hoped that the nation might some day be "one big family of Americans. Not white Americans, not black Americans, not Jewish and Gentile Americans, not Irish or Italian Americans, not Mexican Americans, not Puerto Rican Americans, but just Americans."

Does this mean that King would have agreed with Justice Antonin Scalia's concurring opinion in *Adarand Constructors v. Pena* (1995), in which the Supreme Court deemed minority set-asides unconstitutional? "To pursue the concept of racial entitlement—even for the most admirable and benign of purposes—is to reinforce and preserve for future mischief the way of thinking that produced race slavery, race privilege and race hatred," maintained Scalia in elevating membership in the nation over membership in the racial group. "In the eyes of government, we are just one race here. It is American."

■

It is hard to imagine that King would have agreed with Scalia. Like Douglass before him, King did not let devotion to the ideal of color-blindness prevent him from advocating race-based strategies to address persistent historical inequalities. Those who wish to find in King an ally against affirmative action must contend with evidence such as his overt call for quotas of the kind endorsed by Operation Breadbasket, an SCLC program designed to pressure employers to hire a "fair share" of blacks and to withdraw support from those not doing so. "If a city has a 30 percent Negro population," said King by way of example, "then it is logical to assume that Negroes should have at least 30 percent of the jobs in any particular company, and jobs in all categories, rather than only in menial areas." Proportional representation, which transparently displaced the goal of equal opportunity with the goal of equal results, is the logical endpoint of one version of preferential treatment. Although the premises of affirmative action changed in decades to come—"backward-looking" models of remediation gave way to "forward-looking" models based on the value of "diversity" to institutions and to society at large—in King's era the issue was framed almost exclusively in the conflicting terms of opportunity and compensatory treatment. Whether King would have sought to apply the Operation Breadbasket strategy across disparate employment and educational venues is hard to say, just as no one can be certain where he would have stood on later issues such as school vouchers or reparations for slavery. In fact, it is not simple to know exactly where King stood in 1963, but his seeming enunciation of a colorblind ideal in the Dream speech cannot be judged apart from his place in a wider and already rancorous debate.

In *Why We Can't Wait*, which summed up King's views during the key years of 1963 and 1964, he argued that the nation must incorporate into its planning

> some compensatory consideration for the handicaps [the
> Negro] has inherited from the past. It is impossible to create
> a formula for the future which does not take into account that
> our society has been doing something special against the
> Negro for hundreds of years. How then can he be absorbed
> into the mainstream of American life if we do not do some-
> thing special for him now, in order to balance the equation
> and equip him to compete on a just and equal basis?

Employing an analogy around which Lyndon Johnson would build a major speech in 1965, King addressed the question of equal opportunity in terms of athletic competition. Those who react against compensatory treatment, he argued, misunderstand fairness: "If a man is entered at the starting line in a race three hundred years after another man, the first would have to perform some impossible feat in order to catch up with his fellow runner."

In both his assumption that African Americans were "handicapped" and his use of the "race of life" metaphor, King echoed Du Bois, who maintained in *The Souls of Black Folk* that "a people thus handicapped ought not to be asked to race with the world." In modern usage dating back to the eighteenth century, the "race of life" ideology proposed to replace an aristocratic elite with one based on merit—an "aristocracy of character," in King's words. In the nineteenth century, women and the working class, in particular, called upon the idea in seeking to compete on an equal footing. Although the subject of his July 4, 1861, message to Congress was the South's secession, Abraham Lincoln implicitly addressed black rights and free labor when he argued on that occasion that the very purpose of the Union he meant to preserve was "to elevate the condition of men . . . [and] to afford all, an unfettered start, and a fair chance, in the race of life."

As Isaac Kramnick points out, however, this notion of fair play— "Let the race be fair, let all have an equal chance to win"—might in practice simply make inequality morally acceptable insofar as those handicapped at the outset of the race might need special assistance in order to compete fairly. Such was the view of NAACP Chairman Julian Bond in reaction to the Supreme Court's ruling in the 2007 case of *Parents Involved in Community Schools v. Seattle School District No. 1 et al.*, which outlawed the use of race as a singular criterion for achieving "racial balance" in public schools. In a mixed metaphor that evoked the specter of a return to pre-Montgomery segregated buses, Bond attacked the decision in *Parents Involved* for condemning "minority children to a back seat in the race for life's chances."

The Negro is "America's untouchable," wrote Benjamin Mays in

1956, a view with which King concurred and which led him to another lesson of Gandhian Satyagraha. Providing the recently emancipated untouchables with housing and job opportunities, as well as
preferential treatment in university admission, said Prime Minister
Jawaharlal Nehru, is "our way of atoning for the centuries of injustices we have inflicted upon these people." As King saw it, the
United States likewise had a moral obligation to atone for its past
sins by doing more for "our own handicapped multitudes" than simply bringing them to the starting line. King's position restated at
greater length the one set forth by Bayard Rustin in his "Preamble
to the March on Washington," written in early 1963. Along with
the desegregation of schools, businesses, and transportation, "equal
opportunity" and "merit hiring" might prevent "a further diver-
gence in the relative status of the races," said Rustin, but they would
not overcome "the cumulative handicaps of the Negro worker." Or,
as King put it in a variation on the "race of life" metaphor, "giving a
pair of shoes to a man who has not learned to walk is a cruel jest."

In the very ambiguity of King's epigram, however, lay the conun-
drum of affirmative action. What was needed—what should be provided and what should not be provided—for blacks to compete
fairly in the race of life? How severe was their handicap? How much
"damage" had they suffered, to cite a concept in wide use by the
1960s? The post–World War II consensus that racist attitudes, not
racial traits, were responsible for inequality, coupled with the new
contention that African Americans were victims of a generations-
long "genocide," a term coined in 1944 by the Polish jurist Raphael
Lemkin in response to what came to be known as the Holocaust, established in some quarters the further consensus that blacks as a
people were damaged both materially and psychologically. The
United States "has not literally sought to eliminate the Negro," as
Hitler sought to eliminate the Jews, wrote King in *Where Do We Go*

from Here?, but it has sanctioned a system of segregation that substitutes "a subtle reduction of life by means of deprivation" and inflicts on blacks a form of "spiritual or physical homicide." The essence of the damage doctrine was stated in 1954 by Kenneth Clark, whose views, as noted earlier, were instrumental in *Brown v. Board of Education* that same year. "No nation can afford to subject groups of individuals to the psychological crippling and distortion which are the consequences of chronic racism," wrote Clark, and those consequences will be felt not only by the victims but also by the "dominant or privileged groups."

In other words, both blacks and whites, as groups rather than only as individuals, were damaged by racism, and therefore compensation and debt, like suffering and responsibility, were destined to go hand in hand. The damage thesis advanced by Clark reappeared in King's argument in the Dream speech that one hundred years after the Emancipation Proclamation "the life of the Negro is still sadly crippled by the manacles of segregation and the chains of discrimination," but its foremost statement as a component of civil rights policy was Lyndon Johnson's "To Fulfill These Rights" (his title updated the Truman Committee's report, *To Secure These Rights*), presented as a commencement address at Howard University in 1965. Along with words such as *twisted, battered, stunted, wounded,* and *trapped,* Johnson used the word *crippled* (or *cripple*) four times, most importantly in his assertion that a breakdown of the black family dating from slavery created a "circle of despair and deprivation" in which both African Americans and the nation were put at risk: "When the family collapses it is the children that are usually damaged. When it happens on a massive scale the community itself is crippled."

Johnson then made what appeared to be a statement of the government's commitment to action:

But freedom is not enough. You do not wipe away the scars of centuries by saying: Now you are free to go where you want, and do as you desire, and choose the leaders you please.

You do not take a person who, for years, has been hobbled by chains and liberate him, bring him up to the starting line of a race and then say, "you are free to compete with all the others," and still justly believe that you have been completely fair.

Thus it is not enough just to open the gates of opportunity. All our citizens must have the ability to walk through those gates.

This is the next and the more profound stage of the battle for civil rights. We seek not just freedom but opportunity—not just legal equity but human ability—not just equality as a right and a theory but equality as a fact and equality as a result. . . .

To this end equal opportunity is essential, but not enough. Men and women of all races are born with the same range of abilities. But ability is not just the product of birth. . . . It is the product of a hundred unseen forces playing upon the infant, the child, and the man. . . .

The Negro . . . will have to rely mostly on his own efforts. But he just cannot do it alone.

Like the study from which Johnson's views derived, "The Negro Family: The Case for National Action," in which Assistant Secretary of Labor Daniel Patrick Moynihan contended that "roughly equal results, as compared with other groups," will not come about for blacks without "a new and special effort," Johnson's program was more or less dead on arrival. On the one hand, the Moynihan Report, as it came to be called, was attacked by blacks who found his statements about the social disabilities of the black family condescending and offensive, despite the fact that leaders as different as King, Wilkins, and Elijah Muhammad corroborated them. On the other, as what might have been the centerpiece of the War on Poverty, it fell prey to Johnson's costly escalation of the Vietnam War.

King's call for "something special" was in keeping with the views of Johnson and Moynihan, and they all similarly employed the metaphor of the footrace.* His language also resembled that of CORE Director James Farmer in his congressional testimony of June 1963 about the civil rights bill that Kennedy had submitted and Johnson would ultimately sign. "Negroes have received special treatment all their lives," said Farmer slyly, anticipating King's formulation in *Why We Can't Wait*. "All we are asking for now is some special treatment" to overcome that disadvantage. The model he had in mind was evident in the successful boycott launched by CORE between 1960 and 1963 against such major firms as Pepsi-Cola and Gulf Oil, persuading them to grant blacks preferential treatment until they

---

*King returned to the metaphor on several occasions. Shelby Steele, for example, recalled hearing King say in a Chicago speech of 1964, "When you are behind in a footrace, the only way to get ahead is to run faster than the man in front of you. So when your white roommate says he's tired and goes to sleep, you stay up and burn the midnight oil." This same self-help ethic was evident in *Where Do We Go from Here?*, where King said that even though black runners asked "to do the impossible" might want "to give up in despair," they must strive to "transform [their] minus into a plus, and move on aggressively through the storms of injustice and the jostling winds of our daily handicaps." When King described the betrayal of Reconstruction in the same book, however, his usage, like Johnson's in "To Fulfill These Rights," also pointed toward compensatory treatment: "It was like freeing a man who had been unjustly imprisoned for years, and on discovering his innocence sending him out with no bus fare to get home, no suit to cover his body, no financial compensation to atone for his long years of incarceration and to help him get a sound footing in society; sending him out with only the assertion: 'Now you are free.'" Although the proper means were open to interpretation, King expected the second Reconstruction of the post–*Brown v. Board of Education* years to redress the failures of the first.

had been hired in numbers comparable to their proportion of the local population. (Because CORE's strategy proved a harbinger of policies to come, it later prompted Michael Lind to joke that Martin Luther King, Jr., Day should actually be James Farmer Day.)

When he called in *Why We Can't Wait* for "a massive program by the government of special, compensatory measures," King borrowed even more clearly from Whitney Young's proposal for a ten-year "domestic Marshall Plan," which would repay, in part, the Negro's "collectible claim against the descendants of those who enslaved and exploited him." (The 1947 Marshall Plan had provided some thirteen billion dollars to rebuild European nations devastated by World War II.) Young, too, spoke of a "special effort," which he distinguished from "special privileges." Because equal opportunity alone would not allow blacks to overcome "the handicaps of a tragic history," argued Young, what was needed was a crash program of education, job training, and employment for all the underprivileged. Such a program would serve blacks most, since they were disproportionately poor, but it would, for that same reason, "close rather than widen the nation's racial cleavage."

Young's conception of the issue highlighted two kinds of friction that were destined to accompany the affirmative action debate on into the twenty-first century.

The first was illustrated by differences between King and Roy Wilkins apparent in "What the Marchers Really Want," an article that ran in the *New York Times* just a few days before the March on Washington. "My concept of equality," said King, "means the untrammeled opportunity for every person to fulfill his total individual capacity without any regard to race, creed, color or previous ancestry." He seemed subtly to exceed this paraphrase of the pending civil rights legislation, however, when he added that "the Negro's insistent demand for equality must be approximated, if not totally fulfilled." For Wilkins, in turn, equality meant "the recognition of

individual merit without regard to the color, race, religion or national origin of the individual. . . . Each person is accorded the same
opportunities and treatment as other persons, irrespective of race."
Where King's *approximated* appeared to steer toward a competition
in which equal results would be achieved, Wilkins hewed more
closely to an everyday notion of equal opportunity in which each
person has the same chance to come to the starting line. In King's
language "the Negro" was effectively a group, while in Wilkins's he
was an individual.*

The second kind of friction was identified by Michael Harrington in his influential 1962 study of poverty, *The Other America.*

---

*Another instance of Wilkins's colorblind perspective is worth noting. In the
spring of 1963 James Farmer had a conversation with Vice President Johnson in
which he pushed for a policy of "compensatory preferential treatment." Johnson
agreed, saying, "We have to give minorities an extra push to help them catch up. It's
not fair to ask a man to run a race when the other fellow is halfway around the
track." But he objected to the label *compensatory*, which he thought "a terrible
name." What can we call it? Johnson wondered. "We have to move the nation forward, act positively, affirmatively. That's it: affirmative action." (The concept of
affirmative action dates to the National Labor Relations Act of 1935, where it required an employer found to be practicing discrimination "to cease and desist from
such unfair labor practice, and to take such affirmative action, including reinstate-
ment of employees with or without back pay," as necessary to comply with the act.)
When Farmer recounted the conversation at a meeting of the leaders of the March
on Washington, Young liked the idea, but Wilkins objected to *special* treatment to
make up for *unequal* treatment: "I think that's outside the American tradition and
the country won't buy it. . . . I just want to be treated like everyone else." According
to executive orders issued by Kennedy in 1961 and Johnson in 1965, federal contractors were required to take "affirmative" action to ensure nondiscrimination and
to correct discrimination where it had occurred, "without regard to . . . race, creed,
color, or national origin." However, Johnson's order also created the Office of Federal Contract Compliance, whose internally generated guidelines were soon setting
goals and timetables for minority hiring based on proportional representation and
which in the 1970s adopted further results-oriented procedures such as "race-norm-
ing" (adjusting test scores to take account of race) to remedy the underutilization of
black workers.

Being born black constitutes "the most profound disability that the United States imposes upon a citizen," argued Harrington, and "real emancipation" can be achieved only by "a massive assault upon the entire culture of poverty." Although his colloquy with Wilkins might have suggested otherwise, and although he singled out African Americans in the Dream speech—"One hundred years later, the Negro lives on a lonely island of poverty in the midst of a vast ocean of material prosperity. One hundred years later, the Negro is still languished in the corners of American society"—King reached the same conclusion. The "something special" for African Americans should, on the model of the GI Bill of Rights, be part of a "gigantic Bill of Rights for the Disadvantaged"—all the disadvantaged, white as well as black and other minorities. Although he did not spell out the practical details of his thinking, King's premise was clear in a letter to the editor working with him on *Why We Can't Wait*:

> Any "Negro Bill of Rights" based upon the concept of compensatory treatment as a result of years of cultural and economic deprivation resulting from racial discrimination must give greater emphasis to the alleviation of economic and cultural backwardness on the part of the so-called "poor white." It is my opinion that many white workers whose economic condition is not too far removed from that of his black brother, will find it difficult to accept a "Negro Bill of Rights," which seeks to give special consideration to the Negro in the context of unemployment, joblessness, etc. and does not take into sufficient account their plight (that of the white worker).

Whatever it may have promised in the long run, however, no such plan—not Young's domestic Marshall Plan, not A. Philip Randolph's "Freedom Budget," which called for one hundred billion dollars to be spent over ten years for all those in need, not Johnson's ill-starred War on Poverty—proved feasible in the short run.

"It is both too late and too soon to be color-blind," wrote Nat Hentoff in 1964. Until special efforts could be made on behalf of all the underclass, African Americans alone would be the beneficiaries of "compensatory special efforts." There was the sticking point, and there it would remain for decades to come, with African Americans soon joined by women and other minority groups, including hundreds of thousands of new Hispanic and Asian immigrants and their children, one effect of which was to diminish sharply the initial focus of affirmative action on blacks. Compensatory treatment on economic, rather than racial or ethnic, grounds might seem more justly to approximate the American dream. Few would argue, however, that it would be—or that it has been, where implemented—easier, not to say cheaper. Preference according to "the color of their skin" proved both more urgent and more expedient. In order to see why, and with what consequences, it is necessary to look briefly at the evolution of post–*Brown v. Board of Education* civil rights law.

■

In a well-known passage in *The Morality of Consent* (1975), Alexander Bickel commented that if the Constitution prohibits the exclusion of blacks on racial grounds, it cannot permit the exclusion of whites on the same grounds, "for it must be the exclusion on racial grounds which offends the Constitution, and not the particular skin color of the person excluded." This was the stance taken by Chief Justice John Roberts in his majority opinion in *Parents Involved:* "Accepting racial balancing as a compelling state interest would justify the imposition of racial proportionality throughout American society," contrary to the Court's repeated recognition that at "'the heart of the Constitution's guarantee of equal protection lies the simple command that the Government must treat citizens as individuals, not simply as components of a racial, religious, sexual or national class.'"

Roberts's interpretation would have been anathema to proponents of racial balancing no matter what his predicates, but the fact that he, like Justice Clarence Thomas, appealed directly to *Brown v. Board of Education* was galling to them. In citing *Brown*, however, both Roberts and Thomas looked less to the Court's ruling than to the briefs filed by attorneys for the NAACP Legal Defense Fund, Thurgood Marshall among them. Making no constitutional distinction between segregation and racial balancing, Roberts and Thomas held that *Parents Involved* rested on the same question as *Brown*—namely, "the fact of legally separating children on the basis of race," which the Court found to violate the Constitution in 1954—with Roberts citing one part of the plaintiffs' own colorblind argument ("The Fourteenth Amendment prevents states from according differential treatment to American children on the basis of their color or race") and Thomas another ("That the Constitution is color blind is our dedicated belief"). In recurring to John Marshall Harlan's famous dissent in *Plessy v. Ferguson*—"Our constitution is color-blind, and neither knows nor tolerates classes among citizens. In respect of civil rights, all citizens are equal before the law"—the majority in *Parents Involved* in effect retried *Brown*, responding more strongly to the first prong of the plaintiffs' case, its appeal to the colorblind Constitution, than to the second prong, its appeal to the psychological and material harm done by segregation, which was the foundation of Earl Warren's unanimous opinion.

Roberts and Thomas did not mean that *Brown* was wrongly decided, only that the Warren Court had failed to give credence to the proffered justification of colorblindness. In responding to the arguments of white segregationists that they were the ones harmed by

Brown, in that it usurped their right to free association and threatened them with intermarriage, civil rights advocates had by the late 1960s shifted their arguments from the harm done to blacks as individuals by segregation to the harm done to them by a racial classification, a form of apartheid, that stigmatized them as a group. Whereas this approach to equal protection provided grounds for the compensatory treatment advocated by King, Farmer, Johnson, and others, it also prompted charges by whites of reverse discrimination and thus provided grounds for the Supreme Court, in subsequent decades, to reflect increasingly, if disjointedly, the position of its conservative justices that any classification by race was inherently inequitable. If *Brown* had been based on a colorblind vision of justice rather than racial stigmatization, said this line of argument, it would have established a sounder basis for today's widely accepted doctrine of "strict scrutiny," which holds that racial classifications are "inherently suspect" and thus unconstitutional unless a compelling public interest can be proved.

Whether or not it would have been possible in 1954 for Earl Warren to recruit a verdict in *Brown v. Board of Education* on the basis of colorblindness—especially for the southerners on the Court, Andrew Kull has noted, this would "have raised the Gorgon's head of miscegenation"—the notion nevertheless became a staple of mainstream liberal discourse. Although King's view was more ambiguous than that of Roy Wilkins, neither view was at odds with the language used by President Kennedy in his June 11 speech: "Not every child has an equal talent or an equal ability or an equal motivation, but they should have the equal right to develop their talent and their ability and their motivation, to make something of themselves. We have a right to expect that the Negro community will be responsible, will uphold the law, but they have a right to expect that the law will be fair, that the Constitution will be color blind, as Justice Harlan said at the turn of the century." And neither Wilkins nor King would have disputed the words of the man who would have to muscle the dead president's bill into law. "Until justice is blind to color, until education is unaware of race, until opportunity is unconcerned with the color of men's skins," said then–Vice President Lyndon Johnson in a 1963 Memorial Day speech at Gettysburg, "emancipation will be a proclamation but not a fact."

Like King's belief that the Negro's demands must be "approximated," Johnson's belief that emancipation had to become "a fact" could be understood in colorblind terms. Nevertheless, his 1965 Howard University address moved him closer to the meaning of Bayard Rustin, who argued in an influential essay appearing just a few months earlier that civil rights strategy must henceforth be concerned not with "removing the barriers to full *opportunity* but with achieving the fact of *equality*," presumably, as King said, by doing "something special" for blacks. All such statements were bound to be tentative, if not deliberately vague, however, for the public and the major media were overwhelmingly opposed to "special treatment." As we have seen, *Newsweek*'s 1963 poll showed that 97 percent of whites opposed preferential hiring. On the eve of the March on Washington *Life* magazine likewise cautioned that in advocating quotas, busing, or other kinds of preferential treatment—"something akin to 'war reparations,'" as the editorial put it—activists risked offending "even the most softhearted liberals" and creating a form of reverse discrimination the writer dubbed "Crow-Jimism." These "slide-rule methods of artificial race mixing," warned the writer, playing not so subtly upon the peril of interracial sexuality, "could be as evil as segregation in the long run."

We cannot know the fate of the Civil Rights Act had Kennedy lived—"Kennedy couldn't have gotten the Ten Commandments through Congress," Johnson once cracked to an aide—but suffice it to say that whatever role grief over his death, or King's charisma in the Dream speech, may have played, the bill would have failed, and probably failed miserably, had it deviated from common under-standings of "equal opportunity." During the protracted debate over the bill, southern senators, as well as others, often charged that it would lead to preferences for minorities, a charge that was just as often refuted by the bill's supporters, chief among them Senator Hubert Humphrey. "Contrary to the allegations of some oppo-nents" of Title VII of the Act, which prohibited employment dis-crimination, he said, "there is nothing in it that will give any power to the [Equal Employment Opportunity] Commission or to any court to require hiring, firing, or promotion of employees in order to meet a racial 'quota' or to achieve a certain racial balance." Title VII "forbids discrimination against anyone on account of race," Humphrey continued. "This is the simple and complete truth."*

---

*Even more colorfully, Humphrey offered that if anyone could show him lan-guage in the act providing "that an employer will have to hire on the basis of per-centage or quota related to color, race, religion, or national origin," he would "start eating the pages one after another, because it is not in there," a challenge later quoted by Chief Justice William Rehnquist in his dissenting opinion in *United Steel-workers of America, AFL-CIO-CLC v. Weber* (1979), a reverse-discrimination case in which the Court upheld the remedial proportional hiring of black craft workers. Rehnquist challenged his colleague William Brennan's majority opinion, which also quoted Humphrey's protestations but insisted that the use of *require* rather than *re-quire or permit* in a key passage in Section 703(j) of Title VII—"Nothing contained in this title shall be interpreted to require any employer . . . to grant preferential treat-ment to any individual or to any group because of the race, color, religion, sex, or national origin . . . "—indicated that Congress did not mean to forbid "voluntary race-conscious affirmative action." Comparing the majority opinion to the Or-wellian language of *1984* and the magical escapes of Houdini, Rehnquist replied to Brennan by pointing out that Section 703(j) had been added to prevent the imposi-tion of quotas, there being no need to deal with the voluntary use of preferences be-cause they were plainly excluded by other sections of Title VII (703a and 703d). To Rehnquist's detractors, his argument seemed disingenuous insofar as he, as a law clerk for Supreme Court Justice Robert H. Jackson in the early 1950s, had written a memo opposing the end of segregation on the grounds offered in *Brown v. Board of Education.*

Humphrey's insistence notwithstanding, a combination of factors rendered his disclaimers moot during the minority rights revolution of the ensuing decade. When the Equal Employment Opportunity Commission found itself overwhelmed with a backlog of cases brought by individuals charging discrimination under the Civil Rights Act, it shifted its enforcement strategy from those accused of discrimination to those who were victims of discrimination. Setting aside the question of an employer's intention to discriminate, the commission prohibited practices that had a negative "disparate impact" on the racial group, shown statistically, a benchmark approved by the Supreme Court in *Griggs v. Duke Power Co.* (1971). In the arena of education, the failure of desegregation in the face of southern subterfuges—"there has been entirely too much deliberation and not enough speed," wrote Justice Hugo Black in *Griffin v. Prince Edward County* (1964), when fewer than 2 percent of southern black children attended majority white schools—soon led the Court to approve busing as a means to eliminate dual school systems. Whether in the workplace or the schoolroom, compensatory justice came to be defined not as *desegregation* but rather as *integration*, with some degree of proportional representation—whether described by goals and timetables, by quotas, or later by the nebulous notions of "racial balance" and "diversity"—the expected result.

In language that would be cited in a number of Supreme Court rulings and that typified the evolving consensus in favor of color consciousness, Fifth Circuit Court of Appeals Judge John Minor Wisdom, writing in the school segregation case of *United States v. Jefferson County Board of Education* (1966), ruled that *Brown* required the "affirmative duty of states to furnish fully integrated education to Negroes as a class." In response to the claim by segregationists that *Brown* was an affront to their own constitutional rights, Wisdom determined that one color, one racial classification, was not constitutionally the same as another. The Constitution is "both color blind and color conscious" he argued. "To avoid conflict with the Equal Protection clause, a classification that denies a benefit, causes harm, or imposes a burden must not be based on race. In that sense, the Constitution is color blind." Yet the Constitution is color conscious, he averred, in order "to prevent discrimination being perpetuated and to undo the effects of past discrimination." The decisive criterion is "the relevance of color to a legitimate governmental purpose," such as the integration of public schools. In a bold declaration that made no attempt at obfuscation, Wisdom ruled that "*the only school desegregation plan that meets constitutional standards is one that works,*" a dictum reiterated by the Supreme Court in school busing cases, first in *Green v. County School Board of New Kent County* (1968) and then in *Swann v. Charlotte-Mecklenburg Board of Education* (1971).

Later named Thurgood Marshall's successor as director of the NAACP Legal Defense Fund, Jack Greenberg had contended in 1959 that civil rights organizations, in contrast to labor organizations, "do not aim to perpetuate their group interest since the group interest itself is to eliminate the socially enforced group identity." A decade later, however, both Greenberg and Marshall, who was named to the Supreme Court in 1967, had embraced Wisdom's theory that the Constitution was both colorblind with respect to individual rights and color conscious with respect to the rights of a historically disadvantaged group. As Wisdom intuited, it was not possible to achieve "the fact of equality" or to construct a "plan . . . that works" without addressing the interests of "Negroes as a class." Because "black people have not suffered as individuals but as members of a group," wrote Stokely Carmichael and Charles Hamilton in the 1967 manifesto *Black Power,* "their liberation lies in group action." If the revolutionary agenda failed on the street, it might yet be vindicated by federal agencies and the courts.

Like the shift from individual rights to group rights, the shift from desegregation to integration, when understood not as the right to equal opportunity (the early NAACP strategy) but instead as the right to proportional representation (the CORE strategy adopted by John Minor Wisdom and then the Supreme Court), contravened prevailing liberal views. The change in principle "from discrimination to representation," objected Daniel Bell, turned the "denial of a justly earned place to a person on the basis of an unjust group attribute" into a preference on that same basis. As the debate encompassed a wider and wider array of minority groups, those opposing affirmative action found it contrary to the values of individualism, equal opportunity, and meritocracy, all rudimentary principles underlying and defining most understandings of the American dream, while proponents rejected the doctrine of colorblindness as a mask for racism, whether individual or structural. Discounting popular notions of equal opportunity and equal treatment, they concluded that the idea of "individual merit," because it was predicated on the privilege or disadvantage of membership in a group and necessarily defined by a community's needs, was an artificial concept, and they spoke of opportunity in terms of the "group-disadvantaging principle," according to which a white applicant rejected in favor of a less qualified black applicant might have been treated unfairly as an individual, but her group would not have been disadvantaged.

Following a period of "transitional inequality," in the words of Justice Harry Blackmun's concurring opinion in *Regents of the University of California v. Bakke* (1978), which echoed John Minor Wisdom and borrowed from McGeorge Bundy's variation on the race-of-life metaphor, the goal was to reach a future time when "persons will be regarded as persons, and discrimination of the type we address today will be an ugly feature of history that is instructive but that is behind us." In the meantime, in order to make the race of life more equitable, no racially neutral program could be successful: "In order to get beyond racism, we must first take account of race.

There is no other way. And in order to treat some persons equally, we must treat them differently. We cannot—we dare not—let the Equal Protection Clause perpetuate racial supremacy." The period of transitional inequality, said Blackmun, would end "within a decade, at the most."

Although *Bakke* determined that the separate admissions program for minority students operated by the medical school at the University of California at Davis was unconstitutional, it approved the use of race as a "plus factor" in order to achieve diversity. Striving to be both colorblind and color conscious, *Bakke* thus protected individual whites from harm while at the same time it approved, in limited ways, race-conscious programs designed to aid historically disadvantaged minorities. Noting that it had been twenty-five years since *Bakke* first endorsed this concept, Justice Sandra Day O'Connor avowed in *Grutter v. Bollinger* (2003)—which again employed colorblind discourse while validating programs at the University of Michigan's law school meant to combat racial disadvantage—that another twenty-five years hence the use of racial preferences would no longer be necessary.

Both rulings, responded Linda Chavez, chair of the Center for Equal Opportunity, "stood the Rev. Martin Luther King Jr.'s dream on its head." By adopting the view that the government should guarantee diversity rather than nondiscrimination and by making race and ethnicity proxies for belief and point of view, the Court said in effect that students should not be judged by the "content of their character" but should instead be given a "plus factor" based on the color of their skin. Chavez and others thus saw the "plus factor," like the very idea of diversity, as a beguiling means of reaching proportional representation—an unstated quota that turned membership in the disadvantaged group, what once constituted the stigma of racial classification, into a form of merit, a kind of "character," in its own right.

■

Speaking in 1857, Abraham Lincoln attacked the Supreme Court's decision in the *Dred Scott* case—the decision sent an escaped slave back to his master, accompanied by Chief Justice Roger Taney's infamous words that Negroes were "so far inferior that they had no rights which the white man was bound to respect"—as doing violence to "the plain unmistakable language of the Declaration." By the same token, Lincoln was quick to distinguish among the rights that should or could be afforded to blacks, adding that the authors of the Declaration of Independence did not mean that men "were equal in color, size, intellect, moral developments, or social capacity," nor did they mean to assert "that all were then actually enjoying that equality, nor yet, that they were about to confer it immediately upon them." Lincoln's concessions to the racial prejudices of his day, which virtually disappeared during the years of his presidency, were meant to clear space for his adamant argument, with reference to both the Declaration and the Constitution, against slavery. What the Founding Fathers intended, said Lincoln, was "to set up a standard maxim for free society, which should be familiar to all, and revered by all; constantly looked to, constantly labored for, and even though never perfectly attained, constantly approximated, and thereby constantly spreading and deepening its influence, and augmenting the happiness and value of life to all people of all colors everywhere."

In a 1987 lecture the future Supreme Court justice Clarence Thomas spoke of the need "to recover the moral horizons" of Lincoln's views, as stated in this passage. "Equality of rights, not of possessions or entitlements, offered the opportunity to be free, and self-governing," and the last prominent American political figure to appeal to this "natural law," which "both transcends and underlies time and place, race and custom," contended Thomas, was Martin Luther King, Jr. Like Lincoln and King, moreover, Thomas has fondly cited the Declaration of Independence as "the principle of inherent equality that underlies and infuses our Constitution," as he did in his *Adarand* opinion, from which he derived the consequent belief that the "government cannot make us equal; it can only recognize, respect, and protect us as equal before the law."

King never lost faith in his ability to achieve tangible results—the end of segregation ordinances, new educational and job opportunities for blacks, voting rights—through nonviolent direct action, court decisions, and legislation, but he also recognized that perfect equality, like perfect justice, was an illusion. "Although man's moral pilgrimage may never reach a destination point on earth," he said in the revised version of "The Death of Evil upon the Seashore," one of his more Lincolnian moments, "his never-ceasing strivings may bring him ever closer to the city of righteousness." This is the vision attributed to Lincoln and King by Clarence Thomas. The best that can be achieved, both constitutionally and morally, is to make the law colorblind and ask society to follow suit. Attempting to engineer equal results, rather than equal opportunity, will, in this view, only make colorblindness—"a standard maxim for free society," in Lincoln's phrase, "the city of righteousness," in King's—more elusive.

Those who claim King as a fellow opponent of affirmative action are certainly right if they mean he aspired to a colorblind ideal. Nonviolent direct action will continue, King told Alex Haley in 1965, until "the Negro wins the protections of the Constitution that have long been denied to him; until society, at long last, is stricken gloriously and incurably color-blind," a statement that would have been perfectly at home in the Dream speech. Yet King's very way of envisioning national colorblindness, as a miraculous event, rendered it utopian, and the pessimistic retort belonged to James Farmer, who feared that America would become colorblind only "when *we* [give] up our color." It is doubtful that King, were he alive today, would align himself with the legal opinions of Clarence

Thomas. This does not make those opinions wrong, but it does underscore the degree to which King the icon of colorblindness has been detached from King the moral pragmatist.

Although it left the findings of *Grutter v. Bollinger* intact—the doctrine of diversity in higher education passed the muster of strict scrutiny since race was found to be but one among other factors considered for admission to the University of Michigan's law school—*Parents Involved* revamped the Court's reliance on the race-of-life paradigm and, in the language chosen by John Roberts, reversed the Blackmun dictum: "The way to stop discrimination on the basis of race is to stop discriminating on the basis of race." In his lengthy dissent in *Parents Involved*, Justice Stephen Breyer emphatically rejected this version of colorblind equal protection, arguing that diversity is no less important in elementary and secondary schools than in universities, and that *Brown* held out "the promise of true racial equality—not as a matter of fine words on paper, but as a matter of everyday life in the Nation's cities and schools. . . . It sought one law, one Nation, one people, not simply as a matter of legal principle but in terms of how we actually live."

If Roberts and Thomas sided with King the idealist, we can speculate that King might have sided with Breyer the pragmatist, concerned with "how we actually live" and "the promise of true racial equality" not yet achieved. In this account, race is meritorious not simply as a badge of historical oppression. Rather, it is shorthand, as Orlando Patterson has maintained in his own variation on the "plus factor" argument, for the present-day reality of "surviving an environment in which racism is still an important obstacle," a fact that must be taken into account in assessing "the content of any Afro-American person's character."

Even if this speculation about King's likely view today is correct, however, he still cannot be blithely counted as a proponent of racial preferences—even, perhaps, in Patterson's terms. On the one hand,

King defended the proportional black representation demanded by Operation Breadbasket, believed that employers should be subsidized to establish special training programs for blacks, argued that the requirement of certain educational credentials unfairly kept blacks from getting skilled and semiskilled jobs for which they were otherwise qualified, and maintained that America "owes a debt to justice which it has only begun to pay." In different forms and different venues, such strategies became the common currency of affirmative action, whether by means of goals and timetables, disparate impact findings, or diversity, all of which would probably have enjoyed King's support.

On the other hand, King might have determined, over time, that proportional representation on the basis of race and ethnicity was not the fairest or best way to reach the day when America would be stricken "gloriously and incurably color-blind." Even when he spoke in favor of race-based compensatory treatment, King almost always anchored his arguments in the economic terms set forth in the idea of a Bill of Rights for the Disadvantaged. (One might rather say, in fact, the capitalist terms. Although Cold War constraints may have kept class-based arguments from getting a serious hearing, King argued in *Where Do We Go from Here?* that it would be wise for the nation to take "affirmative action . . . to remove those conditions of poverty, insecurity, and injustice which are the fertile soil in which the seed of Communism grows and develops.") Yet only in reaction to judicial and legislative curbs on race-based preferences did this approach to compensatory treatment begin to gain ground toward the end of the twentieth century. One might say, indeed, that only then did the debate begin to be conducted in King's preferred terms.

No matter what the terms, any strategy for achieving equal opportunity, let alone equality as a fact, will be based on approximation. Like the "promissory note" not yet redeemed, arguably the core image of the Dream speech, the "race of life" that cannot yet be run fairly is appealing in its simplicity and clarity but knotted with problems in real-life application. Past injustices, even present injustices, cannot be remedied as easily as a note past due can be paid, but neither can a fair chance to compete, even one in which offsetting advantages are provided to the disadvantaged, guarantee a race whose conclusion will seem just to all.

The content of one's character might depend in some circumstances and for some prescribed period of time—twenty-five years? twice twenty-five years? two hundred years after the Emancipation Proclamation?—on the color of one's skin. In King's moral universe, however, character always trumps color. Not only are affirmative action strategies focused on those faced with economic hardship more likely to withstand strict scrutiny; they would also seem more closely to approximate King's dream. His aspiration to colorblindness did not contradict his commitment to compensatory treatment—so long as both are seen as matters of economic justice, which included but transcended racial justice, much as his vision of human rights included but transcended black civil rights. And what he said of the mid-1960s civil rights legislation, King would probably have said just as emphatically of affirmative action—that communal justice without must be met by personal initiative and integrity within. The African American "will only be truly free," he maintained the year before his death, "when he reaches down to the inner depths of his own being and signs with the pen and ink of assertive selfhood his own emancipation proclamation."

■

Speculating about where King would have stood on one or another contemporary issue is inevitable, though perhaps we would rather not always know. In a 2006 episode of the animated television series *The Boondocks* entitled "The Return of the King," which aired on the eve of the King holiday, creator Aaron McGruder imagined King waking in the year 2000 from the coma into which he had been plunged after being wounded, rather than killed, in April 1968. Of course, he is a living anachronism, his southern drawl and measured speaking style equally out of place on Fox News and Black Entertainment Television. In the wake of the 9/11 terror attacks, King's pacifism gets him branded a traitor, one of CNN's "ten most unpatriotic Americans." Persuaded to address a meeting of the Black Revolutionary Political Party, which is held in a church but features hustling preachers, obscenity, licentiousness, and drunken fistfights, King denounces the crudeness of black popular culture and asks what purpose his dream has served: "Is this it? This is what I got all those ass-whippings for?" Set off by stained-glass windows in the background, King's vociferous "my people" speech on *The Boondocks* was a distinct echo of comedian Bill Cosby's public condemnations of "ghetto" culture—the first came at an event marking the fiftieth anniversary of *Brown v. Board of Education* in May 2004—for which he was both lionized and demonized.

McGruder's depiction of King was immediately condemned, both for his repeated use of the epithet *nigger*, here the everyday idiom not of white racists but of blacks themselves, and for its portrait of the very behavior that King himself was denouncing. But critics generally ignored the results of the cartoon King's latter-day jeremiad, which brings about a revolution among African Americans, who vow to restore a sense of dignity to the culture and use their economic and political power to better purpose. In cadences evocative of the real King, though in words he would never have uttered in public, McGruder's King speaks as a black man to black people, but he speaks about issues of personal and communal responsibility that transcend skin color. On the day King finally dies, in the year 2020, having moved to Canada like escaped slaves of the past, Oprah Winfrey is elected president.

"The Return of the King" is a fairy tale, an ironic send-up of both black popular culture and its critics. Like other burlesques of King in contemporary comedy, McGruder's capitalized upon the fact that King, arguably the most iconic figure of modern American history, is automatically available for satire. "I had a dream once," laments the cartoon King, "a dream that little black boys and little black girls would drink from the river of prosperity, freed from the thirst of oppression"—a fair imitation of King's inspirational rhetoric instantly deflated by his scandalous resort to street talk. By contrast to the superficial, degenerate world around him, however, this King is a figure about whom there can be no doubt as to the content of his character. Twisted to fit the needs of his creator's imagination, this King is a figure to be admired—indeed, to be revered—a figure whose words are perhaps as close as we can come to what the real King might have said had he awakened from a coma in the early twenty-first century.

For good and for ill, it is a sign of the distance the nation has traveled since 1963 that we tend now to know Martin Luther King, Jr., and his speech at the March on Washington through many distorting lenses—the kaleidoscope of popular culture, the self-aggrandizement of politicians, the wrangling over rights and dollars. And yet having more of King's dream, not less, wanting the blessing of his words on occasions both majestic and trivial, is not such a bad thing. When at last he has his memorial in Washington, D.C., standing directly in the line of sight from the Jefferson Memorial to the Lincoln Memorial, King will be where he belongs. His life was far more than a single speech, but in that speech, no less magnificent today than it was on August 28, 1963, he took the measure of a nation whose soul was in need of redemption and spoke the words it needed to hear.

Who now does not stand in King's shadow?

Appendix

MARTIN LUTHER KING, JR.,
"I HAVE A DREAM"

*Speech delivered at the March on Washington,
August 28, 1963*

I am happy to join with you today in what will go down in history as the greatest demonstration for freedom in the history of our nation.

Fivescore years ago, a great American, in whose symbolic shadow we stand today, signed the Emancipation Proclamation. This momentous decree came as a great beacon light of hope to millions of Negro slaves who had been seared in the flames of withering injustice. It came as a joyous daybreak to end the long night of their captivity.

But one hundred years later, the Negro still is not free. One hundred years later, the life of the Negro is still sadly crippled by the manacles of segregation and the chains of discrimination. One hundred years later, the Negro lives on a lonely island of poverty in the midst of a vast ocean of material prosperity. One hundred years later, the Negro is still languished in the corners of American society and finds himself an exile in his own land. And so we've come here today to dramatize a shameful condition.

In a sense we've come to our nation's capital to cash a check. When the architects of our republic wrote the magnificent words of the Constitution and the Declaration of Independence, they were signing a promissory note to which every American was to fall heir. This note was a promise that all men, yes, black men as well as white men, would be guaranteed the "unalienable Rights of Life, Liberty, and the pursuit of Happiness." It is obvious today that America has defaulted on this promissory note insofar as her citizens of color are concerned. Instead of honoring this sacred obligation, America has given the Negro people a bad check, a check which has come back marked "insufficient funds."

But we refuse to believe that the bank of justice is bankrupt. We refuse to believe that there are insufficient funds in the great vaults of opportunity of this nation. And so we've come to cash this check, a check that will give us upon demand the riches of freedom and the security of justice.

We have also come to this hallowed spot to remind America of the fierce urgency of now. This is no time to engage in the luxury of cooling off or to take the tranquilizing drug of gradualism. Now is the time to make real the promises of democracy. Now is the time to rise from the dark and desolate valley of segregation to the sunlit path of racial justice. Now is the time to lift our nation from the quicksands of racial injustice to the solid rock of brotherhood. Now is the time to make justice a reality for all of God's children.

It would be fatal for the nation to overlook the urgency of the moment. This sweltering summer of the Negro's legitimate discontent will not pass until there is an invigorating autumn of freedom and equality. Nineteen-sixty-three is not an end, but a beginning. And those who hope that the Negro needed to blow off steam and will now be content will have a rude awakening if the nation returns to business as usual. There will be neither rest nor tranquility in America until the Negro is granted his citizenship rights. The whirlwinds of revolt will continue to shake the foundations of our nation until the bright day of justice emerges.

But there is something that I must say to my people, who stand on the warm threshold which leads into the palace of justice: In the process of gaining our rightful place, we must not be guilty of wrongful deeds. Let us not seek to satisfy our thirst for freedom by drinking from the cup of bitterness and hatred. We must forever conduct our struggle on the high plane of dignity and discipline. We must not allow our creative protest to degenerate into physical violence. Again and again, we must rise to the majestic heights of meeting physical force with soul force. The marvelous new militancy which has engulfed the Negro community must not lead us to a distrust of all white people, for many of our white brothers, as evidenced by their presence here today, have come to realize that their destiny is tied up with our destiny. And they have come to realize that their freedom is inextricably bound to our freedom. We cannot walk alone.

And as we walk, we must make the pledge that we shall always march ahead. We cannot turn back. There are those who are asking the devotees of civil rights, "When will you be satisfied?"

We can never be satisfied as long as the Negro is the victim of the unspeakable horrors of police brutality. We can never be satisfied as long as our bodies, heavy with the fatigue of travel, cannot gain lodging in the motels of the highways and the hotels of the cities. We cannot be satisfied as long as the Negro's basic mobility is from a smaller ghetto to a larger one. We can never be satisfied as long as our children are stripped of their selfhood and robbed of their dignity by signs stating "For Whites Only." We cannot be satisfied as long as a Negro in Mississippi cannot vote and a Negro in New York believes he has nothing for which to vote. No, no, we are not satisfied, and we will not be satisfied until justice rolls down like waters and righteousness like a mighty stream.

I am not unmindful that some of you have come here out of great trials and tribulations. Some of you have come fresh from narrow jail cells. Some of you have come from areas where your quest for freedom left you battered by the storms of persecution and staggered by the winds of police brutality. You have been the veterans of creative suffering. Continue to work with the faith that unearned suffering is redemptive. Go back to Mississippi, go back to Alabama, go back to South Carolina, go back to Georgia, go back to Louisiana, go back to the slums and ghettos of our northern cities, knowing that somehow this situation can and will be changed. Let us not wallow in the valley of despair.

I say to you today, my friends, so even though we face the difficulties of today and tomorrow, I still have a dream. It is a dream deeply rooted in the American dream.

I have a dream that one day this nation will rise up and live out the true meaning of its creed: "We hold these truths to be self-evident, that all men are created equal."

I have a dream that one day on the red hills of Georgia, the sons of former slaves and the sons of former slave owners will be able to sit down together at the table of brotherhood.

I have a dream that one day even the state of Mississippi, a state sweltering with the heat of injustice, sweltering with the heat of oppression, will be transformed into an oasis of freedom and justice.

I have a dream that my four little children will one day live in a nation where they will not be judged by the color of their skin but by the content of their character. I have a dream today.

I have a dream that one day down in Alabama, with its vicious racists, with its governor having his lips dripping with the words of "interposition" and "nullification," one day right there in Alabama little black boys and black girls will be able to join hands with little white boys and white girls as sisters and brothers. I have a dream today.

I have a dream that one day every valley shall be exalted, and every hill and mountain shall be made low; the rough places will be made plain, and the crooked places will be made straight; and the glory of the Lord shall be revealed, and all flesh shall see it together.

This is our hope. This is the faith that I go back to the South with. With this faith we will be able to hew out of the mountain of despair a stone of hope. With this faith we will be able to transform the jangling discords of our nation into a beautiful symphony of brotherhood. With this faith we will be able to work together, to pray together, to struggle together, to go to jail together, to stand up for freedom together, knowing that we will be free one day. This will be the day, this will be the day when all of God's children will be able to sing with new meaning:

My country, 'tis of thee, sweet land of liberty, of thee I sing.
Land where my fathers died, land of the pilgrim's pride,
From every mountainside, let freedom ring!

And if America is to be a great nation, this must become true.
And so let freedom ring from the prodigious hilltops of New
  Hampshire.
Let freedom ring from the mighty mountains of New York.
Let freedom ring from the heightening Alleghenies of
  Pennsylvania.
Let freedom ring from the snowcapped Rockies of Colorado.
Let freedom ring from the curvaceous slopes of California.
But not only that: Let freedom ring from Stone Mountain of
  Georgia.
Let freedom ring from Lookout Mountain of Tennessee.
Let freedom ring from every hill and molehill of Mississippi.
  From every mountainside, let freedom ring.

And when this happens, when we allow freedom [to] ring, when we let it ring from every village and every hamlet, from every state and every city, we will be able to speed up that day when all of God's children, black men and white men, Jews and Gentiles, Protestants and Catholics, will be able to join hands and sing in the words of the old Negro spiritual:

Free at last! Free at last!
Thank God Almighty, we are free at last!

Notes

Bibliographical Note

In order to minimize annotation related to familiar aspects of King's life and the civil rights movement, I have provided references only for direct quotations and distinctive events. In recounting basic facts about King and the March on Washington, I have relied in particular on *The Papers of Martin Luther King, Jr.*, ed. Clayborne Carson et al., 6 vols. to date (Berkeley: University of California Press, 1992–), cited below as *Papers*, as well as the following works, cited in more detail below: Coretta Scott King, *My Life with Martin Luther King, Jr.* (1969); David Levering Lewis, *King: A Biography*, 2nd ed. (1978); Stephen B. Oates, *Let the Trumpet Sound: The Life of Martin Luther King, Jr.* (1982); Thomas Gentile, *March on Washington: August 28, 1963* (1983); David J. Garrow, *Bearing the Cross: Martin Luther King, Jr., and the Southern Christian Leadership Conference* (1986); Taylor Branch, *Parting the Waters: America in the King Years, 1954–1963* (1988); Keith D. Miller, *The Voice of Deliverance: The Language of Martin Luther King, Jr., and Its Sources* (1992); Richard Lischer, *The Preacher King: Martin Luther King, Jr., and the Word That Moved America* (1995); Taylor Branch, *Pillar of Fire: America in the King Years, 1963–65* (1998); *The Autobiography of Martin Luther King, Jr.*, ed. Clayborne Carson (1998); Michael Eric Dyson, *I May Not Get There with You: The True Martin Luther King, Jr.* (2000); and Taylor Branch, *At Canaan's Edge: America in the King Years, 1965–68* (2006).

My sources for speeches, sermons, and other writings by King are cited in the notes below. King's Dream speech has been reproduced often, both legally and illegally, in text, audio, and video formats. I have relied on, and reproduced as an appendix, the text of the speech as it appears in *A Call to Conscience: The Landmark Speeches of Dr. Martin Luther King, Jr.*, ed. Clayborne Carson and Kris Shepard (New York: Warner, 2001), while leaving out the interpolated audience remarks and checking it against several audio and video versions. The speech is readily available on a Warner Books compact disk, among other sources, some of which are cited below. On early reprintings of the speech, see Haig Bosmajian, "The Inaccuracies in the Reprintings of Martin Luther King's 'I Have a Dream' Speech," *Communication Education* 31 (1982), 107–14.

Documents relating to plans for the March on Washington, including speeches given by King and others, are in *Speeches by the Leaders: The March on Washington for Jobs and Freedom*, Library of Congress microfilm, Papers of the NAACP, part 21, NAACP relations with the modern civil rights movement, reel 19 (Bethesda, Md.: University Publications of America, 1996), cited below as *Speeches by the Leaders.* I have also compared the texts to one of the original LP recordings, *The Emancipation March on Washington* (Mayco Associates, Mr. Maestro, 1963).

Unless otherwise noted, all biblical quotations refer to the King James Bible, King's usual source. Because they are easily accessed on the Internet at FindLaw and other venues, I have not included references for Supreme Court cases.

In addition to Drew Hansen's indispensable study *The Dream: Martin Luther King, Jr., and the Speech That Inspired a Nation* (2003), I have also benefited in particular from J. Robert Cox, "The Fulfillment of Time: King's 'I Have a Dream' Speech," in *Texts in Context: Critical Dialogues on Significant Episodes in American Political Rhetoric*, ed. Michael C. Leff and Fred J. Kauffeld (Davis, Ga.: Hermagoras, 1989), 181–204; Martha Solomon, "Covenanted Rights: The Metaphoric Matrix of 'I Have a Dream,'" in *Martin Luther King, Jr., and the Sermonic Power of Public Discourse*, ed. Carolyn Calloway-Thomas and John Louis Lucaites (Tuscaloosa: University of Alabama Press, 1993), 66–84; Keith D. Miller and Emily M. Lewis, "Touchstones, Authorities, and Marian Anderson: The Making of 'I Have a Dream,'" in *The Making of Martin Luther King and the Civil Rights Movement*, ed. Brian Ward and Tony Badger (Basingstoke, England: Macmillan, 1996), 147–61; Elizabeth Vander Lei and Keith D. Miller, "Martin Luther King, Jr.'s, 'I Have a Dream' in Context: Ceremonial Protest and the African American Jeremiad," *College English* 62 (September 1999), 83–99; Nathan W. Schlueter, *One Dream or Two? Justice in America and in the Thought of Martin Luther King, Jr.* (Lanham, Md.: Lexington, 2002), 1–29; and David A. Bobbitt, *The Rhetoric of Redemption: Kenneth Burke's Redemption Drama and Martin Luther King, Jr.'s, "I Have a Dream" Speech* (Lanham, Md.: Rowman and Littlefield, 2004). Other sources are included below.

Introduction

p. 1 "the greatest speech": Garry Wills, *Certain Trumpets: The Call of Leaders* (New York: Simon and Schuster, 1994), 219.

p. 2 "one hundred best political speeches": "'I Have a Dream' Leads Top 100 Speeches of the Century" (based on a 1999 survey by researchers at the University of Wisconsin at Madison and Texas A&M University), http://www.news.wisc.edu/releases/3504.html (accessed March 10, 2008).

p. 2 "high school seniors": Diane Ravitch and Chester E. Finn, Jr., *What Do Our 17-Year-Olds Know? A Report on the First National Assessment of History and Literature* (New York: Harper and Row, 1987), 99–100, 270; Sam Dillon, "Survey Finds Teenagers Ignorant of Most Basic History and Literature Questions," *New York Times*, February 27, 2008, http://query.nytimes.com/gst/fullpage.html?res=9B05 E6D61F3CF934A15751C0A96E9C8B63&scp (accessed February 27, 2008).

p. 2 "rhetorical Woodstock": Greil Marcus, *The Shape of Things to Come: Prophecy and the American Voice* (New York: Farrar, Straus and Giroux, 2006), 21.

p. 2 "as good as its Declaration": Thomas P. O'Neill, *Congressional Record 129*, 98th Congress (August 2, 1983), 22236.

p. 3 "wisely choosing its heroes": print advertisement, *New York Times*, January 20, 1986, Y5.

p. 3 "describing nightmare conditions": Jesse Jackson, "Protecting the Legacy: The Challenge of Dr. Martin Luther King, Jr.," in *Straight from the Heart*, ed. Roger D. Hatch and Frank E. Watkins (Philadelphia: Fortress, 1987), 124–25.

p. 4 "like that '63 nonsense": "Fight the Power," music video, directed by Spike Lee, Universal City Studios, 1989. *Do the Right Thing: Bonus Material*, DVD, Criterion Collection, 2001.

p. 4 "how much of King's dream": George Gallup, Jr., ed., *The Gallup Poll: Public Opinion, 1997* (Wilmington, Del.: Scholarly Resources, 1998), 204.

p. 4 "Holy Martin": Scott W. Hoffman, "Holy Martin: The Overlooked Canonization of Dr. Martin Luther King, Jr.," *Religion and American Culture* 10 (Summer 2000), 123–48.

p. 4 "elastic fetish": David Levering Lewis, *King: A Biography*, 2nd ed. (Urbana: University of Illinois Press, 1978), 398.

p. 4 "ten thousand students to date": I Have a Dream Foundation, http://www.ihad.org/html/our_program.htm#Children_We_Serve (accessed March 10, 2008).

p. 5 "When *Newsweek* titled": "Rethinking the Dream," *Newsweek* 125 (June 26, 1995), 18–21.

p. 5 "head of Operation Rescue": Randall Terry, "Operation Rescue: The Civil-Rights Movement of the Nineties," *Policy Review* 47 (Winter 1989), 82–83.

p. 5 "bamboozled blacks": Darryl Fears, "Controversial Ad Links MLK, GOP," *Washington Post*, October 19, 2006, http://www.washingtonpost.com/wp-dyn/content/article/2006/10/18/AR2006101801754.html (accessed March 10, 2008).

p. 6 "dream began to be realized": Hillary Rodham Clinton interviewed on Fox News, January 7, 2008; www.youtube.com/watch?v=v9LhWUsrJnM (accessed March 10, 2008).

p. 6 "Dr. King dreamed the dream": Oprah Winfrey quoted in Dan Balz, "'Our Moment Is Now,' Obama Declares," *Washington Post*, December 10, 2007.

p. 6 "our collective dreams": Barack Obama, *The Audacity of Hope: Thoughts on Reclaiming the American Dream* (New York: Three Rivers, 2006), 362.

p. 6 "paid the price of obtaining": "I Has a Dream," print advertisement, *New York Times*, October 9, 1998.

p. 7 "a really weird dream": Scott Dickers, ed., *The Onion Presents Our Dumb Century* (New York: Three Rivers), 100.

p. 7 "segregation will rule": Unnamed man quoted in "A Cold Reminder," *Economist* 346 (January 24, 1998), 28.

p. 7 "ten-year moratorium": Michael Eric Dyson, *I May Not Get There with You: The True Martin Luther King, Jr.* (New York: Touchstone, 2001), 15.

p. 8 "Before you can inspire": Paul Farhi, "King's 'Dream' Becomes Commercial," *Washington Post*, March 28, 2001, http://www.washingtonpost.com/ac2/wp-dyn?pagename=article&node=&contentId=A2981-2001Mar27 (accessed March 10, 2008).

p. 9 "I Have a Dreamland": Cynthia Tucker, "A Dream Gone Astray," *Atlanta Journal Constitution*, December 18, 1994.

p. 9 "inspired headlines": James Reston, "'I Have a Dream . . . ': Peroration by Dr. King Sums Up a Day the Capital Will Remember," *New York Times*, August 29, 1963; Eugene Patterson, "In Shadow of Abe Lincoln, a Voice Shouts for Freedom," *Atlanta Constitution*, August 29, 1963; editorial, "The Dream Defiled," *Boston Globe*, April 9, 2001; Swati Pandey, "The Dream—For Sale," *Los Angeles Times*, June 18, 2006.

p. 10 "a prophecy of pure hope": Ralph David Abernathy, *And the Walls Came Tumbling Down: An Autobiography* (New York: HarperPerennial, 1990), 280–81, 433.

p. 10 "hasn't changed any votes": Humphrey quoted in Lewis, *King*, 229–30.

ONE

Dreamer—1963

p. 14 "started out reading": King quoted in David J. Garrow, *Bearing the Cross: Martin Luther King, Jr., and the Southern Christian Leadership Conference* (New York: Vintage, 1988), 283.

p. 14 "Tell 'em about the dream": Taylor Branch, *Parting the Waters: America in the King Years, 1954–1963* (New York: Simon and Schuster, 1988), 882.

p. 14 "near my beloved": Joan Baez, *And a Voice to Sing With: A Memoir* (New York: Plume, 1988), 103.

p. 14 "from some higher place": Coretta Scott King, *My Life with Martin Luther King, Jr.* (New York: Avon, 1970), 243, 245.

p. 14 "wept unashamedly": Lerone Bennett, Jr., "Introduction," *The Day They Marched*, ed. Doris E. Saunders (Chicago: Johnson, 1963), 13. Bennett's account also appeared in the November 1963 issue of *Ebony*.

p. 15 "enslaved his audience": "The March's Meaning," *Time* 82 (September 6, 1963), 15.

p. 15 "demagogic speech": William C. Sullivan quoted in Richard Gid Powers, *Secrecy and Power: The Life of J. Edgar Hoover* (New York: Free Press, 1987), 377.

p. 16 "pedestrian by comparison": On the drafting of King's speech, as well as the departures he made from his prepared text, see Drew Hansen, *The Dream: Martin Luther King, Jr., and the Speech That Inspired a Nation* (New York: HarperCollins, 2003), 65–94.

p. 18 "some big words like that": King quoted in David Levering Lewis, *King: A Biography*, 2nd ed. (Urbana: University of Illinois Press, 1978), 12.

p. 18 "the sublime phrascology": James Weldon Johnson, "Preface," *God's Trombones* (1927; rpt. New York: Penguin, 1976), 9.

p. 18 "an African drum": Julius Lester, "The Martin Luther King I Remember," *Evergreen Review* 74 (January 1970), 18.

p. 19 "I see angel's wings": Unnamed woman quoted in Stephen B. Oates, *Let the Trumpet Sound: The Life of Martin Luther King, Jr.* (New York: Mentor, 1985), 76.

p. 19 "warm bodies in the street": Wyatt T. Walker quoted in Aldon D. Morris, *The Origins of the Civil Rights Movement: Black Communities Organizing for Change* (New York: Free Press, 1984), 92.

p. 19 "touching me from the inside": Charles Gratton interview in *Remembering Jim Crow: African Americans Tell about Life in the Segregated South*, ed. William Chafe et al. (New York: New Press, 2001), 8.

p. 19 "well-honed ability": Dan Rather, with Mickey Herskowitz, *The Camera Never Blinks: Adventures of a TV Journalist* (New York: William Morrow, 1977), 96.

p. 19 "conservative militant": August Meier, "On the Role of Martin Luther King," *New Politics* 4 (Winter 1965), 53–54.

p. 19 "radical moderation": Stewart Burns, *To the Mountaintop: Martin Luther King, Jr.'s, Mission to Save America* (San Francisco: HarperCollins, 2004), 220, 222.

p. 19 "unwarranted protest": Joseph H. Jackson quoted in Branch, *Parting the Waters*, 848.

p. 19 "You just can't communicate": King quoted in Garrow, *Bearing the Cross*, 497.

p. 19 "voice out of Bethlehem": Martin Luther King, Jr., "A Testament of Hope" (published posthumously in *Playboy*, January 1969), in *A Testament of Hope: The Essential Writings of Martin Luther King, Jr.*, ed. James Melvin Washington (San Francisco: Harper, 1986), 328.

p. 20 "One day the South": Martin Luther King, Jr., "Letter from Birmingham Jail," in *Why We Can't Wait* (New York: Signet, 1964), 94.

p. 20 "sweltering August afternoon": Martin Luther King, Jr., "A Christmas Sermon on Peace" (December 24, 1967), in *The Trumpet of Conscience* (New York: Harper and Row, 1968), 75–77. Cf. Martin Luther King, Jr., "I've Been to the Mountaintop" (April 3, 1968), in *A Call to Conscience: The Landmark Speeches of Dr. Martin Luther King, Jr.*, ed. Clayborne Carson and Kris Shepard (New York: Warner, 2001), 222.

p. 20 "don't need no damn dreams": Martin Luther King, Jr., "Tough Years Ahead," *Newsweek* 66 (August 30, 1965), 19.

p. 21 "story of shattered dreams": Martin Luther King, Jr., "Unfulfilled Dreams" (March 3, 1968), in *A Knock at Midnight: Inspiration from the Great Sermons of Reverend Martin Luther King, Jr.*, ed. Clayborne Carson and Peter Holloran (New York: Warner, 1998), 191–94.

p. 21 "the fulfillment of a dream": King quoted in Claude Sitton, "Rioting Negroes Routed by Police at Birmingham," *New York Times*, May 8, 1963.

p. 21 "discovered a conscience": King, *Why We Can't Wait*, 109.

p. 21 "your dream has come true": Bayard Rustin quoted in Patrik Henry Bass, *Like a Mighty Stream: The March on Washington, August 28, 1963* (Philadelphia: Running Press, 2002), 136.

p. 22 "she began to intone": James Bevel quoted in Richard Lischer, *The Preacher King: Martin Luther King, Jr., and the Word That Moved America* (New York: Oxford University Press, 1995), 93. The woman in question was Prathia Hall. For an analysis that casts some doubt on the story, see Hansen, *The Dream*, 249–50.

p. 22 "hold hands with your child": Dorothy Cotton speaking in *Martin Luther King, Jr.: The Man and the Dream*, VHS video, prod. Lina Gopaul, Black Audio Films, BBC Television and A&E Network, 1997.

p. 22 "horrid dreams of freedom": Frederick Douglass, "American Slavery" (September 24, 1847), in *The Life and Writings of Frederick Douglass*, ed. Philip S. Foner, 5 vols. (New York: International Publishers, 1950), 1: 276–77.

p. 22 "a wonderful world": W. E. B. Du Bois, *The Autobiography of W. E. B. Du Bois: A Soliloquy on Viewing My Life from the Last Decade of Its First Century* (1968; rpt. New York: International Publishers, 1986), 422–23.

p. 22 "Let America be the dream": Langston Hughes, "Let America Be America Again" (1935), in *The Collected Poems of Langston Hughes*, ed. Arnold Rampersad and David Roessel (New York: Knopf, 1996), 189.

p. 22 "how many dead dreams": Lillian Smith, *Killers of the Dream*, rev. ed. (1961; rpt. New York: Norton, 1978), 20.

p. 23 "he told Harold DeWolf ": King quoted in Hansen, *The Dream*, 153.

p. 23 "last will and testament": James Meredith, *Three Years in Mississippi* (Bloomington: Indiana University Press, 1966), 200–201.

p. 23 "some kind of strange dream": King quoted in Lewis, *King*, 125.

p. 24 "The white majority": "Albany, Georgia—Police State," quoted in A. J. Muste, "Rifle Squads or the Beloved Community," *Liberation* 9 (May 1964), 7–8.

p. 24 "Liberty to all": Abraham Lincoln, "Fragment on the Constitution and the Union" (January 1861), in *The Collected Works of Abraham Lincoln*, ed. Roy P. Basler, 9 vols. (New Brunswick, N.J.: Rutgers University Press, 1953), 4: 169.

p. 25 "great soul": W. E. B. Du Bois, "Abraham Lincoln" (1907), in *The Oxford W. E. B. Du Bois Reader*, ed. Eric J. Sundquist (New York: Oxford University Press, 1996), 249, 252.

p. 25 "American Creed": Gunnar Myrdal, *An American Dilemma: The Negro Problem and Modern Democracy*, 2 vols. (1944; rpt. New Brunswick, N.J.: Transaction, 1996), 1: 4.

p. 26 "ceased to be a cliché": Ralph McGill, *The South and the Southerner* (Boston: Little, Brown, 1963), 16–18.

p. 26 "African American could be president": Robert Kennedy cited in Louis Lomax, *The Negro Revolt* (New York: Signet, 1963), 256.

p. 26 "best exemplifies your idea": Sheldon Appleton, "Martin Luther King in Life . . . and Memory," *Public Perspective*, February–March 1995, 11–13.

p. 26 "When I think of King": Wynton Marsalis quoted in "Celebrities Share What the Rev. Dr. Martin Luther King, Jr., Means to Them," *Jet* 95 (January 25, 1999), 8.

p. 27 "the great dream of America": Martin Luther King, Jr., "What a Mother Should Tell Her Child" (May 12, 1963), quoted in Lischer, *The Preacher King*, 179.

p. 27 "the aspiration of America itself ": Joachim Prinz, speech at the March on Washington (August 28, 1963), in *Speeches by the Leaders*.

p. 27 "In a real sense America": Martin Luther King, Jr., "The Negro and the American Dream" (September 25, 1960), in *Papers*, 5: 508–9.

p. 28 "awoke from a stupor": King, *Why We Can't Wait*, 23–25.

p. 28 "We will say Freedom": King quoted in Lischer, *The Preacher King*, 133.

p. 28 "there comes a time": Martin Luther King, Jr., "MIA Mass Meeting at the Holt Street Baptist Church" (December 5, 1955), in *Papers*, 3: 72–73.

p. 31 "speed up the coming": Martin Luther King, Jr., "Facing the Challenge of a New Age" (December 3, 1956), in *Papers*, 3: 459–63.

p. 31 "reached beyond lawbooks": "Attack on the Conscience," *Time* 69 (February 18, 1957), 17.

p. 32 "cannot look for salvation": Ella Baker quoted in Charles M. Payne, *I've Got the Light of Freedom: The Organizing Tradition and the Mississippi Freedom Struggle* (Berkeley: University of California Press, 1995), 93.

p. 33 "a man on the moon": Martin Luther King, Jr., "Fumbling on the New Frontier," *Nation* 194 (March 3, 1962), 193.

p. 33 "blacks supported Kennedy": "The Negro in America," *Newsweek* 62 (July 29, 1963), 28.

p. 34 "Second Emancipation Proclamation": King quoted in Branch, *Parting the Waters*, 518.

p. 34 "conscience of America": Martin Luther King, Jr., "An Appeal to the President of the United States," in *A Martin Luther King Treasury* (Yonkers, N.Y.: Negro Heritage Library, 1964), 294–95.

p. 34 "moment in the country's history": King, *Why We Can't Wait*, 25.

p. 35 "ill-timed": King quoted in Arthur M. Schlesinger, Jr., *A Thousand Days: John F. Kennedy in the White House* (Boston: Houghton Mifflin, 1965), 970. Cf. King, "Letter from Birmingham Jail," 80.

p. 37 "see the dogs work": Eugene "Bull" Connor quoted in Garrow, *Bearing the Cross*, 249.

p. 37 "get a better education": Wyatt T. Walker quoted in "Birmingham, U.S.A.: 'Look at Them Run,'" *Newsweek* 62 (May 13, 1963), 28.

p. 37 "no Gabriel trumpet": King, *Why We Can't Wait*, 98.

p. 37 "blunt pen of marching ranks": Martin Luther King, Jr., *Where Do We Go from Here: Chaos or Community?* (Boston: Beacon, 1967), 139.

p. 37 "*New York Times* coverage": Julian Bond, "The Media and the Movement: Looking Back from the Southern Front," in *Media, Culture, and the Modern African American Freedom Struggle*, ed. Brian Ward (Gainesville: University Press of Florida, 2001), 31.

p. 38 "their top source of news": Erik Barnouw, *Tube of Plenty: The Evolution of American Television*, 2nd rev. ed. (New York: Oxford University Press, 1990), 314; the ratings had changed from 57 percent for newspapers and 52 percent for television in 1961 to 55 percent for television and 53 percent for newspapers in 1963.

p. 38 "we made it impossible": Unnamed NBC correspondent quoted in Edward Jay Epstein, *News from Nowhere: Television and the News* (1973; rpt. Chicago: Ivan R. Dee, 2000), 219–20.

p. 38 "Public relations": King quoted in Bruce Miroff, *Icons of Democracy: American Leaders as Heroes, Aristocrats, Dissenters, and Democrats* (New York: Basic, 1993), 324.

p. 38 "luminous glare": King, *Why We Can't Wait*, 39. On the role of the press in Birmingham, see also Gene Roberts and Hank Klibanoff, *The Race Beat: The Press, the Civil Rights Struggle, and the Awakening of a Nation* (New York: Knopf, 2006), 301–33, and Davi Johnson, "Martin Luther King Jr.'s 1963 Birmingham Campaign as Image Event," *Rhetoric and Public Affairs* 10 (2007), 1–26. On magazine coverage of civil rights in the spring and summer 1963, the March on Washington in particular, see Richard Lentz, *Symbols, the News Magazines, and Martin Luther King* (Baton Rouge: Louisiana State University Press, 1990), 95–112.

p. 38 "picture of a snarling dog": Eric Sevareid quoted in David Farber, *The Age of Great Dreams: America in the 1960s* (New York: Hill and Wang, 1994), 87.

p. 39 "Now the time has come": John F. Kennedy, "Radio and Television Report to the American People on Civil Rights" (June 11, 1963), in *Public Papers of the Presidents of the United States, 1963* (Washington, D.C.: U.S. Government Printing Office, 1964), 469.

p. 39 "race and color prejudice": King quoted in "What the Marchers Really Want," *New York Times*, August 23, 1963.

p. 39 "unprecedented number of blacks": "The Negro in America," 26, 28; William Brink and Louis Harris, *The Negro Revolution in America* (New York: Simon and Schuster, 1964), 136, 238. In both the survey of blacks and the corresponding survey of whites some of the figures in the Brink-Harris volume differ in small ways from those in *Newsweek*, though each refers to a survey conducted jointly.

p. 40 "figure stood at 80 percent": Allen J. Matusow, *The Unraveling of America: A History of Liberalism in the 1960s* (New York: Harper and Row, 1984), 211.

p. 40 "made irreversible": "Man of the Year," *Time* 83 (January 3, 1964), 25.

p. 40 "remembers having dreamed up": Ralph David Abernathy, *And the Walls Came Tumbling Down: An Autobiography* (New York: HarperPerennial, 1989), 272.

p. 40 "Bevel's proposal": Andrew Young, *An Easy Burden: The Civil Rights Movement and the Transformation of America* (New York: HarperCollins, 1996), 269.

p. 41 "his fire hoses": Bayard Rustin quoted in Thomas Gentile, *March on Washington: August 28, 1963* (Washington, D.C.: New Day, 1983), 22.

p. 41 "people from back home": Roy Wilkins quoted in Jonathan Rosenberg and Zachary Karabell, *Kennedy, Johnson, and the Quest for Justice: The Civil Rights Tapes* (New York: Norton, 2003), 132.

p. 41 "field Negroes in the ghettoes": Calvin Hernton, "Dynamite Growing Out of Their Skulls," in *Black Fire: An Anthology of Afro-American Writing*, ed. LeRoi Jones and Larry Neal (New York: William Morrow, 1968), 99–100.

p. 41 "the people's commemoration": "Proposed Plans for March" (July 2, 1963), in *Speeches by the Leaders.*

p. 42 "at the point of a gun": John F. Kennedy quoted in Schlesinger, *A Thousand Days*, 969.

p. 42 "ain't listening at all": Bob Dylan quoted in Anthony Scaduto, *Bob Dylan* (New York: Grosset and Dunlap, 1971), 151.

p. 43 "a living petition": "Statement by the heads of the ten organizations calling for discipline in connection with the Washington March of August 28, 1963," in *Speeches by the Leaders.*

p. 43 "living, beating heart": King, *Why We Can't Wait,* 123.

p. 43 "slave spirituals and hymns": Here and elsewhere, my citation of the lyrics of slave spirituals and other pre–civil rights movement black music is based on James Weldon Johnson and J. Rosamond Johnson, *The Books of American Negro Spirituals,* 2 vols. in 1 (1925, 1926; rpt. New York: Da Capo, 1969); John Lovell, Jr., *Black Song: The Forge and the Flame: The Story of How the Afro-American Spiritual Was Hammered Out* (1972; rpt. New York: Paragon House, 1986); Gwendolyn Sims Warren, *Ev'ry Time I Feel the Spirit* (New York: Henry Holt, 1997); and *African American Heritage Hymnal* (Chicago: GIA, 2001).

p. 44 "battle hymn of the movement": King: *Why We Can't Wait,* 73.

p. 44 "millions of marching blacks": Adam Clayton Powell, Jr., *Marching Blacks: An Interpretive History of the Rise of the Common Black Man* (New York: Dial, 1945), 182–86.

p. 44 "climb into the unknown": Smith, *Killers of the Dream,* 253.

p. 44 "a black nationalist army": Malcolm X, "The Ballot or the Bullet" (speech of April 3, 1964), in *Malcolm X Speaks: Selected Speeches and Statements,* ed. George Breitman (New York: Grove, 1966), 41.

p. 45 "Armies of Negroes marching": John Adams quoted in Joseph J. Ellis, *Founding Brothers: The Revolutionary Generation* (New York: Vintage, 2002), 241.

p. 45 "We won't stop now": John Lewis's original speech, in John Lewis, with Michael D'Orso, *Walking with the Wind: A Memoir of the Movement* (New York: Harvest, 1998), 221.

p. 46 "*the rainbow sign*": James Baldwin, *The Fire Next Time* (New York: Dell, 1963), 141.

p. 46 "waited twenty-two years": A. Philip Randolph quoted in Lewis, *Walking with the Wind,* 226–27.

p. 46 "A. Philip Randolph Day": "Randolph's Long Dream Realized in D.C. March," *Pittsburgh Courier,* August 31, 1963.

p. 47 "worth a million editorials": A. Philip Randolph, "The March on Washington Movement Presents a Program for the Negro," in *What the Negro Wants,* ed. Rayford W. Logan (Chapel Hill: University of North Carolina Press, 1944), 154. See also Herbert Garfinkel, *When Negroes March: The March on Washington Movement in the Organizational Politics for FEPC* (New York: Atheneum, 1973), and Lucy G. Barber, *Marching on Washington: The Forging of an American Political Tradition* (Berkeley: University of California Press, 2002), 108–78.

p. 47 "build a mammoth machine": A. Philip Randolph, "Call to Negro America," *Black Worker,* May 1941, rpt. in *Reporting Civil Rights,* part 1, *American Journalism, 1941–1963* (New York: Library of America, 2003), 2–3.

p. 47 "a special army": King, *Why We Can't Wait,* 62.

p. 47 "spiritual arsenal of democracy": A. Philip Randolph, "Why Should We March?" (1942), in *A Documentary History of the Negro People of the United States*, ed. Herbert Aptheker, 5 vols. (1974; rpt. New York: Citadel, 1990), 4: 420.

p. 47 "for HITLER's Way": Lynne Olson, *Freedom's Daughters: The Unsung Heroines of the Civil Rights Movement from 1830 to 1970* (New York: Scribner, 2001), 20.

p. 47 "the century-old dream": Myrdal, *An American Dilemma*, 2: 1021–22.

p. 47 *"the United States is not so strong"*: *To Secure These Rights: The Report of the President's Committee on Civil Rights* (Washington, D.C.: United States Government Printing Office, 1947), 148.

p. 48 "a stronger bulwark": Kenneth B. Clark, "Jews in Contemporary America: Problems in Identification" (1954), in *The Psychodynamics of American Jewish Life: An Anthology*, ed. Norman Kiell (New York: Twayne, 1967), 126.

p. 48 "our republican example": Abraham Lincoln, "Speech at Peoria, Illinois" (October 16, 1854), in *Collected Works*, 2: 255.

p. 48 "not Russia that threatens": W. E. B. Du Bois, *An Appeal to the World* (1946), in *The Oxford W. E. B. Du Bois Reader*, 458.

p. 48 "celebration in Moscow": John Rankin quoted in Richard Polenberg, *One Nation Divisible: Class, Race, and Ethnicity in the United States since 1938* (New York: Penguin, 1982), 109.

p. 49 "no absolute moral order": Martin Luther King, Jr., *Stride toward Freedom* (1958; rpt. New York: Harper and Row, 1986), 92–93. King borrowed here and elsewhere in his comments on communism from Robert McCracken's sermon collection *Questions to Ask* (1951). See Keith D. Miller, *The Voice of Deliverance: The Language of Martin Luther King, Jr., and Its Sources* (New York: Free Press, 1992), 100–104.

p. 49 "a pestilence": Randolph, "The March on Washington Movement," 148.

p. 49 "amazing how few Negroes": King speaking in *Citizen King*, prod. Orlando Bagwell and W. Noland Walker, DVD, WGBH Educational Foundation and ROJA Productions, PBS Home Video, 2005.

p. 49 "like a force of nature": Bennett, "Introduction," *The Day They Marched*, 3.

p. 50 "freedom rider and tourist": Willie Leonard quoted in Fred Powledge, "Alabamans Gay on Bus Journey," *New York Times*, August 28, 1963.

p. 51 "300,000 March": *Chicago Defender*, August 29, 1963.

p. 51 "all white, were arrested": Taylor Branch, *Pillar of Fire: America in the King Years, 1963–65* (New York: Simon and Schuster, 1998), 132–33.

p. 52 "pseudo-event": Daniel Boorstin, *The Image: A Guide to Pseudo-Events in America* (1961; rpt. New York: Atheneum, 1980), 39. The book's original subtitle was *What Happened to the American Dream*.

p. 52 "quickly released LPs": On the LPs of the March speeches, see Brian Ward, *Just My Soul Responding: Rhythm and Blues, Black Consciousness, and Race Relations* (Berkeley: University of California Press, 1998), 273–75, and Erwin G. Krasnow, "Copyrights, Performers' Rights, and the March on Civil Rights: Reflections on *Martin Luther King, Jr. v. Mister Maestro*," *Georgetown Law Journal* 53 (1965), 402–29.

p. 53 "the late summer sun": James Reston, "'I Have a Dream . . .': Peroration by Dr. King Sums Up a Day the Capital Will Remember," *New York Times*, August 29, 1963.

p. 53 "public disgrace": David Lawrence, "Day of Disgrace," *Birmingham News*, August 29, 1963.

p. 53 "the best mannered": Kenneth Crawford, "Some Mob," *Newsweek* 62 (September 9, 1963), 31.

p. 53 "so little bitterness": Peter Roberts, "The Big March" (1963), *News of the Day*, included in *Martin Luther King, Jr.: "I Have a Dream*," DVD, MPI Media Group, 2005.

p. 54 "who exhort patience": Excerpts from Randolph and the other speakers, as well as "What We Demand," in *Speeches of the Leaders*.

p. 56 "American slavery": Abraham Lincoln, "Second Inaugural Address" (March 4, 1865), in *Collected Works*, 8: 333.

p. 57 "the nearest thing I've seen": Pauli Murray, *Song in a Weary Throat: An American Pilgrimage* (New York: Harper and Row, 1987), 353–54.

p. 57 "this civil rights stuff": Unnamed woman quoted in Eugene Patterson, "I Have a Dream," *Atlanta Constitution*, August 30, 1963.

p. 57 "a great televised morality play": David Halberstam, "The Second Coming of Martin Luther King," *Harper's* 235 (August 1967), 42–43.

p. 57 "living and breathing history": Mahalia Jackson, with Evan McLeod Wylie, *Movin' On Up* (New York: Hawthorne, 1966), 196–97.

p. 58 "wept like a baby": Bill Clinton quoted in "Bill Clinton's Hidden Life," *U.S. News and World Report* 113 (July 20, 1992), 30.

p. 58 "man's instinctual needs": Herbert Marcuse, *Eros and Civilization: A Philosophical Inquiry into Freud* (1955; rpt. Boston: Beacon, 1962), 3.

p. 58 "freedom to experience everything": Tom Wolfe, *The Electric Kool-Aid Acid Test* (1968; rpt. New York: Bantam, 1999), 143.

p. 59 "first act of the revolution": John Lewis quoted in Harvey Swados, "A Revolution on the March," *Nation* 197 (September 7, 1963), 107.

p. 59 "path of Negro-white unity": King, *Where Do We Go from Here?* 4.

p. 59 "toward two societies": *Report of the National Advisory Commission on Civil Disorders* (New York: Bantam, 1968), 1.

p. 59 "grim clocks were ticking": Roger Wilkins, "The Innocence of August 1963," *Washington Post*, August 28, 1973.

p. 59 "very optimistic moment": Richard Flacks quoted in James Miller, *Democracy Is in the Streets: From Port Huron to the Siege of Chicago* (1987; rpt. Cambridge: Harvard University Press, 1994), 182.

p. 60 "news people got from TV": Fred Freed quoted in Godfrey Hodgson, *America in Our Time* (New York: Vintage, 1978), 146.

p. 60 "talking about his dream": Anne Moody, *Coming of Age in Mississippi* (New York: Laurel, 1968), 307.

p. 60 "beginning of the end": James Farmer, "The March on Washington: The Zenith of the Southern Movement," in *New Directions in Civil Rights Studies*, ed. Armstead L. Robinson and Patricia Sullivan (Charlottesville: University of Virginia Press, 1991), 31.

p. 61 "Farce on Washington": Malcolm X, with Alex Haley, *The Autobiography of Malcolm X* (New York: Grove, 1966), 278–81.

p. 61 "night-club act": Amiri Baraka [LeRoi Jones], "What Does Nonviolence Mean?" (1963), in *Home: Social Essays* (New York: William Morrow, 1966), 138–39, 148.

p. 61 "an abortion": Michael Thelwell, "The August 28th March on Washington," *Présence africaine* (1964), in *Reporting Civil Rights*, part 2, *American Journalism, 1963–1973* (New York: Library of America, 2003), 67.

p. 61 "a giant therapy session": Julius Lester, *Look Out, Whitey! Black Power's Gon' Get Your Mama!* (New York: Grove, 1968), 104.

p. 61 "gentle army": C. E. Wilson, "The Pilgrimage," *Liberator* 3 (October 1963), 5–6.

p. 61 "two events held in Detroit": See Nick Salvatore, *Singing in a Strange Land: C. L. Franklin, the Black Church, and the Transformation of America* (New York: Little, Brown, 2005), 255–64, and Peniel E. Joseph, *Waiting 'Til the Midnight Hour: A Narrative History of Black Power in America* (New York: Henry Holt, 2006), 81–84.

p. 61 "Segregation is a cancer": Martin Luther King, Jr., "Address at the Freedom Rally in Cobo Hall" (June 23, 1963), in *A Call to Conscience*, 62–63, 66, 71; and *The Great March to Freedom: Rev. Martin Luther King Speaks, Detroit, June 23, 1963*, Berry Gordy, Jr., producer, LP, Motown Records, 1963.

p. 62 "King ranked first among": "The Negro in America," 31.

p. 62 "a circus, with clowns": Malcolm X, "Message to the Grass Roots" in *Malcolm X Speaks*, 16, 10–12.

p. 63 "became black": Haki Madhubuti [Don L. Lee], "Black Sketches," *Don't Cry, Scream* (Detroit: Broadside, 1969), 53.

p. 63 "college students in 1963": Tom W. Smith, "Changing Racial Labels: From 'Colored' to 'Negro' to 'Black' to 'African American,'" *Public Opinion Quarterly* 56 (Winter 1992), 499–504.

p. 63 "value of winning access": Bayard Rustin, "From Protest to Politics: The Future of the Civil Rights Movement," *Commentary* 39 (February 1965), 25.

p. 64 "to the Negro demand": Murray Friedman, "The White Liberal's Retreat," *Atlantic Monthly* 211 (January 1963), 46.

p. 64 "pressing their case too hard": George Gallup, "Capital March Opposed 3–1," *Los Angeles Times*, August 27, 1963.

p. 64 "whites strongly favored": "How Whites Feel about Negroes: A Painful American Dilemma," *Newsweek* 62 (October 21, 1963), 45, 57.

p. 65 "this is the moment": Benjamin Mays quoted in Hodgson, *America in Our Time*, 199.

p. 65 "oral tradition in American constitutionalism": Ronald R. Garet, "Proclaim Liberty," *Southern California Law Review* 74 (November 2000), 146.

p. 65 "made the civil rights movement integral": See Bruce Ackerman, "The Living Constitution," *Harvard Law Review* 120 (May 2007), 41–57.

T W O

Freedom Now!

p. 67 "signers of the Constitution": Julius Lester, *Revolutionary Notes* (New York: Richard W. Baron, 1969), 85.

p. 68 "covenant of individual rights": Cf. Martha Solomon, "Covenanted Rights: The Metaphoric Matrix of 'I Have a Dream,'" in *Martin Luther King, Jr., and the Sermonic Power of Public Discourse*, ed. Carolyn Calloway-Thomas and John Louis Lucaites (Tuscaloosa: University of Alabama Press, 1993), 69–74.

p. 69 "A translation of the legacy": Drew Hansen, *The Dream: Martin Luther King, Jr., and the Speech That Inspired a Nation* (New York: HarperCollins, 2003), 91–92.

p. 69 "History would mark it": "The Negro in America," *Newsweek* 62 (July 29, 1963), 15.

p. 69 "how much damage": National Coalition of Blacks for Reparations in America, www.ncobra.com/ncobra_info.htm (accessed March 11, 2008).

p. 70 "we're going to pay the bill": Harper Lee, *To Kill a Mockingbird* (1960; rpt. New York: Warner, 1982), 221.

p. 70 "A bill is coming due": James Baldwin, *The Fire Next Time* (New York: Dell, 1964), 138.

p. 70 "most avid seeker": Julian Mayfield, "Into the Mainstream and Oblivion," in *The American Negro Writer and His Roots: Selected Papers from the First Conference of Negro Writers, March 1959* (New York: American Society of African Culture, 1960), 31.

p. 70 "purchase check of democracy": Robert F. Williams, "Can Negroes Afford to Be Pacifists?" *Liberator* 4 (September 1959), 7.

p. 70 "A bill is owed to us": Malcolm X, "The Black Revolution" (speech of June 1963), in *The End of White Supremacy: Four Speeches*, ed. Imam Benjamin Karin (New York: Arcade, 1971), 75.

p. 70 "deferred-payment plan": Martin Luther King, Jr., *Why We Can't Wait* (New York: Signet, 1964), 128, 31.

p. 71 "bogus freedom checks": Derrick Bell, *Faces at the Bottom of the Well: The Permanence of Racism* (New York: Basic, 1992), 20–21.

p. 71 "we are writing our Declaration": Unnamed man quoted in "The Negro in America," 34.

p. 72 "cesspools of racial injustice": Robert F. Williams, "Speech from Radio Free Dixie" (1963), in *Modern Black Nationalism: From Marcus Garvey to Louis Farrakhan*, ed. William L. Van Deburg (New York: New York University Press, 1997), 96.

p. 72 "one hundredth part": David Walker, *Appeal to the Coloured Citizens of the World* (1829), in *The Ideological Origins of Black Nationalism*, ed. Sterling Stuckey (Boston: Beacon, 1972), 114.

p. 72 "no truer exponents": W. E. B. Du Bois, *The Souls of Black Folk* (1903; rpt. New York: Penguin, 1989), 11.

p. 72 "platform of the Black Panther Party": "Black Panther Party Platform," in *The Black Panthers Speak*, ed. Philip S. Foner (1970; rpt. New York: Da Capo, 1995), 4.

p. 73 "Whose independence?": Elijah Muhammad, *The Fall of America* (Chicago: Muhammad's Temple of Islam No. 2, 1973), 7–8, 68, 70.

p. 73 "old brainwashed Negroes": Malcolm X, *Malcolm X on Afro-American History* (speech of January 24, 1965) (1967; rpt. New York: Pathfinder, 1990), 39–40.

p. 73 "stolen from the lands": "Black Declaration of Independence," in *We, the Other People: Alternative Declarations of Independence*, ed. Philip S. Foner (Urbana: University of Illinois Press, 1976), 164–65.

p. 73 "this mighty Republic": Barry Goldwater, *Where I Stand* (New York: Mc-Graw-Hill, 1964), 9–10, 39.

p. 74 "morally wrong, nonsensical": George Schuyler, "The Case against the Civil Rights Bill" (1963), in *Rac[e]ing to the Right: Selected Essays of George S. Schuyler*, ed. Jeffrey B. Leak (Knoxville: University of Tennessee Press, 2001), 98, 103. The brackets in the title are the editor's.

p. 75 "make an employer love me": Martin Luther King, Jr., *Stride toward Freedom* (1958; rpt. New York: Harper and Row, 1986), 198.

p. 75 "Negroes must be free": A. Philip Randolph, "The March on Washington Movement Presents a Program for the Negro," in *What the Negro Wants*, ed. Rayford W. Logon (Chapel Hill: University of North Carolina Press, 1944), 137.

p. 75 "being against snow": William Faulkner, "American Segregation and the World Crisis," in William Faulkner, Benjamin E. Mays, and Cecil Sims, *The Segregation Decisions* (Atlanta: Southern Regional Council, 1956), 9–11.

p. 76 "contrary to the Constitution": "Declaration of Constitutional Principles," *Congressional Record 102*, 84th Congress (March 12, 1956), 4460.

p. 76 "the cup of genocide": Ross Barnett quoted in William Doyle, *An American*

Insurrection: The Battle of Oxford, Mississippi, 1962 (New York: Doubleday, 2001), 65–66.

p. 77 "This nation was never meant": George Wallace, "The 1963 Inaugural Address of Governor George C. Wallace" (January 14, 1963), http://www.archives .state.al.us/govs_list/inauguralspeech.html (accessed March 11, 2008). The ellipsis is in Wallace's text.

p. 77 "un-American and un-Christian": Martin Luther King, Jr., "Paul's Letter to American Christians" (November 4, 1956), in *Papers*, 3: 418.

p. 78 "force me to cross over": W. A. Criswell quoted in Andrew W. Manis, *Southern Civil Religions in Conflict: Civil Rights and the Culture Wars* (Macon, Ga.: Mercer University Press, 2002), 134.

p. 79 "a secular saint": Jared Taylor, interview with Russell K. Nieli (December 21, 1999), in *Contemporary Voices of White Nationalism in America*, ed. Carol M. Swain and Russ Nieli (New York: Cambridge University Press, 2003), 108–9.

p. 79 "shall be unlawful": "Birmingham's Racial Segregation Ordinances," pamphlet reprinted by Birmingham Civil Rights Institute, Birmingham, Alabama.

p. 79 "story of a white woman": Martin Luther King, Jr., "Loving Your Enemies" (March 7, 1961), in *Papers*, 6: 427.

p. 79 "effect upon the segregator": Diane Nash, "Inside the Sit-Ins and Freedom Rides: Testimony of a Southern Student," in *The New Negro*, ed. Mathew H. Ahmann (Notre Dame, Ind.: Fides, 1961), 47.

p. 79 "break every glass": Unnamed man quoted in Jason Sokol, *There Goes My Everything: White Southerners in the Age of Civil Rights, 1945–1975* (New York: Knopf, 2006), 324.

p. 80 "forever stand like a rock": Statement of Montgomery City Commission quoted in David Levering Lewis, *King: A Biography*, 2nd ed. (Urbana: University of Illinois Press, 1978), 82.

p. 80 "racial characteristics": James J. Kilpatrick quoted in Taylor Branch, *Parting the Waters: America in the King Years, 1954–1963* (New York: Simon and Schuster, 1988), 381.

p. 80 "cultural and the intellectual level": Henry Garrett quoted in "Intermarriage and the Race Problem—As Leading Authorities See It," *U.S. News and World Report* 55 (November 18, 1963), 92–93.

p. 80 "kissing Harry Belafonte": Taylor Branch, *At Canaan's Edge: America in the King Years, 1965–68* (New York: Simon and Schuster, 2006), 164.

p. 80 "not his brother-in-law": King, *Stride toward Freedom*, 206.

p. 80 "*mongrelize* his race": Malcolm X, with Alex Haley, *The Autobiography of Malcolm X* (New York: Grove, 1966), 255.

p. 81 "after the sun goes down": James Baldwin, "Nobody Knows My Name: A Letter from the South" (1959), in *Nobody Knows My Name* (New York: Dell, 1963), 98.

p. 81 "five thousand blacks lynched": Ralph Ginzburg's estimate for the years 1859–1961 in *100 Years of Lynchings* (1962; rpt. Baltimore: Black Classic, 1988), 253–70. Ginzburg also cites a Tuskegee Institute study of 1959 that catalogued 4,733 lynchings since 1882 (244).

p. 81 "crosses this dead line": J. Thomas Heflin quoted in Harvard Sitkoff, *A New Deal for Blacks: The Emergence of Civil Rights as a National Issue* (New York: Oxford University Press, 1978), 269.

p. 82 "I counted pictures": William Bradford Huie, "What's Happened to Emmett Till's Killers?" *Look* 21 (January 22, 1957), 64.

p. 82 "constricted their eyes": Calvin C. Hernton, *Sex and Racism in America* (1965; rpt. New York: Grove Weidenfeld, 1988), 7–8.

p. 82 "Gallup polling": 1958 and 1968 figures in this paragraph are from "Race Relations in the United States and Great Britain" (October 17, 1958), in *The Gallup Poll: Public Opinion, 1935–1971*, 3 vols. (New York: Random House, 1972), 2: 1572; and "Special Survey: Marriage" (November 10, 1968), ibid., 3: 2168. For 2007 figures, see "Race Relations," *The Gallup Poll*, http://www.galluppoll.com/content/default.aspx?ci=1687 (accessed September 21, 2007).

p. 82 "dating a Negro": "How Whites Feel about Negroes: A Painful American Dilemma," *Newsweek* 62 (October 21, 1963), 48.

p. 83 "the court is not talking": "All God's Chillun," *New York Times*, May 18, 1954.

p. 83 "the loveliest and the purest": Tom P. Brady, *Black Monday: Segregation or Amalgamation . . . America Has Its Choice* (Winona, Miss.: Association of Citizens' Councils, 1955), foreword, 44–45.

p. 83 "maelstrom of miscegenation": Theodore Bilbo, *Take Your Choice: Separation or Mongrelization* (Poplarville, Miss.: Dream House, 1947), ii.

p. 84 "nor ever have been": Abraham Lincoln, "Fourth Debate with Stephen A. Douglas at Charleston, Illinois" (September 18, 1858), in *The Collected Works of Abraham Lincoln*, ed. Roy P. Basler, 9 vols. (New Brunswick, N.J.: Rutgers University Press, 1953), 3: 145–46.

p. 84 "There is a natural disgust": Abraham Lincoln, "Speech at Springfield, Illinois" (June 26, 1857), ibid., 2: 405–9.

p. 84 "strategic racism": James Oakes, *The Radical and the Republican: Frederick Douglass, Abraham Lincoln, and the Triumph of Antislavery Politics* (New York: Norton, 2007), 130. On Lincoln's evolving views of natural rights, citizenship rights, and social and political rights, I am also indebted to Oakes, "Natural Rights, Citizenship Rights, States Rights, and Black Rights: Another Look at Lincoln and Race," in *Our Lincoln*, ed. Eric Foner (New York: Norton, forthcoming 2008).

p. 84 "written in the book of fate": Thomas Jefferson, *Autobiography*, in *Basic Writings of Thomas Jefferson*, ed. Philip S. Foner (New York: Wiley, 1944), 439–40.

p. 85 "interracial licentiousness": Merrill D. Peterson, *Lincoln in American Memory* (New York: Oxford University Press, 1994), 45; Forest G. Wood, *Black Scare: The Racist Response to Emancipation and Reconstruction* (Berkeley: University of California Press, 1970), 53–79, plates 1–5.

p. 85 "their wholesale impregnation": Herbert Ravenel Sass, "Mixed Schools and Mixed Blood," *Atlantic Monthly* 198 (November 1956), 45–49.

p. 85 "It's all very well": Dwight D. Eisenhower quoted in James T. Patterson, *Brown v. Board of Education: A Civil Rights Milestone and Its Troubled Legacy* (New York: Oxford University Press, 2001), 82.

p. 85 "take a Negro child by the hand": Martin Luther King, Jr., "My Trip to the Land of Gandhi" (July 1959), in *Papers*, 5: 236.

p. 86 "black and white dolls": Kenneth B. Clark and Mamie Clark, "Racial Identification and Preference in Negro Children," in *Readings in Social Psychology* (New York: Henry Holt, 1947), 169–78.

p. 86 "Clark's data demonstrated": A. James Gregor, "The Law, Social Science, and School Segregation: An Assessment," *Western Reserve Law Review* 14 (September 1963), 621–36; Richard Kluger, *Simple Justice: The History of Brown v. Board of Education and Black America's Struggle for Equality* (New York: Random House, 1975), 353–57.

p. 87 "no basic political right": Hannah Arendt, "Reflections on Little Rock," *Dissent* 6 (Winter 1959), 49–55.

p. 87 "absolutely no conception": Ralph Ellison interviewed by Robert Penn Warren in *Who Speaks for the Negro?* (New York: Vintage, 1965), 344.

p. 87 "maimed a little every day": Martin Luther King, Jr., *Where Do We Go from Here: Chaos or Community?* (Boston: Beacon, 1967), 108.

p. 87 "seventeen-year-olds": David Farber, *The Age of Great Dreams: America in the 1960s* (New York: Hill and Wang, 1994), 57.

p. 87 "a boy on a man's errand": Thurgood Marshall quoted in Branch, *Parting the Waters*, 190.

p. 88 "beautiful children of God": Martin Luther King, Jr., "Eulogy for the Young Victims of the Sixteenth Street Baptist Church Bombing" (September 18, 1963), in *A Call to Conscience: The Landmark Speeches of Dr. Martin Luther King, Jr.*, ed. Clayborne Carson and Kris Shepard (New York: Warner, 2001), 95–96.

p. 88 "great Christian movement": Alice Collins quoted in Larry Still, "Where Was God When Bomb Hit?" *Jet* 24 (October 3, 1963), 26.

p. 88 "Children are little people": Charles Conley Lynch quoted in Wyn Craig Wade, *The Fiery Cross: The Ku Klux Klan in America* (New York: Touchstone, 1988), 326–27.

p. 89 "Rip Van Winkle slumber": King, *Why We Can't Wait*, 47, 84–85, 90.

p. 89 "a time warp of history": Ralph Ellison, "An Extravagance of Laughter" (1985), in *Going to the Territory* (New York: Random House, 1986), 154–56.

p. 90 "tracked down by the Zeitgeist": King, *Stride toward Freedom*, 44.

p. 90 "want their rights as Americans": Roy Wilkins, "Undergirding the Democratic Ideal," *Crisis* 58 (December 1951), 650.

p. 90 "ninety-odd years ago": Thurgood Marshall interview in *Eyes on the Prize: America's Civil Rights Years, 1954–1965*, Henry Hampton producer, Blackside, Inc., PBS/WGBH Television, 1987.

p. 90 "foremost interpreter": Louis Lomax, *The Negro Revolt* (New York: Signet, 1963), 102.

p. 91 "I come to say to you": Martin Luther King, Jr., "Address at the Conclusion of the Selma to Montgomery March" (March 25, 1965), in *A Call to Conscience*, 131.

p. 91 "TELL ME HOW LONG": Langston Hughes, "Ask Your Mama" (1961), in *The Collected Poems of Langston Hughes*, ed. Arnold Rampersad and David Roessel (New York: Knopf, 1996), 475.

p. 92 "the door of frustration": William H. Pipes, *Say Amen, Brother! Old-Time Negro Preaching: A Study in American Frustration* (1951; rpt. Detroit: Wayne State University Press, 1992), 118, 42.

p. 92 "At first I sang the words": Mahalia Jackson, with Evan McLeod Wylie, *Movin' On Up* (New York: Hawthorne, 1966), 198–99.

p. 93 "Abused and scorned": Martin Luther King, Jr., "Letter from Birmingham Jail," in *Why We Can't Wait* (New York: Signet, 1964), 93.

p. 93 "It's been too hard living": Sam Cooke, "A Change Is Gonna Come," and Cooke quoted in Peter Guralnick, liner notes, *Sam Cooke: Portrait of a Legend, 1951–1964*, CD, ABKCO Records, 2003.

p. 94 "never time in the future": James Baldwin, "Faulkner and Desegregation" (1956), in *Nobody Knows My Name*, 106.

p. 94 "questions of Rabbi Hillel": Prinz, speech at the March on Washington, *Speeches of the Leaders*.

p. 94 "If those historic gentlemen": Lena Horne, "Now!" *Here's Lena Now*, Budd Granoff Productions, LP, 20th Century–Fox Records, 1964.

p. 95 "a simple declaration": Horne quoted in Woody L. Taylor, "King's Address a Fitting Climax," *Pittsburgh Courier*, September 7, 1963.

p. 95 "Fuck that dream": Unnamed man quoted in John A. Williams, *This Is My Country, Too* (New York: Signet, 1966), 149.

p. 96 "versions of this peroration": See Martin Luther King, Jr., "Facing the Challenge of a New Age" (1956 version), in *Papers*, 3: 462–63; Martin Luther King, Jr., "Desegregation and the Future" (December 15, 1956) in *Papers*, 3: 478–79; Martin Luther King, Jr., "Facing the Challenge of a New Age" (January 1, 1957), in *Papers*, 4: 88–89; and Martin Luther King, Jr., "A Realistic Look at the Question of Progress in the Area of Race Relations" (April 10, 1957), in *Papers*, 4: 178–79.

p. 97 "preacher's habit": Richard Lischer, *The Preacher King: Martin Luther King,*

Jr., and the Word That Moved America (New York: Oxford University Press, 1995), 93–118. On the question of King's plagiarism, see Theodore Pappas, *Plagiarism and the Culture War: The Writings of Martin Luther King, Jr., and Other Prominent Americans*, rev. ed. (Tampa, Fla.: Hallberg, 1998), and Eugene D. Genovese, *The Southern Front: History and Politics in the Cultural War* (Columbia: University of Missouri Press, 1995), 157–91.

p. 97 "voice-merging": Keith D. Miller, *The Voice of Deliverance: The Language of Martin Luther King, Jr., and Its Sources* (New York: Free Press, 1992), 26, 83, 112–37, and for King's use of Carey in particular, 146–48. Miller first took up King's borrowing from Carey in "Voice-Merging and Self-Making: The Epistemology of 'I Have a Dream,'" *Rhetoric Society Quarterly* 19 (Winter 1989), 28–29.

p. 97 "We, Negro-Americans": Archibald J. Carey, Jr., "An Address to the Republican National Convention," in *Rhetoric of Racial Revolt*, ed. Roy L. Hill (Denver: Golden Bell, 1964), 149–54. During the Montgomery bus boycott, King wrote to Carey requesting that he chair a committee of religious and civic leaders to lobby National City Lines, Inc., the Chicago-based owner of the Montgomery bus company. See "To Archibald James Carey, Jr." (December 27, 1955), in *Papers*, 3: 93–94. On later occasions, Carey offered King advice about dealing with the FBI. David J. Garrow, *Bearing the Cross: Martin Luther King, Jr., and the Southern Christian Leadership Conference* (New York: Vintage, 1988), 425, 454.

p. 100 "Jesus and the adulteress": Howard Thurman, *Jesus and the Disinherited* (New York: Abingdon-Cokesbury, 1949), 106.

p. 100 "bided my time": Robert Hayden, "The Ballad of Nat Turner," in *Collected Poems*, ed. Frederick Glaysher (New York: Liveright, 1985), 58.

p. 100 "whooping, shouting": Alex Haley, *Roots* (New York: Dell, 1977), 682.

p. 100 "Johnson told Roy Wilkins": Lyndon Johnson quoted in Robert Dallek, *Flawed Giant: Lyndon Johnson and His Times, 1961–1973* (New York: Oxford University Press, 1998), 113.

p. 100 "want to be free everywhere": King quoted in David Levering Lewis, *King: A Biography*, 2nd ed. (Urbana: University of Illinois Press, 1978), 125.

p. 101 "every corner of our land": "Pledge" postcard, *Speeches of the Leaders*.

p. 101 "ring the mighty Bell": H. R. H. Moore, "The Liberty Bell" (1844), displayed at the Liberty Bell site in Philadelphia and available at http://www.ushistory .org/libertybell/quotes.html (accessed March 11, 2008).

p. 101 "Lift every voice and sing": James Weldon Johnson, "Lift Every Voice and Sing," in *Complete Poems*, ed. Sondra Kathryn Wilson (New York: Penguin, 2000), 109–10.

p. 102 "Injustice anywhere": King, "Letter from Birmingham Jail," 77.

p. 102 "A breakdown of law": King, *Stride toward Freedom*, 199.

p. 102 "dog buried his fangs": King, *Where Do We Go from Here?* 68.

p. 103 "the rights of every man": John F. Kennedy, "Radio and Television Report to the American People on Civil Rights" (June 11, 1963), in *Public Papers of the Presidents of the United States, 1963* (Washington, D.C.: U.S. Government Printing Office, 1964), 468.

p. 103 "not a geographic term": Prinz, speech at the March on Washington, *Speeches of the Leaders.*

p. 104 "powerful appeal founded": Eugene Patterson, "In Shadow of Abe Lincoln, a Voice Shouts for Freedom," *Atlanta Constitution*, August 29, 1963.

THREE
Soul Force

p. 105 "God Almighty": Martin Luther King, Jr., *Stride toward Freedom* (1958; rpt. New York: Harper and Row, 1986), 160.

p. 105 "substitute tired feet": Ibid., 69–70.

p. 106 "could have ever argued": Andrew Young quoted in Charles V. Hamilton, *The Black Preacher in America* (New York: William Marrow, 1972), 132–33.

p. 106 "Inherent in the [minister's] call": Martin Luther King, Jr., "Recommendations to the Dexter Avenue Baptist Church for the Fiscal Year 1954–1955" (September 5, 1954), in *Papers*, 2: 287.

p. 107 "the presence of the Divine": King, *Stride toward Freedom*, 134–35.

p. 107 "the year of our Lord": Martin Luther King, Jr., *Why We Can't Wait* (New York: Signet, 1964), ix; Abraham Lincoln, "Emancipation Proclamation" (January 1, 1863), in *The Collected Works of Abraham Lincoln*, ed. Roy P. Basler, 9 vols. (New Brunswick, N.J.: Rutgers University Press, 1953), 6: 28.

p. 107 "to *all* His creatures": Abraham Lincoln, "Speech at Lewistown, Illinois" (August 17, 1858), in *Collected Works*, 2: 546.

p. 108 "a mere carpenter": Ralph Cooper, narrator on *The Emancipation March on Washington*, Mayco Associates, LP, Mr. Maestro, 1963.

p. 109 "you are not niggers": Howard Thurman, *Jesus and the Disinherited* (New York: Abingdon-Cokesbury, 1949), 50–51; Martin Luther King, Jr., "Six Talks Based on *Beliefs That Matter* by William Adams Brown," in *Papers*, 1: 281.

p. 109 "story of the children of Israel": R. Nathaniel Dett, ed., *Religious Folk-Songs of the Negro as Sung at Hampton Institute* (Hampton, Va.: Hampton Institute Press, 1927), xiii. On the Exodus in African American culture, see, for example, Theophus H. Smith, *Conjuring Culture: Biblical Formations of Black America* (New York: Oxford University Press, 1994), 55–80; Albert J. Raboteau, *A Fire in the Bones: Reflections on African-American Religious History* (Boston: Beacon, 1995), 17–36; and Eric J. Sundquist, *Strangers in the Land: Blacks, Jews, Post-Holocaust America* (Cambridge: Harvard University Press, 2005), 95–169.

p. 110 "the Israel of our time": Herman Melville, *White-Jacket; or, The World in a Man-of-War*, ed. Harrison Hayford et al. (Evanston: Northwestern University Press, 1970), 150–51.

p. 110 "his almost chosen people": Abraham Lincoln, "Address to the New Jersey Senate at Trenton, New Jersey" (February 21, 1861), in *Collected Works*, 4: 236.

p. 110 "promised land of sweeter beauty": W. E. B. Du Bois, *The Souls of Black Folk* (1903; rpt. New York: Penguin, 1989), 7.

p. 110 "a dream deferred"; "always just ahead": Langston Hughes, "Montage of a Dream Deferred" and "Promised Land," in *The Collected Poems of Langston Hughes*, ed. Arnold Rampersad and David Roessel (New York: Knopf, 1996), 426, 592.

p. 110 "black chillun o'God": Claude Brown, *Manchild in the Promised Land* (1965; New York: Signet, 1967), vii–viii.

p. 111 "It is always difficult": Martin Luther King, Jr., "Give Us the Ballot" (May 17, 1957), in *Papers*, 4: 215.

p. 111 "whenever Pharaoh wanted": Martin Luther King, Jr., "I've Been to the Mountaintop" (April 3, 1968), in *A Call to Conscience: The Landmark Speeches of Dr. Martin Luther King, Jr.*, ed. Clayborne Carson and Kris Shepard (New York: Warner, 2001), 210. Cf. Martin Luther King, Jr., *Where Do We Go from Here: Chaos or Community?* (Boston: Beacon, 1967), 124.

p. 112 "every revolutionary movement": King, *Where Do We Go from Here?* 12, 32.

p. 112 "I was on fire": John Lewis, with Michael D'Orso, *Walking with the Wind: A Memoir of the Movement* (New York: Harvest, 1998), 45–46.

p. 112 "a mystical identity": Coretta Scott King, *My Life with Martin Luther King, Jr.* (New York: Avon, 1970), 321.

p. 112 "the Red Sea of injustice": King, *Why We Can't Wait*, 73.

p. 112 "Before King": James Gray quoted in Jason Sokol, *There Goes My Everything: White Southerners in the Age of Civil Rights, 1945–1975* (New York: Knopf, 2006), 67.

p. 112 "checked back there Easter": Dick Gregory, "Speech at St. John's Baptist Church" (May 20, 1963), in *Say It Plain: A Century of Great African American Speeches*, ed. Catherine Ellis and Stephen Drury Smith (New York: New Press, 2005), 43.

p. 112 "just want to do God's will": King, "I've Been to the Mountaintop," 233.

p. 113 "cross is something that you bear": King quoted in David J. Garrow, *Bearing the Cross: Martin Luther King, Jr., and the Southern Christian Leadership Conference* (New York: Vintage, 1988), 564.

p. 113 "law written upon stone": Martin Luther King, Jr., "The Significant Contributions of Jeremiah to Religious Thought" (November 24, 1948), in *Papers*, 1: 184–85.

p. 113 "demythologized the American covenant": Richard Lischer, *The Preacher King: Martin Luther King, Jr., and the Word That Moved America* (New York: Oxford

University Press, 1995), 172–84. See also David L. Chappell, *A Stone of Hope: Prophetic Religion and the Death of Jim Crow* (Chapel Hill: University of North Carolina Press, 2004), 46–47, and David A. Bobbitt, *The Rhetoric of Redemption: Kenneth Burke's Redemption Drama and Martin Luther King, Jr.'s, "I Have a Dream" Speech* (Lanham, Md.: Rowman and Littlefield, 2004), 8–9, who argues that the Dream speech, by following a "guilt-purification-redemption" arc, enacts a symbolic national rebirth that is a secular version of the sinful being redeemed through the sacrifice of Christ.

p. 114 "Write this word": Margaret Walker, "At the Lincoln Monument in Washington, August 28, 1963," in *This Is My Century: New and Collected Poems* (Athens: University of Georgia Press, 1989), 69.

p. 115 "a wave of crimes": Ernest Vandiver quoted in Taylor Branch, *Parting the Waters: America in the King Years, 1954–1963* (New York: Simon and Schuster, 1988), 267.

p. 115 "outrage the sense of decency": Alabama Code, 1962, Title 14, Section 407, cited in Dan T. Carter, *The Politics of Rage: George Wallace, the Origins of the New Conservatism, and the Transformation of American Politics* (New York: Simon and Schuster, 1995), 163–64.

p. 116 "Christ furnished the spirit": King, *Stride toward Freedom*, 85.

p. 116 "army of peace volunteers": David Levering Lewis, *King: A Biography*, 2nd ed. (Urbana: University of Illinois Press, 1978), 101.

p. 117 "holding on to the Truth": M. K. Gandhi, *Non-Violent Resistance (Satyagraha)* (1951; rpt. New York: Schocken, 1961), 3–4. On Gandhi's influence among African Americans, see Sudarshan Kapur, *Raising Up a Prophet: The African-American Encounter with Gandhi* (Boston: Beacon, 1992), and Daniel Immerwahr, "Caste or Colony? Indianizing Race in the United States," *Modern Intellectual History* 4 (2007), 275–301.

p. 117 "the true place": Henry David Thoreau, "Resistance to Civil Government" (1849), in *Walden and Resistance to Civil Government*, ed. William Rossi (New York: Norton, 1992), 234–35.

p. 117 "beloved community": Martin Luther King, Jr., "My Trip to the Land of Gandhi" (July 1959), in *Papers*, 5: 233; Josiah Royce, *The Problem of Christianity*, 2 vols. (New York: Macmillan, 1913), 1: 172.

p. 117 "world house": King, *Where Do We Go from Here?* 170.

p. 117 "white man to his knees": James Weldon Johnson quoted in George M. Fredrickson, *Black Liberation: A Comparative History of Black Ideologies in the United States and South Africa* (New York: Oxford University Press, 1995), 232.

p. 117 "grandchildren of slaves": Mahatma Gandhi, "To the American Negro," *Crisis* 36 (July 1929), 225.

p. 118 "the greatest Christian": Martin Luther King, Jr., "Palm Sunday Sermon on Mohandas K. Gandhi" (March 22, 1959), in *Papers*, 5: 147, 156.

p. 119 "moral jiu-jitsu": Richard B. Gregg, *The Power of Non-Violence* (Philadelphia: Lippincott, 1934), 41–54.

p. 119 "supreme political artist": Ved Mehta, "Gandhiism Is Not Easily Copied," *New York Times Magazine*, July 9, 1961, 8, 44.

p. 119 "rivers of blood": King, *Stride toward Freedom*, 103.

p. 119 "these young people": "Reverend Martin Luther King, Jr." (King speaking in Birmingham, May 1963), *Sing for Freedom: The Story of the Civil Rights Movement through Its Songs*, CD, Smithsonian/Folkways Records, 1990.

p. 120 "We act today in full concert": quoted in Lewis, *King*, 178.

p. 120 "the blood of the martyr": Martin Luther King, Jr., "Facing the Challenge of a New Age" (1956 version), in *Papers*, 3: 462.

p. 120 "a sense of drama": King quoted in Robert Weisbrot, *Freedom Bound: A History of America's Civil Rights Movement* (New York: Plume, 1991), 134.

p. 120 "the Bible": Eldridge Cleaver, "Psychology: The Black Bible," in *Postprison Writings and Speeches*, ed. Robert Scheer (New York: Random House, 1969), 18.

p. 120 "a new language": Frantz Fanon, *The Wretched of the Earth*, trans. Constance Farrington (1961; rpt. New York: Grove, 1968), 36–37. For King's rejection of Fanon's philosophy, see *Where Do We Go from Here?* 55, 65–66.

p. 120 "the knife of violence": King, *Why We Can't Wait*, 22–26.

p. 121 "try my best to kill you": Anne Moody, *Coming of Age in Mississippi: An Autobiography* (1968; rpt. New York: Dell, 1976), 318.

p. 121 "machine gun in her hand": Christopher McNair quoted in Stephen B. Oates, *Let the Trumpet Sound: The Life of Martin Luther King, Jr.* (New York: Mentor, 1985), 262.

p. 121 "insurrectionist brothers": King, *Where Do We Go from Here?* 56.

p. 121 "hopelessness of physical defense": W. E. B. Du Bois, *The Souls of Black Folk* (1903; rpt. New York: Penguin, 1989), 166.

p. 121 "hot-headedness": King, "Facing the Challenge of a New Age" (1956 version), 3: 461.

p. 121 "truths of two opposites": King, *Stride toward Freedom*, 213.

p. 121 "not alien to Black Power": James H. Cone, *Black Theology and Black Power* (1969; rpt. New York: HarperCollins, 1989), 38.

p. 122 "doctrine of hatred": Kenneth B. Clark, "The New Negro in the North," in *The New Negro*, ed. Mathew H. Ahmann (Notre Dame, Ind.: Fides, 1961), 36–37.

p. 122 "If the white people realize": Malcolm X quoted in Coretta Scott King, *My Life with Martin Luther King, Jr.* (New York: Avon, 1970), 259.

p. 122 "get a shotgun": Malcolm X, "With Mrs. Fannie Lou Hamer" (December 20, 1964), in *Malcolm X Speaks: Selected Speeches and Statements*, ed. George Breitman (New York: Grove, 1966), 108.

p. 122 "shed a little blood": King, interview with Donald T. Ferron (February 4, 1956), in *Papers*, 3: 125.

p. 122 "If the oppressors bomb": King, "Facing the Challenge of a New Age" (1956 version), 3: 462.

p. 123 "such creative tension": Martin Luther King, Jr., "Letter from Birmingham Jail," in *Why We Can't Wait* (New York: Signet, 1964), 79–80.

p. 123 "negative peace": Martin Luther King, Jr., "Love, Law, and Civil Disobedience," in *A Testament of Hope: The Essential Writings and Speeches of Martin Luther King, Jr.*, ed. James Melvin Washington (San Francisco: Harper, 1986), 49–50.

p. 123 "where the law cannot reach them": King, *Stride toward Freedom*, 215.

p. 123 "Speaking at Morehouse": Stokely Carmichael, "Pan-Africanism" (April 1970), in *Stokely Speaks: Black Power Back to Pan-Africanism* (New York: Random House, 1971), 189–90.

p. 123 "Miracle Sunday": On the conflicting accounts of this event, see Diane McWhorter, *Carry Me Home: Birmingham, Alabama: The Climactic Battle of the Civil Rights Revolution* (New York: Simon and Schuster, 2001), 387–88.

p. 123 "genuine Christian witness": Ralph David Abernathy, *And the Walls Came Tumbling Down: An Autobiography* (New York: HarperPerennial, 1990), 257.

p. 123 "relate to the trans-physics": King, "I've Been to the Mountaintop," 212.

p. 124 "the gift of the people": Andrew Young, *An Easy Burden: The Civil Rights Movement and the Transformation of America* (New York: HarperCollins, 1996), 183.

p. 124 "the fear down [South]": Phyllis Martin quoted in Robert Sherman, "Sing a Song of Freedom," *Saturday Review* 46 (September 28, 1963), 65.

p. 124 "don't wanta hear no talk": Charles Sherrod quoted in Young, *An Easy Burden*, 183.

p. 125 "gospel-pop sound": Brian Ward, *Just My Soul Responding: Rhythm and Blues, Black Consciousness, and Race Relations* (Berkeley: University of California Press, 1998), 204; Leroi Jones [Amiri Baraka], "The Changing Same (R&B and New Black Music)," in *Black Music* (New York: William Morrow, 1967), 208.

p. 125 "egalitarian America": Ward, *Just My Soul Responding*, 124, 140, 142. For the role of popular music and jazz in the civil rights movement see also Peter Guralnick, *Sweet Soul Music: Rhythm and Blues and the Southern Dream of Freedom* (New York: Harper and Row, 1986); Craig Werner, *A Change Is Gonna Come: Music, Race, and the Soul of America* (New York: Plume, 1998); and Scott Saul, *Freedom Is, Freedom Ain't: Jazz and the Making of the Sixties* (Cambridge: Harvard University Press, 2003).

p. 125 "freedom jazz players": Ron Carter quoted in Robert K. McMichael, "'We Insist—Freedom Now!': Black Moral Authority, Jazz, and the Changeable Shape of Whiteness," *American Music* 16 (Winter 1998), 397.

p. 125 "a music of integration": Sonny Rollins quoted in Ira Gitler, *Swing to Bop:*

An Oral History of the Transition of Jazz in the 1940s (New York: Oxford University Press, 1985), 303–4.

p. 125 "I can't play it right": Charles Mingus, liner notes to *Best of Charles Mingus* (1970), quoted in Charles Hersch, "'Let Freedom Ring': Free Jazz and African American Politics," *Cultural Critique* 32 (Winter 1995–96), 104.

p. 126 "Bull turned the hoses": Duke Ellington, "King Fit the Battle of Alabam," *My People*, Bob Thiele producer, CD, Sony Music, 1990.

p. 126 "the music that moved": Movement music came from the grass roots but was made available to a wider audience on albums such as *Nashville Sit-In Story* (1960) and *We Shall Overcome: Songs of the Freedom Riders and the Sit-Ins* (1961), as well as in a variety of published collections, including Edith Fowke and Joe Glazer, *Songs of Work and Protest* (New York: Dover, 1973, originally published as *Songs of Work and Freedom* (1960); Guy Carawan and Candie Carawan, eds., *Sing for Freedom* (Bethlehem, Pa.: Sing Out, 1990), originally published as *We Shall Overcome: Songs of the Freedom Movement* (1963), and *Freedom Is a Constant Struggle: Songs of the Freedom Movement* (1968); and Pete Seeger and Bob Reiser, eds., *Everybody Says Freedom* (New York: Norton, 1989). A compendium of recorded music is available on *Voices of the Civil Rights Movement: Black American Freedom Songs, 1960–1966*, CD, Smithsonian Folkways Recordings, 1997.

p. 127 "Pete Seeger performed it": Garrow, *Bearing the Cross*, 98.

p. 127 "dates to the period": Eileen Southern, *The Music of Black Americans: A History* (New York: Norton, 1971), 238–39.

p. 128 "I sat struck dumb": Nina Simone, with Stephen Cleary, *I Put a Spell on You: The Autobiography of Nina Simone* (New York: Pantheon, 1991), 89–90.

p. 128 "my country is full of lies": Nina Simone, "Mississippi Goddam," *The Solid Gold Collection*, CD, Union Square Music, 2005.

p. 130 "we can not dedicate": Abraham Lincoln, "Address Delivered at the Dedication of the Cemetery at Gettysburg" (November 19, 1863), in *The Collected Works of Abraham Lincoln*, ed. Roy P. Basler, 9 vols. (New Brunswick, N.J.: Rutgers University Press, 1953), 7: 18.

p. 131 "his substantial quotations": My analysis of King's use of biblical passages draws on the annotations in *The Zondervan KJV Study Bible*, ed. Kenneth Barker (Grand Rapids, Mich.: Zondervan, 2002), and *The Jewish Study Bible*, ed. Adele Berlin and Marc Zvi Brettler (New York: Oxford University Press, 2004). On King's use of Second Isaiah, see also Keith D. Miller, "Second Isaiah Lands in Washington, D.C.: Martin Luther King's 'I Have a Dream' as Biblical Narrative and Biblical Hermeneutic," *Rhetoric Review* 26 (2007), 405–24.

p. 131 "the maladjusted": Martin Luther King, Jr., "The Christian Way of Life in Human Relations, Address Delivered at the General Assembly of the National Council of Churches" (December 4, 1957), in *Papers*, 6: 327. On King's use of Amos in relation to Lincoln, see also Greil Marcus, *The Shape of Things to Come: Prophecy and the American Voice* (New York: Farrar, Straus and Giroux, 2006), 25–30.

p. 133 "tradition of the black jeremiad": David Howard-Pitney, *The Afro-American Jeremiad: Appeals for Justice in America* (Philadelphia: Temple University Press, 1990), 145.

p. 134 "tell them we climbed": Jeff Stetson, *The Meeting* (1984; rpt. New York: Dramatists Play Service, 1990), 33.

p. 136 "a popular black preacher": John Jasper, "The Stone Cut Out of the Mountain," in *Lift Every Voice: African American Oratory, 1787–1900*, ed. Philip S. Foner and Robert James Branham (Tuscaloosa: University of Alabama Press, 1998), 636.

p. 136 "stone of their individuality": James Baldwin, *The Fire Next Time* (New York: Dell, 1964), 134.

p. 137 "mountain of despair has dwindled": Alice Walker, "Choosing to Stay at Home: Ten Years after the March on Washington" (1973), in *In Search of Our Mothers' Gardens* (New York: Harcourt Brace Jovanovich, 1983), 168.

p. 137 "three Hebrew boys": Martin Luther King, Jr., "Transformed Nonconformist" (November 1954), in *Papers*, 6: 197.

p. 137 "askin' God to get us ready": King, 1962 sermon in Albany, Georgia, quoted in Pat Watters, *Down to Now: Reflections on the Southern Civil Rights Movement* (New York: Pantheon, 1971), 203.

p. 138 "the key passage": Martin Luther King, Jr., "Notecards on Books of the Old Testament," in *Papers*, 2: 165.

p. 139 "a nearly identical variation": See Abraham Joshua Heschel, *The Prophets* (New York: Harper and Row, 1962), 212, and Susannah Heschel, "Theological Affinities in the Writings of Abraham Joshua Heschel and Martin Luther King, Jr.," in *Black Zion: African American Religious Encounters with Judaism*, ed. Yvonne Chireau and Nathaniel Deutsch (New York: Oxford University Press, 2000), 173. King also used the same formulation in a revised version of his 1954 sermon "Transformed Nonconformist," drafted in 1962 or 1963 for inclusion in his sermon collection *Strength to Love* (from which it was ultimately trimmed during the editorial process), as well as in "Letter from Birmingham Jail." See King, "Draft of Chapter II, 'Transformed Nonconformist,'" *Papers*, 6: 475, and King, *Why We Can't Wait*, 88.

p. 140 "the prophetic insight": Walter Rauschenbusch, *Christianity and the Social Crisis* (New York: Macmillan, 1924), 363.

p. 141 "A mighty stream": Abraham Joshua Heschel, "The Religious Basis of Equal Opportunity—The Segregation of God," in *Race: Challenge to Religion*, ed. Mathew Ahmann (Chicago: Henry Regnery, 1963), 63–65, 70–71. Heschel's words also appeared in *The Prophets*.

p. 141 "entrance to the Memorial": On plans for the Martin Luther King, Jr., National Memorial, see www.mlkmemorial.org (accessed March 12, 2008).

FOUR
Lincoln's Shadow

p. 142 "hand-to-hand combat": Marian Anderson, *My Lord, What a Morning* (1956; rpt. Madison: University of Wisconsin Press, 1992), 189.

p. 143 "almost in the shadow": *Washington Times-Herald* editorial, January 15, 1939, quoted in Alan Keiler, *Marian Anderson: A Singer's Journey* (New York: Scribner, 2000), 207.

p. 144 "became the principal site": On the Memorial's history and use, see Scott A. Sandage, "A Marble House Divided: The Lincoln Memorial, the Civil Rights Movement, and the Politics of Memory, 1939–1963," *Journal of American History* 80 (June 1993), 135–67, and Christopher A. Thomas, *The Lincoln Memorial and American Life* (Princeton: Princeton University Press, 2002).

p. 144 "Capital of Babylon": "Call for Revolutionary People's Constitutional Convention" (June 19, 1970), in *The Black Panthers Speak*, ed. Philip S. Foner (1970; rpt. New York: Da Capo, 1995), 267.

p. 144 "in his stone temple": James Reston, "'I Have a Dream . . . ': Peroration by Dr. King Sums Up a Day the Capital Will Remember," *New York Times*, August 29, 1963.

p. 145 "At the end of the Mall": "Living Petition," *Washington Post*, August 29, 1963. The editorial refers to the abolitionist James Sloan Gibbons's poem "We Are Coming Father Abraham, Three Hundred Thousand More," written in response to Lincoln's 1862 call for more troops and later set to music by Stephen Foster and others.

p. 145 "Genius, like justice": Harold Ickes quoted in Keiler, *Marian Anderson*, 212.

p. 146 "there must be some design": B. Rush Plumly quoted in Allen C. Guelzo, *Lincoln's Emancipation Proclamation: The End of Slavery in America* (New York: Simon and Schuster, 2004), 208.

p. 146 "tinged by wish-fulfillment": Benjamin Quarles, *Lincoln and the Negro* (New York: Oxford University Press, 1962), unpaginated foreword and 148.

p. 147 "familiar religious cadences": Christopher Lasch, *The True and Only Heaven: Progress and Its Critics* (New York: Norton, 1991), 393.

p. 147 "Lincoln Memorial Address": Neil Schmitz, "Doing *The Gettysburg Address:* Jefferson / Calhoun / Lincoln / King," *Arizona Quarterly* 62 (Summer 2006), 145. On King's joining of the Emancipation Proclamation and the Gettysburg Address, see also Nathan W. Schlueter, *One Dream or Two? Justice in America and in the Thought of Martin Luther King, Jr.* (Lanham, Md.: Lexington, 2002), 11–14, and Mark Vail, "The 'Integrative' Rhetoric of Martin Luther King Jr.'s 'I Have a Dream' Speech," *Rhetoric and Public Affairs* 9 (2006), 64–66.

p. 148 "a new form of slavery": Martin Luther King, Jr., "The Death of Evil upon the Seashore" (May 17, 1956), in *Papers*, 3: 256–62; Martin Luther King, Jr., *Strength to Love* (1963; rpt. Philadelphia: Fortress, 1981), 77–86. For King's use of Phillips Brooks's sermon "Egyptians Dead upon the Seashore" and other sources, see Keith D. Miller, *The Voice of Deliverance: The Language of Martin Luther King, Jr., and Its Sources* (New York: Free Press, 1992), 14–28.

p. 148 "a fire-bell in the night": Thomas Jefferson, "Letter to John Holmes" (April 22, 1820), in *The Portable Thomas Jefferson*, ed. Merrill D. Peterson (New York: Viking, 1975), 568.

p. 149 "In giving freedom to the slave": Abraham Lincoln, "Annual Message to Congress" (December 1, 1862), in *The Collected Works of Abraham Lincoln*, ed. Roy P. Basler, 9 vols. (New Brunswick, N.J.: Rutgers University Press, 1953), 5: 537.

p. 149 "Unquestionably the first of January": Frederick Douglass, "January First, 1863" (January 1863), in *The Life and Writings of Frederick Douglass*, ed. Philip S. Foner, 5 vols. (New York: International Publishers, 1950), 3: 306.

p. 150 "strong, unequivocal belief": Martin Luther King, Jr., *Where Do We Go from Here: Chaos or Community?* (Boston: Beacon, 1967), 75–78.

p. 151 "far country of segregation": Martin Luther King, Jr., "The Christian Doctrine of Man" (March 12, 1958), in *Papers*, 6: 337.

p. 151 "the electric cord": Abraham Lincoln, "Speech at Chicago, Illinois" (July 10, 1858), in *Collected Works*, 2: 499–500.

p. 152 "new birth of freedom": Abraham Lincoln, "Address Delivered at the Dedication of the Cemetery at Gettysburg," in *Collected Works*, 7: 23.

p. 152 "central act of my administration": Abraham Lincoln quoted in Quarles, *Lincoln and the Negro*, 151.

p. 152 "naturally anti-slavery": Abraham Lincoln, "To Albert G. Hodges" (April 4, 1864), in *Collected Works*, 7: 281.

p. 153 "the genuine abolition ground": Frederick Douglass, "Oration in Memory of Abraham Lincoln" (April 14, 1876), in *Life and Writings*, 4: 316.

p. 154 "thus liberated": Abraham Lincoln, "Annual Message to Congress" (December 3, 1861), in *Collected Works*, 5: 48.

p. 154 "And upon this act": Abraham Lincoln, "Emancipation Proclamation," in *Collected Works*, 6: 30.

p. 154 "virtually a Second Declaration": Guelzo, *Lincoln's Emancipation Proclamation*, 203–4.

p. 154 "four score and seven years ago": Lincoln, "Address Delivered at the Dedication of the Cemetery at Gettysburg," 23.

p. 154 "transforming the proposition": On this widely discussed idea see, for example, William J. Wolf, *The Almost Chosen People: A Study of the Religion of Abraham Lincoln* (Garden City, N.Y.: Doubleday, 1959), 170–71; Glen E. Thurow, "The Gettysburg Address and the Declaration of Independence," in *Abraham Lincoln: The Gettysburg Address and American Constitutionalism*, ed. Leo Paul S. Alvarez (Dallas: University of Dallas Press, 1976), 68–72; and Garry Wills, *Lincoln at Gettysburg: The Words That Remade America* (New York: Touchstone, 1992), 86–89, 139–47.

p. 155 "quarrel among equals": Unnamed minister quoted in Robert James Branham and Stephen J. Hartnett, *Sweet Freedom's Song: "My Country, 'Tis of Thee" and Democracy in America* (New York: Oxford University Press, 2002), 100–101.

p. 155 "have our Fourth of July": Peter Osborne, "It Is Time for Us to Be Up and Doing" (July 5, 1832), in *Lift Every Voice: African American Oratory, 1787–1900*, ed. Philip S. Foner and Robert James Branham (Tuscaloosa: University of Alabama Press, 1998), 124.

p. 155 "worse than Egyptian bondage": Nathaniel Paul, "The Abolition of Slavery" (July 5, 1827), in *Negro Orators and Their Orations*, ed. Carter G. Woodson (1925; rpt. New York: Russell and Russell, 1969), 64–77.

p. 156 "a thin veil": Frederick Douglass, "The Meaning of July Fourth for the Negro" (July 5, 1852), in *Life and Writings*, 2: 181–204. In *My Bondage and My Freedom*, the speech was titled "What to the Slave Is the Fourth of July?"

p. 156 "imitates only the heroes": Frederick Douglass, *My Bondage and My Freedom*, ed. WIlliam S. Andrews (Urbana: University of Illinois Press, 1987), 119.

p. 157 "tremendous struggle": Frederick Douglass, "The Slaveholders' Rebellion" (July 4, 1862), in *Life and Writings*, 3: 243–48.

p. 157 "Douglass had long been pressing": On Douglass, Lincoln, and emancipation, see James Oakes, *The Radical and the Republican: Frederick Douglass, Abraham Lincoln, and the Triumph of Antislavery Politics* (New York: Norton, 2007), 133–208.

p. 157 "fundamental Act of Union": Thomas Jefferson, "From the Minutes of the Board of Visitors, University of Virginia, 1822–1825," in *Public and Private Papers* (New York: Vintage, 1990), 153.

p. 157 "not we the white people": Frederick Douglass, "The Constitution of the United States: Is It Pro-Slavery or Anti-Slavery?" (March 26, 1860), in *Life and Writings*, 2: 477.

p. 157 "covenant with death": William Lloyd Garrison, speech of July 4, 1854, quoted in *William Lloyd Garrison and the Fight against Slavery: Selections from "The Liberator,"* ed. William E. Cain (Boston: Bedford, 1995), 36.

p. 158 "carefully excluded from the Constitution": Frederick Douglass, "The Present and Future of the Colored Race in America" (May 1863), in *Life and Writings*, 3: 354.

p. 158 "covert language": Abraham Lincoln, "Seventh and Last Debate with Stephen A. Douglas at Alton, Illinois" (October 15, 1858), in *Collected Works*, 3: 306–7.

p. 159 "this magical omnipotence": Abraham Lincoln, "Message to Congress in Special Session" (July 4, 1861), in *Collected Works*, 4: 434.

p. 159 "not a mystical hope": Wills, *Lincoln at Gettysburg*, 144, 147.

p. 160 "more than all the victories": Unnamed soldier, writing in the Portland, Maine, *Press,* January 14, 1863, quoted in Kenneth A. Bernard, *Lincoln and the Music of the Civil War* (Caldwell, Idaho: Caxton, 1966), 90.

p. 160 "Heartbreak Day": Eileen Southern, *The Music of Black Americans: A History* (New York: Norton, 1971), 237.

p. 161 "Let the first of January": Absalom Jones, "A Thanksgiving Sermon . . . on Account of the Abolition of the African Slave Trade," in *Early Negro Writing, 1760–1837,* ed. Dorothy Porter (Boston: Beacon, 1971), 337, 340–41.

p. 161 "other days competed for the honor": On African American holidays, see Leonard I. Sweet, "The Fourth of July and Black Americans in the Nineteenth Century: Northern Leadership Opinion within the Context of Black Experience," *Journal of Negro History* 61 (1976), 256–75; William H. Wiggins, Jr., *O Freedom! Afro-American Emancipation Celebrations* (Knoxville: University of Tennessee Press, 1987), 25–47; and Geneviève Fabre, "African-American Commemorative Celebrations in the Nineteenth Century," in *History and Memory in African-American Culture,* ed. Geneviève Fabre and Robert O'Meally (New York: Oxford University Press, 1994), 72–91.

p. 162 "time of times": Henry M. Turner quoted in Quarles, *Lincoln and the Negro,* 142.

p. 162 "lay hands on another": Ralph Waldo Emerson, "Boston Hymn" (1863), in *Collected Poems and Translations* (New York: Library of America, 1994), 165.

p. 162 "at which future visionaries": Washington *Morning Chronicle,* January 2, 1863, quoted in John Hope Franklin, *The Emancipation Proclamation* (Garden City, N.Y.: Doubleday, 1963), 119.

p. 163 "Nor shall I ever forget": Douglass, "Oration in Memory of Abraham Lincoln," in *Life and Writings,* 4: 315.

p. 163 "sang songs of jubilee": Quarles, *Lincoln and the Negro,* 143–44; Oakes, *The Radical and the Republican,* 176–77.

p. 165 "same typological progression": David Brion Davis, "The Emancipation Moment," in *Lincoln, the War President,* ed. Gabor S. Boritt (New York: Oxford University Press, 1992), 64–73; Ronald R. Garet, "Proclaim Liberty," *Southern California Law Review* 74 (November 2000), 160–64.

p. 165 "If there were one day": Phillips Brooks quoted in Merrill D. Peterson, *Lincoln in American Memory* (New York: Oxford University Press, 1994), 8.

p. 166 "American document of freedom": Franklin, *The Emancipation Proclamation,* vi.

p. 166 "the Civil War centennial": Michael Kammen, *Mystic Chords of Memory: The Transformation of Tradition in American Culture* (New York: Knopf, 1991), 590–610.

p. 166 "One hundred years ago today": John F. Kennedy, "Remarks Recorded for the Ceremony at the Lincoln Memorial Commemorating the Emancipation Proclamation" (September 22, 1962), in *Public Papers of the Presidents of the United States, 1962* (Washington, D.C.: U.S. Government Printing Office, 1963), 702.

p. 167 "the image of a man": Archibald MacLeish, "At the Lincoln Memorial," in *New and Collected Poems, 1917–1976* (Boston: Houghton Mifflin, 1976), 432–35. All ellipses are MacLeish's.

p. 168 "I have often inquired": Abraham Lincoln, "Speech in Independence Hall, Philadelphia, Pennsylvania" (February 22, 1861), in *Collected Works*, 4: 240.

p. 169 "faith statement": H. Richard Niebuhr, *Radical Monotheism and Western Civilization* (Lincoln: University of Nebraska Press, 1960), 83.

p. 169 "sort of a Gettysburg Address": King, speaking to Al Duckett, one of his ghostwriters, quoted in David J. Garrow, *Bearing the Cross: Martin Luther King, Jr., and the Southern Christian Leadership Conference* (New York: Vintage, 1988), 676n59.

F I V E

Whose Country 'Tis of Thee?

p. 170 "as old as the scriptures": John F. Kennedy, "Radio and Television Report to the American People on Civil Rights" (June 11, 1963), in *Public Papers of the Presidents of the United States, 1963* (Washington, D.C.: U.S. Government Printing Office, 1964), 469.

p. 171 "deeply felt faith": Whitney M. Young, Jr., *To Be Equal* (New York: Mc-Graw-Hill, 1966), 245.

p. 171 "absurd and nonsensical": Addison Gayle, Jr., "Nat Turner vs. Black Nationalists," *Liberator* 8 (February 1968), 5–7.

p. 172 "be able to laugh": Malcolm X quoted in Peter Goldman, *The Death and Life of Malcolm X* (New York: Harper and Row, 1973), 25.

p. 172 *"Screams off key"*: Amiri Baraka, *The Slave*, in *Selected Plays and Prose of Amiri Baraka / Leroi Jones* (New York: William Morrow, 1979), 105–6.

p. 172 "sweet land of slavery": Charles Mingus quoted in Scott Saul, *Freedom Is, Freedom Ain't: Jazz and the Making of the Sixties* (Cambridge: Harvard University Press, 2003), 325–26.

p. 172 "the musician Mos Def": David Hajdu, "Songbook Man," *New Republic* 236 (March 19, 2007), 45.

p. 172 "You got your thirty-eight": Coretta Scott King, *My Life with Martin Luther King, Jr.* (1969; New York: Avon, 1970), 140.

p. 173 "love our white brothers": Martin Luther King, Jr., *Stride toward Freedom* (1958; rpt. New York: Harper and Row, 1986), 137–38.

p. 174 "a man without a country": Julian Mayfield, "Into the Mainstream and

Oblivion," in *The American Negro Writer and His Roots: Selected Papers from the First Conference of Negro Writers, March 1959* (New York: American Society of African Culture, 1960), 33.

p. 174 "the song's early history": I am much indebted for information about the song and examples of its use in the following pages to Robert James Branham and Stephen J. Hartnett, *Sweet Freedom's Song: "My Country, 'Tis of Thee" and Democracy in America* (New York: Oxford University Press, 2002), 14–162.

p. 177 "America, it is to thee": J[ames]. M[onroe]. Whitfield, "America," in *America and Other Poems* (Buffalo, N.Y.: James S. Leavitt, 1853), 9.

p. 177 "took and waved the flag": Thomas Wentworth Higginson, *Army Life in a Black Regiment* (1870; rpt. East Lansing: Michigan State University Press, 1960), 30–31.

p. 179 "forgot about the President": John E. Washington, *They Knew Lincoln* (New York: Dutton, 1942), 82–88; Bernard, *Lincoln and the Music of the Civil War,* 91–93.

p. 179 "Gettysburg gospel": Gabor Boritt, *The Gettysburg Gospel: The Lincoln Speech That Nobody Knows* (New York: Simon and Schuster, 2006), 181–89. See also David W. Blight, *Race and Reunion: The Civil War in American Memory* (Cambridge: Harvard University Press, 2001), 6–15, 383–91.

p. 180 "commemorative of the great charter": *The Lincoln Memorial in Washington* (Washington, D.C.: U.S. Government Printing Office, 1927), 15.

p. 180 "restoration of the brotherly love": Ibid., 86.

p. 181 "The grip that swung": Edwin Markham, "Lincoln, the Man of the People," ibid., 83.

p. 181 "the Pilgrim Fathers set foot": Robert Russa Moton, "The Negro's Debt to Lincoln," ibid., 78–81.

p. 181 "Moton had his speech censored": Adam Fairclough, "Civil Rights and the Lincoln Memorial: The Censored Speeches of Robert R. Moton (1922) and John Lewis (1963)," *Journal of Negro History* 82 (Autumn 1997), 408–16.

p. 182 "champion of human liberty": Ida B. Wells, "Lynch Law in All Its Phases," in Mildred I. Thompson, *Ida B. Wells-Barnett: An Exploratory Study of an American Black Woman, 1893–1930* (Brooklyn, N.Y.: Carlson, 1990), 171–87.

p. 185 "pack-jammed with colored folks": Mahalia Jackson, with Evan McLeod Wylie, *Movin' On Up* (New York: Hawthorne, 1966), 128–29.

p. 185 "voice of exile": W. E. B. Du Bois, *The Souls of Black Folk* (1903; rpt. New York: Penguin, 1989), 205, 208.

p. 186 "land on Plymouth Rock": Malcolm X, with Alex Haley, *The Autobiography of Malcolm X* (New York: Grove, 1966), 201. Malcolm's aphoristic statement echoed lyrics about Puritans arriving in a modern America in Porter's "Anything Goes" ("'Stead of landing on Plymouth Rock, / Plymouth Rock would land on them").

p. 186 "inspired by the example of Lincoln": Martin Luther King, Jr., "The Negro and the Constitution" (May 1944), in *Papers*, 1: 109–11.

p. 187 "black sons of bitches": Martin Luther King, Jr., interview with Alex Haley (1965), in *The Playboy Interviews*, ed. Murray Fisher (New York: Ballantine, 1993), 84.

p. 188 "This is my country": Ralph Bunche, "The United Nations in 1963," in *The Negro Speaks: The Rhetoric of Contemporary Black Leaders*, ed. Jamye Coleman Williams and McDonald Williams (New York: Noble and Noble, 1970), 27.

p. 188 "some people don't think": "This Is My Country," Curtis Mayfield and the Impressions, *The Very Best of the Impressions*, CD, Rhino Entertainment, 1997.

p. 188 "the vast majority of us": Billy Graham quoted in Scott A. Sandage, "A Marble House Divided: The Lincoln Memorial, the Civil Rights Movement, and the Politics of Memory, 1939–1963," *Journal of American History* 80 (June 1993), 163.

p. 188 "truly the Negro's country": Carl T. Rowan, "Martin Luther King's Tragic Decision," *Reader's Digest* 46 (September 1967), 42.

p. 188 "This is your home": James Baldwin, *The Fire Next Time* (New York: Dell, 1964), 21.

p. 189 "give back to Africa": Marcus Garvey, "Speech Delivered on Emancipation Day at Liberty Hall, New York City" (January 1, 1922), in *Philosophy and Opinions of Marcus Garvey*, ed. Amy Jacques-Garvey, 2 vols. in 1 (1925; rpt. New York: Atheneum, 1977), 1: 81–82.

p. 189 "colored autonomous state": Cyril V. Briggs, "The African Blood Brotherhood" (1920), in *Modern Black Nationalism: From Marcus Garvey to Louis Farrakhan*, ed. William L. Van Deburg (New York: New York University Press, 1997), 34–35.

p. 189 "a home on this earth": Elijah Muhammad, speech of May 31, 1959, quoted in E. U. Essien-Udom, *Black Nationalism: A Search for an Identity in America* (Chicago: University of Chicago Press, 1962), 257.

p. 189 "Malcolm X met": Malcolm X, speech at Audubon Ballroom, Harlem, February 15, 1965, in Malcolm X, *The Final Speeches*, ed. Steve Clark (New York: Pathfinder, 1992), 117.

p. 190 "Republic of New Africa": Milton R. Henry quoted in Robert Sherrill, "We Want Georgia, South Carolina, Louisiana, Mississippi, and Alabama—Right Now . . . We Also Want Four Hundred Billion Dollars Back Pay," *Esquire* 71 (January 1969), 72–75, 146–48.

p. 190 "people were seeking a home": Chester Himes, *Cotton Comes to Harlem* (1965; rpt. New York: Vintage, 1988), 26.

p. 190 "My 'old country'": Roger Wilkins, "What Africa Means to Blacks," *Foreign Policy* 15 (Summer 1974), 131–32.

p. 191 "brave revolutionaries": Maya Angelou, *All God's Children Need Traveling Shoes* (New York: Random House, 1986), 121–27.

p. 191 "who truly had his tongue": Alice Walker, "Choosing to Stay at Home:

Ten Years after the March on Washington" (1973), in *In Search of Our Mothers' Gardens* (New York: Harcourt Brace Jovanovich, 1983), 159–62.

p. 192 "live in the land of our birth": Frederick Douglass, "Letter to Thomas Auld" (appended to *My Bondage and My Freedom* as "Letter to My Old Master"), in *The Life and Writings of Frederick Douglass*, ed. Philip S. Foner, 5 vols. (New York: International Publishers, 1950), 1: 339.

p. 192 "a great American": Mrs. Medgar [Myrlie] Evers, with William Peters, *For Us, the Living* (Garden City, N.Y.: Doubleday, 1967), 324–29.

S I X
Not by the Color of Their Skin

p. 195 "a virtual job qualification": Dinesh D'Souza, *The End of Racism* (New York: Free Press, 1995), 165.

p. 195 "affirmative action pie": William Bradford Reynolds, "An Experiment Gone Awry," in *The Affirmative Action Debate*, ed. George C. Curry (Cambridge, Mass.: Perseus, 1996), 133.

p. 195 "bridge that was necessary": Alveda C. King, quoted in "The Niece of Martin Luther King, Jr., Is a Staunch Opponent of Affirmative Action," *Journal of Blacks in Higher Education* 22 (Winter 1998–99), 49.

p. 195 "Twenty-two years ago": Ronald Reagan, "Radio Address to the Nation on Civil Rights" (June 15, 1985), in *Public Papers of the Presidents of the United States, 1985* (Washington, D.C.: U.S. Government Printing Office, 1988), 773. See also Nicholas Laham, *The Reagan Presidency and the Politics of Race: In Pursuit of Colorblind Justice and Limited Government* (Westport, Conn.: Praeger, 1998), 74–75, 82–87.

p. 196 "Both measures stand": Robert Dole quoted in Lydia Chávez, *The Color Bind: California's Battle to End Affirmative Action* (Berkeley: University of California Press, 1998), 116.

p. 196 "patron saint": Ward Connerly, *Creating Equal: My Fight against Race Preferences* (San Francisco: Encounter, 2000), 196.

p. 196 "ill-conceived television ad": Chávez, *The Color Bind*, 218–19, 227–28, 230.

p. 197 "misrepresenting his beliefs": Coretta Scott King quoted in Edward W. Lempinen and Robert B. Gunnison, "King Ad for Prop. 209 on Hold," *San Francisco Chronicle*, October 24, 1996.

p. 198 "wilted under the pressure": Connerly, *Creating Equal*, 196.

p. 198 "an American icon": Jonah Goldberg, "The Clay Feet of Liberal Saints," *Los Angeles Times*, January 5, 2006.

p. 198 "for nobody can doubt": Martin Luther King, Jr., "MIA Mass Meeting at Holt Street Baptist Church" (December 3, 1955), in *Papers*, 3: 72.

p. 199 "representing my people": Marian Anderson, *My Lord, What a Morning* (1956; rpt. Madison: University of Wisconsin Press, 1992), 189.

p. 199 "the sweat of my people": Duke Ellington, "My People," *My People*, Bob Thiele producer, CD, Sony Music, 1990.

p. 199 "forced outward by pity": Zora Neale Hurston, *Dust Tracks on a Road: An Autobiography*, ed. Robert Hemenway (1942; rpt. Urbana: University of Illinois Press, 1984), 215.

p. 199 "must not let the fact": Martin Luther King, Jr., *Stride toward Freedom* (1958; rpt. New York: Harper and Row, 1986), 223. See also, for example, Martin Luther King, Jr., "Some Things We Must Do" (December 5, 1957), in *Papers*, 4: 335–37.

p. 200 "Men and women who want": Marcus Garvey, "Lessons from the School of African Philosophy," in *Marcus Garvey: Life and Lessons*, ed. Robert A. Hill (Berkeley: University of California Press, 1987), 233.

p. 200 "gospel of the tooth-brush": Booker T. Washington, *Up from Slavery* (1901; rpt. New York: Penguin, 1986), 174–75.

p. 200 "talked much of character": W. E. B. Du Bois, *The Autobiography of W. E. B. Du Bois: A Soliloquy on Viewing My Life from the Last Decade of Its First Century* (1968; rpt. New York: International Publishers, 1986), 277.

p. 200 "culture of personality": Warren I. Sussman, "'Personality' and the Making of Twentieth-Century Culture," in *Culture as History: The Transformation of American Society in the Twentieth Century* (New York: Pantheon, 1984), 271–85.

p. 200 "character of Abraham Lincoln": W. E. B. Du Bois, "Abraham Lincoln" (1907), rpt. in *The Oxford W. E. B. Du Bois Reader*, ed. Eric J. Sundquist (New York: Oxford University Press, 1996), 255.

p. 200 "one of the greatest characters": Martin Luther King, Jr., "Accepting Responsibility for Your Actions" (July 26, 1953), in *Papers*, 6: 140–41.

p. 201 "character came through": C. T. Vivian quoted in Flip Schulke and Penelope McPhee, *King Remembered* (New York: Pocket Books, 1986), 67.

p. 201 "abnormal fraudulent self": David J. Garrow, *The FBI and Martin Luther King, Jr.* (New York: Penguin, 1983), 125–26.

p. 201 "indelible stamp of the Creator": Martin Luther King, Jr., *Where Do We Go from Here: Chaos or Community?* (Boston: Beacon, 1967), 97.

p. 201 "aristocracy of character": Martin Luther King, Jr., "Eulogy for the Young Victims of the Sixteenth Street Baptist Church Bombing," in *A Call to Conscience: The Landmark Speeches of Dr. Martin Luther King, Jr.*, ed. Clayborne Carson and Kris Shepard (New York: Warner, 2001), 97.

p. 202 "Do nothing with us": Frederick Douglass, "What the Black Man Wants" (April 1865), in *The Life and Writings of Frederick Douglass*, ed. Philip S. Foner, 5 vols. (New York: International Publishers, 1950), 4: 164.

p. 202 "Mere connection with what is known": Washington, *Up from Slavery*, 40–41.

p. 202 "transformation of character": Ralph Ellison, "If the Twain Shall Meet" (1964), in *Going to the Territory* (New York: Vintage, 1987), 102.

p. 203 "not his color but his integrity": King, *Where Do We Go from Here?* 49.

p. 203 "one big family of Americans": Martin Luther King, Jr., "The American Dream" (July 4, 1965), in *A Knock at Midnight: Inspiration from the Great Sermons of Reverend Martin Luther King, Jr.*, ed. Clayborne Carson and Peter Holloran (New York: Warner, 1998), 92.

p. 203 "30 percent Negro population": King, *Where Do We Go from Here?* 144.

p. 204 "some compensatory consideration": Martin Luther King, Jr., *Why We Can't Wait* (New York: Signet, 1964), 134.

p. 205 "a people thus handicapped": W. E. B. Du Bois, *The Souls of Black Folk* (1903; rpt. New York: Penguin, 1989), 9.

p. 205 "elevate the condition of men": Abraham Lincoln, "Message to Congress in Special Session" (July 4, 1861), in *The Collected Works of Abraham Lincoln*, ed. Roy P. Basler, 9 vols. (New Brunswick, N.J.: Rutgers University Press, 1953), 4: 438.

p. 205 "Let the race be fair": Isaac Kramnick, "Equal Opportunity and the Race of Life" (1981), in *Dogmas and Dreams: Political Ideologies in the Modern World*, ed. Nancy S. Love (Chatham, N.J.: Chatham House, 1991), 97, 101.

p. 205 "a back seat in the race": Julian Bond quoted in Leslie Fulbright, "Debate Mixed over Effect of the Schools Decision," *San Francisco Chronicle*, June 29, 2007, http://sfgate.com/cgi-bin/article.cgi?f=/c/a/2007/06/29/MNGMIQO4401.DTL (accessed March 13, 2008).

p. 205 "America's untouchable": Benjamin E. Mays, "The Moral Aspects of Segregation," in William Faulkner, Benjamin E. Mays, and Cecil Sims, *The Segregation Decisions* (Atlanta: Southern Regional Council, 1956), 13–17.

p. 206 "our way of atoning": Jawaharlal Nehru quoted in King, *Why We Can't Wait*, 135.

p. 206 "handicapped multitudes": King, *Why We Can't Wait*, 136.

p. 206 "relative status of the races": Bayard Rustin, "Preamble to the March on Washington" (1963), in *Time on Two Crosses: The Collected Writings of Bayard Rustin*, ed. Devon W. Carbado and Donald Weise (San Francisco: Cleis, 2003), 111–13.

p. 206 "eliminate the Negro": King, *Where Do We Go from Here?* 70.

p. 207 "No nation can afford": Kenneth B. Clark, "Jews in Contemporary America: Problems in Identification" (1954), in *The Psychodynamics of American Jewish Life: An Anthology*, ed. Norman Kiell (New York: Twayne, 1967), 111–12. On the concept of racial "damage" see Daryl Michael Scott, *Contempt and Pity: Social Policy and the Image of the Damaged Black Psyche, 1880–1996* (Chapel Hill: University of North Carolina Press, 1997).

p. 207 "circle of despair and deprivation": Lyndon Johnson, "Commencement Address at Howard University: 'To Fulfill These Rights'" (June 4, 1965), in *Public Papers of the Presidents of the United States, 1965* (Washington, D.C.: U.S. Government Printing Office, 1966), 635–40.

p. 208 "roughly equal results": Daniel Patrick Moynihan, "The Negro Family: The Case for National Action," in *The Moynihan Report and the Politics of Controversy*, ed. Lee Rainwater and William T. Yancey (Cambridge: MIT Press, 1967), unpaginated introduction.

p. 209 "When you are behind in a footrace": King quoted in Shelby Steele, *The Content of Our Character: A New Vision of Race in America* (New York: St. Martin's, 1990), 138.

p. 209 "to do the impossible": King, *Where Do We Go from Here?* 120, 79.

p. 209 "Negroes have received": Farmer quoted in Hugh Davis Graham, *The Civil Rights Era: Origins and Development of National Policy* (New York: Oxford University Press, 1990), 109.

p. 210 "James Farmer Day": Michael Lind, *The Next American Nation: The New Nationalism and the Fourth American Revolution* (New York: Free Press, 1995), 111.

p. 210 "domestic Marshall Plan": Whitney Young, "Should There Be 'Compensation' for Negroes?" *New York Times Magazine*, October 6, 1963, 43, 128–29.

p. 210 "My concept of equality": King and Wilkins quoted in "What the Marchers Really Want," *New York Times*, August 23, 1963.

p. 211 "compensatory preferential treatment": James Farmer, *Lay Bare the Heart: An Autobiography of the Civil Rights Movement* (New York: New American Library, 1985), 222.

p. 212 "most profound disability": Michael Harrington, *The Other America: Poverty in the United States* (New York: Macmillan, 1962), 72, 79.

p. 212 "gigantic Bill of Rights": King, *Why We Can't Wait*, 137.

p. 212 "Negro Bill of Rights": King quoted in David J. Garrow, *Bearing the Cross: Martin Luther King, Jr., and the Southern Christian Leadership Conference* (New York: Vintage, 1988), 312.

p. 212 "Freedom Budget": Bayard Rustin, "'Black Power' and Coalition Politics," *Commentary* 42 (September 1966), 39–40.

p. 213 "too soon to be color-blind": Nat Hentoff, *The New Equality* (New York: Viking, 1964), 111–14.

p. 213 "it must be the exclusion": Alexander M. Bickel, *The Morality of Consent* (New Haven: Yale University Press, 1975), 132–33.

p. 214 "plaintiffs' own colorblind argument": For the briefs cited by Roberts and Thomas, see "Briefs for Appellants . . . on Reargument," in *Landmark Briefs and Arguments of the Supreme Court of the United States: Constitutional Law*, ed. Philip B.

Kurland and Gerhard Casper (Arlington, Va.: University Publications of America, 1975), 49: 514–748, quotations at 528, 578.

p. 215 "shifted their arguments": My discussion here and following is indebted to Andrew Kull, *The Color-Blind Constitution* (Cambridge: Harvard University Press, 1992), 151–210, and Reva B. Siegel, "Equality Talk: Antisubordination and Anticlassification Values in Constitutional Struggles over *Brown*," *Harvard Law Review* 117 (March 2004), 1470–1547.

p. 215 "rather than racial stigmatization": Edward J. Erler, "Sowing the Wind: Judicial Oligarchy and the Legacy of *Brown v. Board of Education*," *Harvard Journal of Law and Public Policy* 8 (Spring 1985), 410–13.

p. 215 "Gorgon's head of miscegenation": Kull, *The Color-Blind Constitution*, 159.

p. 215 "Not every child has an equal": John F. Kennedy, "Radio and Television Report to the American People on Civil Rights" (June 11, 1963), in *Public Papers of the Presidents of the United States, 1963* (Washington, D.C.: U.S. Government Printing Office, 1964), 471.

p. 216 "Until justice is blind to color": Lyndon B. Johnson, "Remarks by Vice President, Memorial Day, Gettysburg, Pennsylvania" (May 30, 1963), Press Release, Statements File, Box 80, Lyndon Baines Johnson Library, http://www.lbjlib.utexas.edu/johnson/archives.hom/speeches.hom/630530.asp (accessed March 13, 2008).

p. 216 "removing the barriers": Bayard Rustin, "From Protest to Politics: The Future of the Civil Rights Movement," *Commentary* 39 (February 1965), 25–27.

p. 216 "akin to 'war reparations'": "The Longer March to Real Equal Rights," *Life* 55 (August 23, 1963), 4.

p. 216 "Ten Commandments": Lyndon Johnson quoted in Maurice Isserman and Michael Kazin, *America Divided: The Civil War in the 1960s* (New York: Oxford University Press, 2000), 103.

p. 217 "Contrary to the allegations": Hubert Humphrey, *Congressional Record 110*, 88th Congress (March 30, 1964), 6549.

p. 217 "start eating the pages": Hubert Humphrey, *Congressional Record 110*, 88th Congress (April 9, 1964), 7420.

p. 217 "Rehnquist's detractors": Richard Kluger, *Simple Justice: The History of Brown v. Board of Education and Black America's Struggle for Equality* (New York: Random House, 1975), 605–9.

p. 218 "minority rights revolution": See, for example, Graham, *The Civil Rights Era*, 233–54, and John D. Skrentny, *The Minority Rights Revolution* (Cambridge: Harvard University Press, 2002), 85–142.

p. 219 "color blind and color conscious": *United States v. Jefferson County Board of Education*, 372 F.2d. 836 (1966), 846–47, 876.

p. 219 "perpetuate their group interest": Jack Greenberg, "Race Relations and Group Interests in the Law," *Rutgers Law Review* 13 (Spring 1959), 503.

p. 219 "liberation lies in group action": Stokely Carmichael and Charles V. Hamilton, *Black Power: The Politics of Liberation in America* (New York: Vintage Random, 1967), 53–54.

p. 220 "discrimination to representation": Daniel Bell, "On Meritocracy and Equality," *Public Interest* 27 (Summer 1972), 37–39.

p. 220 "individual merit": Kenneth L. Karst and Harold W. Horowitz, "Affirmative Action and Equal Protection," *Virginia Law Review* 60 (October 1974), 956–59, 965.

p. 220 "group-disadvantaging principle": Owen M. Fiss, "Groups and the Equal Protection Clause," *Philosophy and Public Affairs* 5 (Winter 1976), 147–70.

p. 220 "McGeorge Bundy's variation": Writing the year before *Bakke*, Bundy had argued: "Still, it seems clear that to take race into account today is better than to let the door swing almost shut because of the head start of others. . . . To get past racism, we must here take account of race. There is no other present way." McGeorge Bundy, "The Issue before the Court: Who Gets Ahead in America?" *Atlantic Monthly* 240 (November 1977), 54.

p. 221 "dream on its head": Linda Chavez, "A Turning Point in the Civil Rights Struggle," *Chronicle of Higher Education*, July 4, 2003, B10.

p. 221 "making race and ethnicity proxies": Cf. David Hollinger, *Postethnic America: Beyond Multiculturalism*, rev. ed. (New York: Basic, 1996), 183–89, and Peter Wood, *Diversity: The Invention of a Concept* (San Francisco: Encounter, 2003), 118–20, 134–37.

p. 222 "plain unmistakable language": Abraham Lincoln, "Speech at Springfield, Illinois" (June 26, 1857), in *Collected Works*, 2: 405–6.

p. 222 "recover the moral horizons": Clarence Thomas, "Why Black Americans Should Look to Conservative Policies," in *The Heritage Lectures* (Washington, D.C.: Heritage Foundation, 1987), 8.

p. 223 "man's moral pilgrimage": Martin Luther King, Jr., "The Death of Evil upon the Seashore," in *Strength to Love* (1963; rpt. Philadelphia: Fortress, 1981), 83–84.

p. 223 "incurably color-blind": King, interview with Alex Haley (1965), in *The Playboy Interviews*, ed. Murray Fisher (New York: Ballantine, 1993), 125.

p. 223 *"we* [give] up our color": James Farmer, *Freedom—When?* (New York: Random House, 1965), 87.

p. 224 "surviving an environment": Orlando Patterson, *The Ordeal of Integration: Progress and Resentment in America's "Racial" Crisis* (Washington, D.C.: Civitas/Counterpoint, 1997), 156.

p. 225 "owes a debt to justice": Martin Luther King, Jr., "An Address by Dr. Martin Luther King, Jr." (October 29, 1965), in *The Moynihan Report*, 404, 406, 408–9.

p. 225 "those conditions of poverty": King, *Where Do We Go from Here?* 189.

p. 226 "will only be truly free": Ibid., 43.

p. 227 "ten most unpatriotic Americans": "The Return of the King," Aaron Mc-Gruder, writer and executive producer, Adult Swim TV, *The Boondocks: The Complete First Season*, DVD, Rebel Base in association with Sony Pictures Television, 2007.

Acknowledgments

My first and greatest debt is to my research assistant, T. Austin Graham, whose diligence and inspiration, as well as his reading of the manuscript, led me in many fruitful directions. I would also like to thank friends and colleagues for reading various parts of the book in manuscript. Whether or not they agree with the use I have made of their excellent advice, I am indebted to George Bornstein, William Cain, Sharon Cameron, Michael Colacurcio, Gregg Crane, Keith Gandal, David Hollinger, Kenneth Karst, Wayne Mixon, Cynthia Nash, James Oakes, Robert Post, and David Zarefsky. In addition, I learned a great deal from readers for Yale University Press, including Keith D. Miller, whom I am especially pleased to be able to thank by name. I had the opportunity to present early versions of my argument to audiences at the University of Kansas, Kansas State University, the University of Michigan, Purdue University, and the Sewanee School of Letters and I am grateful for the responses I received. I am likewise thankful for the research assistance, sabbatical leave, and library support, especially that of Miki Goral, provided by the University of California at Los Angeles.

For everything that makes a new life new, I am happy to share this book with Sharifa Oppenheimer.

My thanks go to Mark Crispin Miller for first asking me to write for the Icons of America series. At Yale University Press I have benefited from the encouragement and wise counsel of Jonathan Brent; the generous assistance of Annelise Finegan and Susan Laity; and the expert copy-editing of Daniel Heaton.

I am pleased to acknowledge that some material appeared first in a different form as "King's 'Dream'—Whose Country 'Tis of Thee?" *Michigan Quarterly Review* 46 (Fall 2007), 572–94. I am grateful, as well, to the copyright holders for permission to reprint the following:

"I Have a Dream" reprinted by arrangement with The Heirs to the Estate of Dr. Martin Luther King, Jr., c/o Writers House, LLC, as agent for the proprietor, New York, NY. Copyright © 1963 by Dr. Martin Luther King, Jr.; copyright renewed © 1991 by Coretta Scott King.

Excerpts from Archibald MacLeish, "At the Lincoln Memorial," from *Collected Poems, 1917–1982* by Archibald MacLeish. Copyright © 1985 by the Estate of Archibald MacLeish. Reprinted by permission of Houghton Mifflin Company. All rights reserved.

Excerpts from Margaret Walker, "At the Lincoln Monument in Washington, August 28, 1963," from *This Is My Century: New and Collected Poems* by Margaret Walker. Copyright © 1989 by Margaret Walker Alexander. Reprinted by permission of the University of Georgia Press.

Index